WONDER AND GENEROSITY

Wonder
&
Generosity
Their Role in Ethics and Politics

Marguerite La Caze

SUNY
PRESS

Published by State University of New York Press, Albany

© 2013 State University of New York

For information, contact State University of New York Press, Albany, NY
www.sunypress.edu

Production by Ryan Morris
Marketing by Michael Campochiaro

Library of Congress Cataloging-in-Publication Data
La Caze, Marguerite, 1964–
  Wonder and generosity : their role in ethics and politics / Maguerite La Caze.
     p. cm.
  Includes bibliographical references and index.
  ISBN 978-1-4384-4675-2 (hardcover : alk. paper) 1. Generosity. 2. Wonder. 3. Political
ethics. I. Title.
  BJ1533.G4L39 2013
  179'.9—dc23
                                    2012026096

10 9 8 7 6 5 4 3 2 1

To my parents, Charles and Val La Caze

Contents

Acknowledgments

Writing this book has been a real pleasure and has involved endless discussions and support over years. Much of the work has been presented at conferences, and I would like to thank audiences at the Australasian Society for Continental Philosophy, the Society for Philosophy in the Contemporary World, Women's Studies, Feminist Ethics and Social Theory, International Association of Women Philosophers, Women in Philosophy, Derrida Roundtable, Australasian Association for Philosophy, Benevolence, and Society for European Philosophy conferences for lively discussions. I have also presented sections to the philosophy seminar at University of Queensland, at the UQ-UNE weekend, the philosophy department at the University of New South Wales, the Centre for Applied Philosophy and Public Ethics, ANU, and I gained a great deal from those discussions. Thank you.

I am grateful to the Australian Research Council for their support through an Australian Research Fellowship in the years 2003–07. The School of History, Philosophy, Religion and Classics and the Centre for the History of European Discourses have supported research activities for the European Philosophy Research Group, and I appreciate that very much. Colleagues and friends in the school have discussed the issues with me, provided advice, and supported my research, including Michelle Boulous Walker, Gil Burgh, Phil Dowe, Gary Malinas, Michael Lattke, and Clive Moore. Lorraine Code, Rosalyn Diprose, Max Deutscher, Michael Levine, Frances Gray, Michèle Le Dœuff, Paul Formosa, and Andrew Schaap have all very kindly given helpful feedback. Damian Cox, as always, has talked with me every step of the way and commented on drafts unstintingly, showing a level of generosity that I deeply acknowledge. My family members and friends were tireless in their support and so I am indebted to them for that.

Teaching has also been important to development of the book and I especially thank the students in my Ethics and the Passions course the last few years for their insights. Anonymous reviewers have helped improve my thinking at many points, so thanks to all of them. I would also like to thank a number of journals and presses for permission to reprint work that the chapters are based on: Wiley-Blackwell for "The Encounter between Wonder and Generosity," *Hypatia: A Journal of Feminist Philosophy* 17, no.3 (2002): 1–19, and "Love, That Indispensable Supplement: Irigaray and Kant on Love and Respect," *Hypatia: A Journal of Feminist Philosophy* 20, no.3 (2005): 92–114; Cornell for "If You Say So: Feminist Philosophy and Anti-Racism," in *Racism in Mind*, ed. Michael Levine and Tamás Pataki (Ithaca: Cornell University Press, 2004), 261–78; Sage for "At the Intersection: Kant, Derrida, and the Relation between Ethics and Politics," *Political Theory: An International Journal of Political Philosophy* 35, no. 6 (2007): 781–805; *Philosophy Today* for "Not Just Visitors: Cosmopolitanism, Hospitality, and Refugees," *Philosophy Today* 48, no.3 (2004): 313–24; Springer for "Should Radical Evil be Forgiven?" in *Forensic Psychiatry: Influences of Evil,* ed. Tom Mason (Totowa: Humana Press, 2005), 273–93; and Palgrave for "The Asymmetry between Apology and Forgiveness," Feature Article: Theory and Practice, *Contemporary Political Theory* 5, no.4 (2006): 447–68. Finally, I would like to express my gratitude to three anonymous reviewers for SUNY Press for insightful suggestions and to Andrew Kenyon, Acquisitions Editor, philosophy, for SUNY, for his encouragement and professionalism.

Introduction

This book concerns the ethical and political significance of two passions: wonder and generosity. Wonder is based on accepting others' differences, and generosity is based on self-respect and mutual respect. When both are cultivated, they supplement each other and form the basis for an ethics and politics. This ethics and politics includes both an acceptance of sexual and cultural difference, for example, and a recognition of our common humanity. My starting point is a study of the important insights into responding to difference raised by Luce Irigaray in *An Ethics of Sexual Difference* (1993a). I began thinking about these questions when reading her incredibly suggestive and fruitful essay "Wonder: A Reading of Descartes, *The Passions of the Soul.*" In that essay Irigaray argues that Descartes is right to place wonder as the first of all the passions and that wonder can provide the basis for an ethics of sexual difference because it is prior to judgment and so free of hierarchical relations. Wonder is surprise at what is unusual, what stands out against a background of familiar, everyday experiences. It is different from other passions. Other passions are a reaction to what we find pleasant or distasteful about an object, whereas wonder is a direct response to an object as it is.

Wonder involves recognizing others as different from ourselves in that it is a response to what is unfamiliar and a way of finding the unfamiliar in the familiar. Thus, wonder provides a basis for a response to others that accepts their difference. As is well known, Irigaray believes that the most important difference between human beings is the difference between the sexes, a difference that traditional ethics such as utilitarianism or Kant's ethics do not fully recognize or fully understand. In my view, the response of wonder should be extended to other kinds of differences between human beings. Ethnic, cultural, and racial differences are all grounds for wonder.

However, wonder alone cannot provide the basis of the ethics and politics of respect for difference because it introduces the risk of regarding others as exotic or strange. I argue that we also need an ethical basis for respect for commonality or similarity. In *The Passions of the Soul* (1989), Descartes argues that *generosité,* or appropriate self-esteem or respect, is the proper basis for ethics. Generosity involves regarding others as essentially similar to ourselves, in that we share a common basis for action and responsibility—that is, free will. This idea of a respect for what is common between human beings needs to work with the idea of wonder in a complex way. Wonder and generosity are responses that we can cultivate in ourselves and so they have a normative dimension and can become virtues. My project focuses on wonder and generosity in order to develop a positive guide to ethics and to political change. This is a different approach from focusing on the problem of violence that characterizes so much of recent history and continental thought, and also from approaches, for example, neo-Hegelian ones, that take struggle between adversaries to be the basis of ethical and political thinking.

Wonder and generosity are central to ethical responses in ethics and politics. By recognizing the way in which others are similar to us and accepting the ways they are different, we gain a better understanding of the relevance of the passions to both ethics and politics. Given the past prevalent neglect of otherness, it is important to emphasize passions that accept difference, such as wonder. Nevertheless, difference can only be properly appreciated in relation to commonality and similarity. Overlooking the interplay between regarding others as similar to ourselves and recognizing their differences from us has limited our understanding of relationships and how to deal with injustice, oppression, and evil.

The questions the book begins with are philosophical questions concerning our conceptualization of passions and their possible cultivation, after which an account of respect for others and love is developed. On my account, passions are responses to others that have the potential to be cultivated and altered and so to become virtues. Since they have this potential, an ethics of the passions can then be connected to political context. I focus on the way passions have to be understood in their positive contribution to ethical thought and action and to public discussion and political thought more generally. This account of the passions is developed to examine questions concerning the injustice of sexist and racist oppression and equality and difference approaches to these injustices.

In later chapters I make my general account more concrete by examining particular situations such as the treatment of refugees and asylum seekers, responses to acts of radical evil, and official apologies and refusals to apologize for past injustices to African and native North Americans and indigenous Australians. Much of the debate internationally has focused on notions of equality, and is framed in terms such as equal treatment and equal opportunity, rather than thinking about how specific issues and the concerns of oppressed groups such as indigenous people and asylum seekers can be recognized and responded to. One could say that generosity has been focused on to the exclusion of wonder. I draw on examples from the United States, UK, Canada, and Australia concerning the treatment of asylum seekers and past racist practices against indigenous peoples and other groups. I show how these cases are of general significance, both conceptually and practically. I also discuss the ethical issues that emerge from radical evil, exemplified by crimes against humanity such as the Shoah, torture, and abuse.

In an earlier book, *The Analytic Imaginary* (2002), I argued that there has been an overemphasis on similarities between people and a reliance on the power of individual imaginative projection (imagining oneself in the place of others) to decide ethical and other issues on behalf of others. Traditional ethics have held that imagining oneself in the place of others is in itself sufficient to develop ethical sensitivity. While I hold that the development of such empathic capacities can be extremely useful, relying on them alone can mean the overlooking of the specifics of others' situations. I develop this idea further through the notion of wonder as a way of conceptualizing how we can accept the limits of our capacities to imagine ourselves in the places of others.

An understanding of the passions is central to a philosophically satisfactory account of ethics and politics, and I clarify this role by examining the work of significant historical and contemporary attempts to treat the passions as vital to ethics and politics in this way. Descartes and Kant are the two primary historical figures whose work I discuss, and modern and contemporary philosophers who also contribute to this area include Simone de Beauvoir, Hannah Arendt, Luce Irigaray, and Jacques Derrida. I am both influenced by and critical of these thinkers. I find these philosophers thoroughly interconnected in very interesting ways, as will become evident as the book progresses. My approach is to use their work to elaborate the

most significant concepts, to extend their arguments and relate them to
urgent current ethical and political issues.

Descartes's delineation of the nature of wonder and generosity and
Irigaray's elaboration of the role of wonder in thinking about sexual difference provide an excellent starting point for thinking about ethics. Furthermore, Descartes gives a useful account of how we should cultivate virtuous
passions in ourselves and live a virtuous life. Nevertheless, I find a turn to
Immanuel Kant's work on ethics important for a number of reasons. Descartes does not concern himself with the political context in which we
live the good life and his ethics is notoriously conservative. For the kind of
ethics I wish to develop, one that takes into account oppression and aims to
overcome it, Descartes's ethics can only take us so far.

Thus, in later chapters I turn to Kant, and Derrida's reworking of Kant.
Kant develops a political philosophy and takes seriously the question of the
relation between ethics and politics. Kant also has a more detailed moral
psychology than Descartes, particularly as he develops it in the *Metaphysics of Morals* (1996a), with a complex account of respect and love and their
relation to each other. One can see Descartes as anticipating elements of
Kant and Kant, conversely, as elaborating features in Descartes's thought in
his ethics. In contrast to Descartes, Kant gives an account of love as a general
ethical concept, at least in the sense of benevolence or practical love. Kant also
introduces the idea that respect involves a certain "distance" from the other,
which I argue is crucial to understanding both respect and love.

While respect is generally taken to be essential to the ethical life, love is
often thought to be an optional extra or supplement. The question I reflect
on is what role love should play in our ethical life. Philosophers who accept
that love is at least relevant to ethics disagree over the nature of love and
whether love is basic to ethics. Moreover, many philosophical analyses of
love do not take seriously the effect of social and political context on the
experience of love. I examine Irigaray's and Kant's work on love since both
have significant sensitivity to the importance of love in ethics and politics.
Both Kant's discussion of respect as a basis for ethics and Irigaray's work
on love, especially in *An Ethics of Sexual Difference* (1993a) are well known.
However, the surprising similarities between their views have not been
remarked upon. Both Kant and Irigaray stress the relationship between love
and respect, both recognize (to different extents) the importance of self-
love, and both confront the ideal of the unity of lovers and the conception
of love as a means.

However, there are pertinent differences in their respective positions. Kant is interested in love as a duty, whereas Irigaray takes love as a passion to be relevant to ethics. Kant focuses on love as benevolence, whereas Irigaray focuses on the openness of love. Kant is concerned with love in the form of friendship, but Irigaray does not draw a distinction in kind between the love of friendship and eroticism. Furthermore, Irigaray discusses the sort of political conditions needed for genuine respect and love to thrive, which is central to my concerns. This examination of respect and love as concepts enables me to elaborate on my initial discussion of wonder and generosity by linking them with other passions and with politics.

In chapter 3, I discuss the relationship between sexual differences and other differences between human beings and the problematic ways in which people tend to respond to these differences, both in terms of prejudices and in attempts to overcome them. Wonder and generosity can help us understand analyses of the relations between sexism and other forms of oppression and discrimination and how they can be overcome. Recent scholars, most notably Elizabeth Spelman in *Inessential Woman* (1988), have found that feminist texts, including those of Irigaray, have neglected class and race in their stress on sexual and gender differences. One important criticism is that some feminists, through their focus on sexism, have overlooked the specificity of other oppressions such as those of race and class and have obscured black women's and men's experience. It is important not to take for granted that either racism or sexism is more basic or more pervasive than the other. My discussion concentrates on what can be gleaned from analysis of the analogies between racism and sexism themselves. I argue that one can avoid the difficulties faced by these kinds of analogies and articulate an understanding of the relations between race, sex, and class that is sensitive to the differences between them. This leads me to a clarification of the role of wonder and generosity in defeating oppression. Wonder and generosity are connected to issues of racism and sexism because these racist and sexist attitudes involve the assumption of the power to determine when difference and similarity are relevant and so what kind of responses are appropriate. Wonder and generosity need to be combined in flexible ways to counter prevalent forms of oppression.

As a way into these issues, I discuss Irigaray's more recent texts, such as *Between East and West* (2002a) where she approaches the question of cultural differences directly. I also examine those works where she pays attention to the nature of class, for example in "Women on the Market" (1985b), to work toward developing an understanding of the relation between sexual and other differences. Ultimately, I conclude that while one can use Irigaray's work to further reflection on these issues, her own texts do not take the questions very far. Although I find Irigaray's sexual difference constructive, her work needs to be related to conceptions of equality, including making more explicit the way equality is relevant to her conception of sexual difference. She also neglects in some respects the relations between sexist oppression and other forms of oppression. Thinking about the connections between sexist and other kinds of oppression help us to understand their complexity and to see how wonder and generosity can contribute to a new ethics and politics. We need to go beyond Irigaray at the same time as utilizing her understanding of wonder, love, and respect. We need a way of seeing the interaction between equality and difference approaches.

An adequate philosophical conception of these problems is one that takes into account the specificities of particular oppressions while noting that there is a basic similarity of structure to sexist and racist attitudes, which means there are also general structures in experiences of oppression. One common feature of sexist and racist attitudes is that those in power determine the relevance of sex and race. This insight, first discussed by Simone de Beauvoir in *The Second Sex* (1997a) in relation to individuals in personal contexts, is an important key to understanding ethics and political issues. I find Beauvoir's work constructive in seeing how we can develop Irigaray's ideas and give a complex account of the structure and experience of different oppressions, their interaction, and assess strategies for resisting oppression. Beauvoir's analysis demonstrates how one can combine equality and difference approaches to these questions and suggests how it is that wonder and generosity are essential to overcoming forms of oppression. Adequate responses to sexist and racist oppression cannot be based purely on acknowledgment of difference or purely on acknowledgment of commonality. Being forced to choose between denying one's sex or race and affirming it all times is oppressive, as is living according to others' conception of whether one's sex or race is relevant. Both racism and sexism are experienced in different contexts and simultaneously, so it is important to take into account the specificities and overlaps between different forms of oppression, and the inflections of wonder and generosity in different situations.

The argument sketched here spans the first three chapters. How many important issues cross the divide between ethics and politics and how many ethical matters can genuinely be resolved depends on political circumstances. For this reason, it is essential to consider the question of how we should conceive the proper relation between ethics and politics. I examine the work of Kant, Derrida, and Arendt here as I find them to be the most significant and articulate on this question. Kant's well-known view, presented in his political essays, is that there is no genuine conflict between ethics and politics because ethics restricts the range of action in the political arena. Similarly, Derrida argues in his later work, such as *Adieu to Emmanuel Levinas* (1999), that politics must be derived from ethics.

I compare their views on the relation between ethics and politics in order to develop a conception of an ethical politics. Kant believes that ethics is based on what is possible while Derrida sets up impossible, unconditional guides for ethics such as unconditional hospitality, or unconditional forgiveness. Kant focuses on the issues of enforcing that part of ethics that can be compelled, whereas Derrida goes farther than Kant in arguing for a role for ethical virtues in politics. In examining Kant's and Derrida's views I take into account Arendt's worry about the risks of moralism in politics and her view that political life raises its own special concerns. In addition to ethics constraining politics, political conditions should enable an ethical politics or make it more likely that wonder, generosity, and love will thrive.

In chapter 5, we can see how this ethical politics, using Kant's and Derrida's insights, works in relation to a significant contemporary issue. I examine the usefulness of the concepts of cosmopolitanism and hospitality for thinking about the treatment of asylum seekers and refugees who are subject to mandatory, arbitrary, and prolonged detention in a number of countries. It should be noted that hospitality is an act or series of acts, not a passion, even though it involves the openness and warmth of responses and even though hospitability can be considered a virtue. I discuss the concept of hospitality in the context of the ethical and political philosophy of cosmopolitanism. Many recent thinkers have argued that we can use the concept of cosmopolitanism to articulate the ideal relationship between nations, and to help overcome the difficulties of asylum seekers and refugees. Both Kant's view of cosmopolitanism and the right to universal hospitality in "Toward Perpetual Peace" (1996a) and Derrida's deconstruction of the concept of hospitality in *On Cosmopolitanism and Forgiveness* (2001a) and *Of Hospitality* (2000) are important to this debate. I examine the differences between their uses of the concepts, in particular Derrida's distinction between conditional and unconditional hospitality. I also develop Arendt's notion of the "right to have rights," referred to in *The Origins of Totalitarianism* (1976) in order to reframe approaches to asylum seeker and refugee issues. My question here is whether the concept of hospitality is adequate to respond to the difficulties asylum seekers face. We need an open response of wonder to cultural and racial difference, and a respect for asylum seekers' basic rights and rights to have a voice in public affairs.

To this point, the focus of the book is on how wonder and generosity can be understood in order to develop an ethical politics that is both just and virtuous and that can help to overcome sexist and racist oppression. However, some experiences, that is, experiences of evil, seem to raise the question of the adequacy of wonder and generosity and love as ethical responses. Evil raises a difficulty or limit case for the concept of wonder, as evil is a difference that it seems wrong to say we should wonder at in the same way we wonder at sexual and cultural differences. As we learn and become familiar with things we come to understand that some things are worthy of wonder and some are not. There may be differences we see in others that we should regard as horrible, such as when people do not show others even the most basic respect or try to destroy their lives. Nor do the perpetrators wonder at differences in others; rather they exaggerate and penalize imagined differences. Moreover, they do not treat their victims with generosity or respect. Thus, we are unlikely to feel wonder at them or their actions and it is controversial as to whether we should feel generosity or respect for them. Our initial reaction to evil may be wonder in the sense of being surprised, but then we have to make some kind of judgment about it. In chapter 6 I address the question as to how we should respond: with such attitudes as horror or contempt and a refusal to forgive, or with forgiveness.

I briefly revisit Descartes's work in *The Passions of the Soul* (1989) here, to see how he conceived the relation between generosity and evil. His view of generosity as an acceptance of others' capacity for free will implies that respect is as relevant a response to an evil person as it is to a good person. This idea, that respect should be universal even for those who commit evil, is an important influence on contemporary understandings of how we should react to evil. Nevertheless, Descartes appears to have little sense of the depths of possible evil such as those of the twentieth century. One of the most important questions that arises concerning evil within an ethics of wonder, generosity, and love is whether we should forgive evil, especially in the very worst cases. Cases of extreme or radical evil really test our ability to respect and love others. Certain acts and even certain individuals appear unforgivable and provide the "hard cases" for forgiveness, so I concentrate on them in this chapter. I examine the issues of whether we should forgive the unforgivable and on what basis we might be able to do so through the work of Arendt, Jean Améry, Vladimir Jankélévitch, and Derrida.

On Arendt's account of radical evil in *The Origins of Totalitarianism* (1976) as incomprehensible or lacking in the usual human motivations, radical evil raises particular problems for the possibility of forgiveness, since we cannot explain or excuse radical evil in the usual ways. Arendt argues that radical evil transcends human concerns and so it is beyond human forgiveness. Her primary example of radical evil is the murder of millions of people by the Nazis during World War II. I argue that Arendt's view of the unforgivability of radical evil also applies to the banal evil she describes in *Eichmann in Jerusalem* (1994b). Jankélévitch also argues that the most extreme crimes are unforgivable. Améry maintains that we should hold onto our resentments after suffering extreme evil unless there is a profound change in the attitudes of former torturers and their supporters and bystanders. Another example that shows the limits of forgiveness, as well as the way that brutality can undermine the generosity of the victim, is domestic violence. This example raises the question of shame, which may be experienced by both victims of evil and in some cases, the perpetrators themselves. In contrast to these philosophers, Derrida contends in *On Cosmopolitanism and Forgiveness* (2001a) that true or genuine forgiveness is forgiveness of the unforgivable or the forgiveness of radical evil. I interpret Derrida as implicitly endorsing this pure forgiveness, although he does not explicitly argue for that position.

Arendt's and Derrida's positions seem very different since Arendt is concerned with the politics of forgiveness and Derrida is primarily concerned with its logic. Yet what they share is the view that both radical evil and forgiveness are beyond the human. Against this view I argue that, sadly, radical evil is all too human and so is our response, whether it involves forgiveness or not. We need to respond to evil in a way that recognizes the harm that has been done but that also at least allows the possibility of a "loving" response in terms of forgiveness.

The discussion of forgiveness in chapter 6 leads to the issue of how to regard official apologies for past wrongs, particularly in contexts of racist oppression. Many governments have made official apologies for previous governments' unjust and even evil policies and practices, such as slavery. However, some governments have either refused to apologize or resisted apologizing, primarily on the grounds that they are not responsible for the actions taken by previous governments. In their arguments about guilt, responsibility, and forgiveness, Arendt and Derrida seem to lend some credibility to the arguments for the refusal. Arendt's criticisms of the notion of collective guilt in many of her postwar writings seem to undermine the argument for official apologies since such apologies are believed to rely on such collective guilt. The way Derrida unties forgiveness from apology in his deconstruction of forgiveness seems to imply that apologizing is not necessary for forgiveness. Reconciliation as a response to past wrongs is also often criticized from all sides of politics as suggesting—very implausibly—that there was prior unity between the oppressors and the oppressed, wrongdoing by both parties, and a vision of a future impossible harmony.

My aim in chapter 7 is to answer these objections and explain what these apologies mean. Apology and forgiveness are claimed to be symmetrical either because they are both based on respect, as both perfect duties, or as both capable of being public acts. None of these claimed symmetries stand up to close scrutiny. We do, however, need a better understanding of the relation between a public apology and the processes of reconciliation. Official apologies, on my account, do not have to and should not incorporate a corresponding expectation of forgiveness. Furthermore, apologies of this kind are an obligation of generosity or respect, whereas forgiveness on the part of aboriginal Australians or descendents of slaves, for example, is not an obligation. This is because forgiveness is an act of love and cannot be required as a duty in these cases. Although forgiveness cannot be expected in cases of injustice of this kind I still believe it is possible to work toward reconciliation, as long as reconciliation is understood in the right way. I suggest that these basic gestures of generous respect, interconnected with wonder at difference, are the beginning of a different and more constructive politics that comes to include forms of love. Respect is the condition of love and we must make forms of love more likely to flourish. I begin with wonder, as philosophy is said to begin in wonder.

1

Wonder and Generosity

To arrive at the constitution of an ethics of sexual difference, we must at least return to what is for Descartes the first passion: *wonder*.

—Luce Irigaray

As I mentioned in the introduction, the passions of wonder and generosity provide my starting point for thinking about the role of the passions in ethical and political questions. In her book *The Ethics of Sexual Difference* (1993a), Luce Irigaray reads texts in the history of philosophy by Plato, Aristotle, Spinoza, Merleau-Ponty, and Levinas in a productive and sympathetic, although not uncritical, way for what they can contribute to this new ethics that incorporates the passions. For her, the question of sexual difference is the philosophical question of our age (1993a, 5). In a very suggestive reading of René Descartes's *The Passions of the Soul* (1989), she argues that Descartes is right to place wonder as the first of all the passions and that wonder can provide the basis for an ethics of sexual difference. However, unsurprisingly, Descartes himself is not thinking of sexual difference in relation to wonder, although he does discuss sexual difference in the context of desire (1989, 67–69). Furthermore, he believed that a different passion, generosity, by which he means proper self-respect that leads to respect for others, is the true basis for ethics. In this chapter, I discuss this meeting between Irigaray and Descartes and what I see as the implications of the encounter. As concepts, wonder and generosity are enormously fruitful because they provide us with a way to think about how to respond to both difference and similarity and their relation. Through my reading of both Irigaray's and Descartes's texts, I argue that we should respond to other differences, beyond sexual difference, with wonder; that the passions of wonder and generosity need to be brought together to ground an ethics; and that wonder and generosity must be understood as responses or attitudes that we can cultivate in ourselves, rather than simply fleeting passions.

The Passion of Wonder

Irigaray's earliest work, including *Speculum of the Other Woman* (1995a) and *This Sex Which Is Not One* (1985b), provides a complex critique and analysis of the exclusion of the feminine in Western thought. In other works, especially *An Ethics of Sexual Difference* (1993a), she concentrates on articulating a feminist ethics that takes women and men to be specific in their needs, interests, and rights. This is what she means by an ethics of sexual difference. Her critique of the Western philosophical tradition aims to overcome splits between reason and passion, mind and body, and the sensible and the transcendental. In an unexpected turn, Irigaray argues that wonder can be the basis for an ethics of sexual difference: "To arrive at the constitution of an ethics of sexual difference, we must at least return to what is for Descartes the first passion: *wonder*" (1991a, 171).[1] Of course, she believes that other passions such as desire and love are important, as we will see in the following chapter, but wonder plays a distinctive founding role in her thought concerning sexual difference and ethics. Wonder is surprise at the extraordinary, and Irigaray believes that it is the ideal way to regard others, because it is prior to judgment, and thus free of hierarchical relations. Wonder involves recognizing others as different from ourselves. Generosity, in contrast, is based on respect for the self and involves regarding others as essentially similar to ourselves, as we shall see. To understand the force of Irigaray's claim, we need to examine what Descartes means by wonder.

Descartes believes that all passions are based on wonder (in French, *l'admiration*) and five other primary passions—desire, hate, love, sadness, and joy. All other (secondary) passions are composed of some combination of these six. These passions of the soul, or emotions as we tend to call them, are a subset of the full range of passions, which includes perceptions and sensations, or passions of the body (1989, 56, 32–34). Descartes called them passions because he saw them, in general, as reactions to actions of the body (the brain) and distinct from actions or thoughts of the soul. Wonder is the first of all passions, according to Descartes, since:

> When the first encounter with some object surprises us, and we judge it to be new, or very different from what we knew in the past or what we supposed it was going to be, this makes us wonder and be astonished at it. And since this can happen before we know in the least whether this object is suitable to us or not, it seems to me that Wonder is the first of all the passions. It has no opposite, because if the object presented has nothing in it that surprises us, we are not in the least moved by it and we regard it without passion. (Descartes 1989, 52)[2]

According to Descartes, wonder is a sudden surprise of the soul (or mind) which is related only to impressions in the brain, which represents some things as rare. A particular object seems so worthy of attention that we are transfixed by it, without making a judgment about whether it is good or evil. It is only later, when we decide whether it is good and pleasing or bad and painful, that we feel love or hate toward it. So, wonder is the first or primary passion for several reasons. First, wonder is primary because unlike the other passions, it is prior to judgment and comparison—we experience wonder without knowing whether the object is good or evil, whether it is useful or not, or even what kind of a thing it is. Second, wonder is the first of all passions as it has no opposite.[3] Third, wonder is fundamental in being united to most other passions since they involve surprise—otherwise, we would not be moved by the object (Descartes 1989, 52–53, 103). For example, indignation involves wonder because we are surprised by things not being done in the way we believe they ought to be done.

Wonder may appear to be a rather intellectual or "cool" passion, a view Descartes seems to accept since he says that it affects only the brain, rather than the heart and the blood (1989, 57–58). Nevertheless, he argues that wonder still has great power to move us due to the surprise it involves.[4] Descartes contends that wonder is a useful passion for it leads us to learn and remember things through the strengthening force of surprise. We do not necessarily remember unfamiliar things that appear again, unless the original idea is reinforced by wonder (or through greater understanding). Wonder is a response to the rare and extraordinary; things appear to be rare and extraordinary if they are unfamiliar or unexpected (1989, 59). Only wonder makes us notice those things that are rare; other passions make us notice things that seem good or evil to us. Once we have recognized the rarity of the object, we can go on to investigate and understand its nature

(1989, 59, 61). This investigation will usually dispel the wonder, as we learn, for example, how something works or why it happens.

This description of wonder raises the question: If we have made no judgment about the object, a defining feature of wonder, how can we recognize it as rare or extraordinary? In the Fourth Meditation, Descartes argues that a judgment occurs when the will either affirms or denies some perception of the understanding or intellect (1984, 40–41). All the passions dispose the soul to will whatever actions the passions have prepared the body for (1989, 40). For example, the feeling of fear inclines us to will the body to run away from what we fear. Judgments also influence the soul to will particular actions and ideally, our passions will reinforce accurate judgments. My view of how we can understand responding to an object with wonder before we have formed a judgment about the object is that objects worthy of wonder stand out against the undifferentiated background of those everyday and familiar things that we can easily categorize. Against this background, we can perceive that something is different or unfamiliar without making a judgment or assenting to anything particular about it.

From Descartes's standpoint, it is valuable to be born with some capacity for wonder, which disposes us to learn more, and we should cultivate an ideal or appropriate propensity to wonder (1989, 60–61). On the one hand, given that wonder is thus connected with intelligence and curiosity, those who have little capacity to wonder are unlikely to be knowledgeable.[5] On the other hand, he warns against having too much wonder, claiming that an excess of wonder and wondering about things that are beneath our consideration is always detrimental. Such an extreme of wonder Descartes calls astonishment (L'estonnement) (1989, 58). Wondering at everything could be said to be akin to wondering at nothing because there is no distinction between what is worthy of wonder and what is not. Descartes believes that those who lack confidence in their own judgment will wonder to excess, for they wonder at things of no importance and cannot pass beyond wonder to the stage of reflection. This excess of wonder can develop into a habit if we do not correct it and gain a more extensive knowledge of things.

Furthermore, wondering too much can stall or distort the use of our reason since there is no discrimination between what is rare and what is commonplace. Descartes argues that it is easy to counteract the danger of wondering to excess by gaining more knowledge and thinking about things that seem most rare and strange (1989, 61). Wonder usually decreases over time, because the more we encounter rare things about which we wonder, the more we become used to them and understand them and find that the things that we encounter later are common and familiar. A clear example is small children, who find so much of what they experience evocative of wonder and for whom this surprise gradually diminishes as they grow older and more educated. Descartes suggests, as I will discuss farther on in the chapter, that the most worthy objects of lasting wonder are God and that which, in us, is most similar to God's qualities, our free will.

Wonder's relation to education and philosophy is quite clear from Descartes's account, but understanding how wonder can form the basis of an ethics of sexual difference requires attention to Irigaray's appropriation of the concept of wonder. Irigaray finds a connection between Descartes's account of the passions and psychoanalysis, saying, "Situating the passions at the junction of the physical and the psychological, he [Descartes] constructs a theory of the *ego's* affects which is close to Freud's theory of the drives" (1993a, 80). However, Descartes is not thinking about sexual difference in relation to wonder, just as Freud does not think of wonder, "the passion that Freud forgot?" (1993a, 80).[6] Irigaray is thinking about both in order to situate an ethics of sexual difference.

Wonder and the Ethics of Sexual Difference

The idea of an ethics of *sexual difference* is distinctive, because traditional ethical theories have rarely theorized the ethical relevance of the existence of two sexes. Previous ethics have either assimilated women to men, seen women only in relation to men, or claimed that there is one neutral subject, the human being, for whom ethical principles will always be the same. For example, utilitarianism concerns the greatest happiness of the greatest number of human beings; ethical rules or principles, as in Kant's ethics, are supposed to apply to everyone, regardless of sex; and John Rawls's theory of justice sets sex and gender aside as irrelevant to moral deliberation (1975, 537). Of course, sexual difference *has* been recognized in misogynist ways in the history of philosophy, as in Aristotle's politics (1984, 1259b1–60a31).[7] However, this approach to sexual difference is not what Irigaray has in mind. She also criticizes Emmanuel Levinas for his representation of the feminine as "the reverse side of man's aspiration towards the light, as its negative" (1991a, 179).[8] For her, Levinas does not recognize the specificity of femininity but only the feminine as it is viewed by men.

In contrast to these approaches, what Irigaray is proposing is a *non-hierarchical* recognition of sexual difference, where each sex is thought of as autonomous and self-defined, so that women are not understood through a male paradigm of humanity (1993a, 5–19). If the idea that women and men are different is taken seriously, then it is clear there must be more than one set of interests, values, and perspectives in culture. Feminists have pointed out that there are ethical and political issues of particular concern to women, such as reproductive freedom, maternity leave, child care and work, and rape, for example. Women may reason differently about ethical problems—for instance, Carol Gilligan argues that women tend to rely on an ethic of care rather than justice in trying to resolve moral dilemmas (1993). Most importantly, it cannot be taken for granted that men can represent women's interests or make decisions on women's behalf. Irigaray's idea of an ethics based on wonder challenges the view that ethical subjects of different sexes can be substituted for each other.

On Irigaray's account of ethics, wonder provides the model for the way in which the sexes should respond to each other. Her conception is that the other, male or female, should surprise us, and appear very different from what we expected (1993a, 74). We should not assume that we know everything about the other. As Irigaray puts it, "Wonder might allow them [the sexes] to retain an autonomy based on their difference, and give them a space of freedom or attraction, a possibility of separation or alliance" (1993, 13).[9] The advantage of wonder is that it goes beyond what is or is not considered suitable for us. If the other "suited us" completely in the sense of being enough like us not to surprise, we would have reduced the other to ourselves, as it would be to understand and respond to them only on our own terms. In regarding the other with wonder, their existence resists assimilation or reduction to sameness or self and we are able to accept differences in them. Irigaray describes the response of wonder: "In order for it to affect us, it is necessary and sufficient for it to surprise, to be new, *not yet assimilated or disassimilated as known*" (1993a, 75). Something is "disassimilated as known" if it is not absorbed or incorporated into the subject. What sets the object of wonder apart is that it cannot be circumscribed or defined (1993a, 81).

Irigaray argues that then wonder awakens our passion, our attraction to what is not known, and curiosity toward what we have not encountered or made ours (1993a, 75). Irigaray's understanding of the nature of wonder is consonant with that of other philosophers, such as R. W. Hepburn, who in his well-known essay on wonder, puts the point aptly: "I give myself to wonder in ways not too fancifully analogous to how I give myself in a friendship, entrusting myself to another in an open and therefore vulnerable way" (1984, 134). Wonder is a way of responding directly to the other, rather than imposing or projecting our own views or self-understanding on them. With the other passions, the subject's judgment affirms an object as having a particular nature—lovable, hateful, or beautiful. But wonder is a direct response to the object.[10] Irigaray says that wonder involves a realization that the self is not alone. Furthermore, she thinks that this realization that one is not the only (type of) being in the world involves a loss of (perceived) power, because the existence and independence of the other has to be recognized.[11] The experience of wonder implies acknowledgment that the other cannot be possessed (1993a, 75).

Irigaray remarks on the connection between wonder and knowledge and creativity, by stating that wonder is the passion that inaugurates love and art and thought (1993a, 82). Similarly, Amélie Oksenberg Rorty notes in her discussion of the importance of the body in Descartes's thought that "[i]t is the emotions, and particularly the emotion of wonder, that energize science and give it directions" (1992, 386). The passions in general provide us with some sense of what is important to us, and wonder does this without evaluating the object. On Descartes's account, we will not know whether something is really important until we have investigated it. However, Irigaray claims that in wonder, the subject welcomes as desirable what it does not know or what is foreign to it and so sexual difference can be understood in these terms and an ethics can be developed (1993a, 79). The idea of desirability being connected to wonder in this way seems to be a significant shift from Descartes's view, as he believes that wonder does not entail a particular judgment about whether the object is desirable or not (1989, 52). Irigaray takes him to be saying that "difference attracts" (1993a, 79) and that wonder involves a kind of attraction and curiosity toward what we do not fully understand. What Descartes says is that in wonder the object seems worthy of consideration and attention because of its rarity, which does not necessarily imply desirability, though it implies some impetus toward further understanding (1989, 59). Whether this is sufficient for Irigaray's ethics is a question that we need to look into further.

In Irigaray's view, the relation between those who differ, especially sexually, has to be reworked through the notion of wonder (1993a, 12, 74). She argues that sexual difference is ontological, and so fundamental to ordering society.[12] Her claims about wonder have to be understood as normative rather than descriptive, as it cannot be said that women and men do respond to each other with wonder in general. Women and men currently respond to each other in many different ways, some of which could be considered to be closer to this wondering attitude and others much farther from it. I take seriously Descartes's view that wonder does not have a precise opposite, due to its basic nonjudgmental nature.

However, not having a direct opposite means that wonder can have a range of contrary passions and attitudes, some that we might see as more positive than others. These contraries could include complete indifference or nonrecognition of the extraordinariness of the other. Both sexes could adopt this indifference to the other sex by separating themselves from or avoiding members of it. Other extremes could include the contempt, hatred, or fear evidenced in the worst kind of misogyny. This approach regards differences with scorn or horror and tries to harm the other. More benign attitudes can include awe or adoration that both sexes may feel for the other, yet without wonder this perspective would impose an idea of what the other is. For example, one may take oneself as a model and project that onto the other sex or invent a fantasy of sexual stereotypes and treat the other in those terms. Romantic love as it is depicted in countless Hollywood films is an everyday case in point. What makes each of these disparate passions contrary to wonder is that they do not respond to the other as they are; rather, they project or impose the passion on them, whether it be awestruck worship or scorn. As I will go on to discuss in this and the following chapter, a failure to respect the other only compounds the failure of wonder. I take it that Irigaray is articulating an account of a response to the other for both sexes that overcomes the range of problems in each of these attitudes.

The culture that we live in is one that consists in experiences of a range of these relations of passions between men and women, as well as some relations that may come close to regarding each other with wonder, although that is difficult in a culture where women are oppressed. In *I love to you*, Irigaray suggests that such encounters are possible, if only ephemerally, even now, as she describes her discussion of mixed-sex politics with Italian politician Renzo Imbeni and a crowd of both their supporters. She writes that "a miracle took place" in reference to the discussion as a whole and in relation to him. For her, the experience was one where they did not give up their identities and as an encounter it is one characterized "by the need for the recognition of another who will never be mine" (1996, 7–11). While one might question her interpretation of this particular event, one can see how it works as a kind of image of wondering and respectful relations.

Thus, I see Irigaray's recommendation as that women and men *should* respond to each other with wonder. At this stage, it is not quite clear what it means to regard the other sex with wonder, particularly on the basis of

Descartes's account of wonder. We are supposed to wonder at something rare to us, yet how can the other sex be rare? Irigaray could mean that in each encounter with the other sex we should regard them with wonder; or that we should always have the response of wonder; or that we should approach special relationships with wonder; or that when we think about sexual difference, we should think about it with wonder, in terms of something extraordinary, for sexual difference is extraordinary. Most plausibly, Irigaray's recommendation must refer to each encounter with the other as taking place in wonder. And this seems to be Irigaray's view: "Thus man and woman, woman and man are always meeting as though for the first time because they cannot be substituted one for the other" (1993a, 12–13). Consequently, the attitude of wonder permeates every encounter. Wonder, on this account, does not mean simply curiosity; rather, it leads to an appreciation of the other's qualities. Hepburn argues that there is an appreciative-contemplative aspect to wonder (1984, 134–35), and in this sense, wonder recognizes and affirms the value of the other.

As Irigaray argues, sexual difference is not quantitative (1993a, 76), even though it is traditionally measured by such standards, notoriously in the case of Freud's notion of penis envy (1961, 243–58), which Irigaray has criticized to great effect in *Speculum of the Other Woman* (1985a) and elsewhere. Nor is sexual difference a question of better or worse, as both adoration and contempt toward the other sex are inappropriate (1993a, 13). Wonder is the passion that can express this relation since wonder does not involve judgment and comparison. Then one can accept that the other has different experiences, and different ethical considerations may be relevant. Since wonder takes the object as it is, the other is prior in a way that they are not in the case of other passions.[13] We should encounter the other with wonder and recognize their uniqueness as not just a difference from ourselves, and accept their independence from us. Then the other will strike us as new, unfamiliar, and original like the stars, a great artwork, or the universe.[14] The other is accepted in their irreducible alterity, in terms of their priority for the subject. Irigaray argues that in wonder, there is an acceptance and respect of both sexual specificities (1993a, 74). Wonder seems to be ideal to express the kind of openness to otherness that so holds Irigaray's interest. However, the concept of wonder alone may not be rich enough to incorporate or generate the notion of respect and acceptance of others, which also concerns Irigaray, and this is an issue I will return to farther on in the chapter. For now, I will leave this concern aside to focus on the importance of wonder.

According to Irigaray, any meeting between the sexes always results in effects or products, although this fecundity has not been understood or developed (1993a, 14). Men and women must always leave a remainder not reducible to their relation, which explains the attractions of the encounter. The products of the couple are not only children, although one of Irigaray's important points is that this particular form of creativity should be valued in a way it traditionally has not been (1993a, 11, 14). The nature of these new products will only emerge as the ethics of sexual difference becomes a reality, though they would clearly include artistic and theoretical products. The two sexes create their own ideals, which are different. She claims that "man and woman is the most mysterious and creative couple" (1995a, 112). Her view makes for a fascinating comparison with Freud's view of the mother-son relation as the most satisfying one (1964, 133) and Plato's view of male homosexuals as forming the most creative couples (1999, 208e–209d).

Irigaray believes that the ethics of sexual difference can generate a different relation between subjects, the subject and the world, and between the subject and God (1993a, 8). An acceptance of sexual difference requires a revolution in all spheres of existence: not just ethics, but also aesthetics, language, and our understanding of history and religion. In more recent work, Irigaray argues that such an ethics of sexual difference can only exist in a context where sexual difference is recognized in law: "We have to rethink the whole of the law in such a way that it is just to two genres different in their needs, their desires and their properties" (1991a, 201). She believes that specific rights for women and men must be defined and enshrined in law—how she sees this is as a change in "the mode of relationship between one and the other, between man and woman on the civil and affective plane" (1995, 111). While these are clearly important considerations, and I believe that Irigaray is right to connect personal ethics with legal and political institutions, a discussion of the relation between law and ethics would take me into the concerns of the following chapters. More central here is the question of whether the ethics based on wonder should apply only to sexual difference.

Wonder and Other Differences

The focus on sexual difference in Irigaray's view of ethics raises the question of whether her view can and should be extended to other kinds of differences between human beings. This point has tended to be a controversial one among commentators. On the positive side, Tina Chanter, in *The Ethics of Eros,* claims that Irigaray's attempt to think about difference in a nonhierarchical way "extends to a rethinking of all our relations, not only with other people, but with nature" (1995, 143). Furthermore, Mary Bloodsworth argues that since Irigaray is concerned with rethinking dualisms, her work can be used to disrupt racial dualism (1999, 77). Still, Irigaray's view is a little more complicated than that, insofar as she sees sexual difference as fundamental. For example, she says that sexism is "the most unconscious form of racism" (1993b, 120). Racism can be understood here to mean discrimination or prejudice in general. She also says that "sexual difference is the most radical difference and the one most necessary to the life and culture of the human species" (1992, 3). One criticism that has been raised against Irigaray is that there is a bias toward heterosexuality in her view, particularly in her claim that the encounter between man and woman is the most productive of encounters. Moreover, she has become more emphatic on this point, stating in an interview that homosexuality is an earlier stage of development than heterosexuality (1998, 19). Such a stance raises problems for the formulation of an ethics. On this issue, Elizabeth Grosz notes that gay and lesbian theorists are right to be concerned about this aspect of her views (1994a, 348), which institute a new hierarchy that is simply a reversal of the Platonic view.[15] It is odd because such a reversal parallels the complete rejection of heterosexuality Irigaray warns against in *This Sex Which Is Not One* (1985b, 33). These comments suggest that Irigaray accepts a hierarchy in types of differences, an anomaly in a supposedly nonhierarchical ethics.

However, in her book *Intersecting Voices,* Iris Marion Young argues that Irigaray's view of wonder "can easily be extended . . . to any structured social difference, whether of sex, class, race, or religion" (1997, 45).[16] Young develops this idea by maintaining that people should regard each other as "irreversible," or not mirrors of each other. Instead, we should accept the differences of the other, adopt a stance of "moral humility," acknowledge that our relations with others are asymmetrically reciprocal, and not attempt to espouse their standpoint and speak on their behalf (1997, 49). I support Young's stance that wonder, as openness to difference, can and should be extended beyond the realm of sexual difference.

A more adequate feminist ethics is one that takes into account a range of ethically relevant differences. A range of differences between human beings appear worthy of wonder, such as ethnic and cultural differences, generational differences, and differences in sexuality. The response of wonder cannot be confined to the relation between the sexes but should be extended to all our relations with others. Although sexual difference is extremely important, it should not overshadow and obscure other differences. A range of different groups have issues that are of special concern to them, a concern that others should recognize. For example, land rights affect indigenous groups in ways they do not affect other people, and disabled people are aware of needs that people who are not disabled cannot be. These kinds of differences should be taken into account when formulating an ethics and when reasoning about specific issues, and members of these groups should be recognized as having distinct points of view that only they can articulate. I discuss in more detail how we can conceptualize these differences in ethical and political contexts in chapter 3, and explore questions regarding the special concerns of asylum seekers and refugees, victims of extreme wrongdoing, and indigenous peoples in chapters 5, 6, and 7 respectively.

Relations across and within these difference will also have their own remainder or products. Irigaray's insight that the oppression of women has obscured women's creative potential and that this potential will only be realized when women are recognized as subjects holds true for other oppressed groups as well.[17] In relation to the couple, the different world Irigaray envisages will ensure that homosexual couples, for example, will also be fruitful in ways not yet experienced.

One of the central assumptions of many ethical theories is a belief in the power of the individual to imagine themselves in the place of others and to make judgments on their behalf on that basis.[18] Although it is important to develop our capacity to respond sympathetically to the experience of others through the imagination, limits to this ability ought to be recognized and understood. Where the experience of others is different to our own, we may not be able to imagine what that experience feels like, or we may be apt to project our own experience onto theirs. Extending the notion of wonder beyond sexual difference involves an acceptance of the difference of others and the limits on our ability to understand their experience. Wonder is an ideal notion to encapsulate this acceptance, yet wonder too has its limitations.

The Limits of Wonder

Irigaray's focus on wonder concerns relations between the sexes, and even when generalized to other differences, the focus remains on relations with others, rather than self-concern. Having a sense of one's own value is extremely important, particularly for women in a sexist society and for oppressed peoples generally. Robin S. Dillon provides an illuminating discussion of the ways in which women's basal self-respect is often damaged (1997, 226–49).[19] Irigaray is very much aware of this problem and concerned with self-respect and self-love. On her account, we cannot understand ourselves as simply a reflection of other's views of us. Such an approach would reintroduce the notion of "mirroring" or symmetry, of which Young is rightly so critical, into our ethical relations. While the mirroring Young is concerned with is the mirroring that occurs when we project our own self-understanding onto others, the mirroring involved in assimilating others' views of us can also be harmful. A consideration of Descartes's special sense of generosity in tandem with Irigaray's concern with these questions will provide a starting point for thinking about respect and love and in general.

Irigaray's account of wonder considered alone, while extremely appealing, seems to stretch the concept of wonder beyond its scope in order to include the concepts needed to develop such an ethics. Wonder, in my view, cannot both be prior to judgment *and* involve an attraction to and respect for the other. I believe the idea that our response to others must involve wonder is very important, but that alone it cannot yield respect, acceptance of autonomy, and so on. Irigaray notes in an interview that the relation between men and women she has in mind is one of reciprocal respect, autonomy, and also reciprocal affection (1995a, 111), which indicates that wonder has to be combined with other appropriate passions and responses to bring about the kind of changes envisaged. In the following chapter, I will outline the role of respect and love in developing an ethics of the passions. Here, my focus is on the relation between wonder and generosity.

Young has pointed out some of the problems with Irigaray's account of wonder, saying:

> This concept of wonder is dangerous. It would not be difficult to use it to imagine the other person as exotic. One can interpret wonder as a kind of distant awe before the Other that turns their transcendence into a human inscrutability. Or wonder can become a kind of prurient curiosity. I can recognize my ignorance about the other person's experience and perspective and adopt a probing, investigative mode toward her. Both stances convert the openness of wonder into a dominative desire to know and master the other person. (1997, 56)

The risk or danger is wonder leading to other more inappropriate attitudes through curiosity or through excessive reverence. Yet one could argue that a wonder of this kind is not a proper or true wonder, which is open to the difference of other. Part of the difficulty here is trying to speak of wonder in isolation and also not being clear about the object of wonder. Wonder as initially understood by Descartes leads to curiosity and scientific investigation of the world. Applying wonder in this sense to human relations could lead to both sexes treating the other like objects that need to be probed and manipulated. What both this and the attitude of "distant awe" are lacking is an openness to change in the other, an openness that needs to be articulated.

Young's solution is that we need a respectful stance of wonder, yet as I will argue, the danger implies that wonder must be *combined* with respect. We cannot expect that a single passion uncoupled with other important passions can constitute an appropriate response to the other. Irigaray herself is conscious of this issue. In another essay in *An Ethics of Sexual Difference,* "Love of Same, Love of Other," she notes that "[t]he Other can only exist if it can draw on the well of sameness for its matter. . . . If this were not so, that Other would be so other that we could in no way conceive it" (1993a, 97–98). Irigaray comments in relation to the issue of love between women "*no love of other without love of same*" (1993a, 104). She also indicates a need for common goals: "These two subjects [the sexes] share the common goal of preserving the human species and developing its culture, while granting respect to the differences" (1995b, 12). This problem can be fruitfully overcome by taking a closer look at Descartes's passions and his concept of generosity and bringing it into dialogue with Irigaray's reading of wonder.

The ethics Irigaray suggests can only be developed if we clarify how we can move beyond wonder, to esteem and respect, rather than arrogance or contempt, or reverential awe. Once we pass beyond surprise, something must prevent us from moving to an inappropriate attitude toward the strangeness of the other. Irigaray understands wonder as comprising a set of appropriate responses to difference. However, while wonder is a very rich concept, it needs to be linked to other passions and responses to provide a basis for respect for difference. She suggests that herself; my argument here is that we can deepen the reading of Irigaray through examining Descartes's approach to ethics. On Descartes's conception, wonder is a more neutral term, and this very neutrality is what commends wonder to us as an initial response to difference. Irigaray is not alone in envisaging a greater role for wonder in our ethical lives. Hepburn argues that a range of moral attitudes have an affinity to wonder, such as respect, compassion, gentleness, and humility, because they are only a "short step" away from wonder and follow from its other-regarding aspect (1984, 145–46). Yet we need an account of how these correlates can be developed from wonder in order to make a genuine ethics possible.

Generosity and Ethics

Descartes's account of generosity, and of how the passions should be cultivated and restrained provides some means for understanding how an ethics linked to the passions could be developed.[20] He argues that "all the good and evil of this life depend on them [the passions] alone" (1989, 134). Due to the passions, Descartes believes, we desire things that are useful for us and are repelled by what is harmful (1989, 51–52). The mind has a practical concern with self-preservation, and the passions can help us to avoid pain and to pursue pleasure. In giving an account of the usefulness of the passions, Descartes attempts to explain how we move beyond wonder and live ethically.

The passions that follow wonder, according to Descartes, are either esteem or disdain and scorn. They are united with wonder depending on whether it is the greatness or the meanness of an object that we wonder at. Once an object is esteemed or disdained for its worth or lack of worth, wonder is no longer pure in the sense of being nonjudgmental, and becomes part of the realm of opposites, as do most passions. In Descartes's view, esteem and disdain or scorn are species of wonder—when we do not wonder at the greatness or meanness of an object, we do not make more or less of it than reason tells us—so we then esteem or disdain it without passion. Once comparisons are made between ourselves and others, ideally magnanimity or *generosité* will follow, or otherwise wonder could be followed by pride or vicious humility (1989, 102–103).[21] We either regard the other as an equal, which is appropriate, or we conceive of ourselves as superior or inferior to others, both, for Descartes (and for Irigaray), inappropriate responses.

The key to leading a good life, for Descartes, comes through cultivating the passion of *generosité,* or generosity, which has a very special meaning in his work, quite different from its current use in English.[22] Generosity is a species of wonder combined with love and joy, which involves having proper pride or rightful self-regard (1989, 103, 107). Generosity is esteem of ourselves, an appropriate judgment about our worth that should be developed as a habit. It has the following features: (1) knowing that nothing is really ours except the freedom to control our willing, and that we should only be praised and blamed for using that freedom well or badly; and (2) feeling within ourselves a strong constant resolution to use our free will well—to always have the will to carry out what we think is the best course of action (1989, 103, 121–22). For Descartes, this is to pursue virtue in a perfect manner. What we esteem in ourselves is a virtuous will. My view is that Descartes's conception of esteem here is close to what we today call respect and that becomes apparent in his account.[23]

Generosity is the key to all the virtues and a way of overcoming the disruptions of the passions, giving us control over them. It is similar to "nobility" or Aristotelian "great-souledness" or "pride," although it is more egalitarian, because Aristotle believes that there are very large differences between what people are worth, and only a great person should think they are great (1995, 1123b1–15).[24] On Descartes's understanding, people of generosity are "easily convinced" that others also have the same capacity to exercise free will for good or evil ends. If we have generosity, he argues, we will not prefer ourselves to others because others can also use their free will as we do (1989, 105). This is what he calls virtuous humility. Descartes accepts that it is possible to lose the basis for self-regard through laziness or cowardice, and people may have an improper pride due to such things as wealth and title, or even for no reason at all (1989, 105–106). Nevertheless, we should esteem ourselves and others for the possession of free will and the resolve to use it well.

This self-esteem is thought by Descartes to make it possible to have the right kind of regard for others: if we value ourselves appropriately, then we will respond to others appropriately (1989, 104). Descartes is rather insightful on this point. Robin Dillon argues that for the person lacking in basic self-respect, the "all-consuming project is to find some value for herself; other things, other people, matter only in relation to her worthlessness. But to be blessed with secure basal self-respect is to be able [to] move through life oblivious to issues of self-worth—for these issues have already been resolved—to be free to attend to the independent value of other people and things" (1997, 242). We can understand the esteem Descartes refers to as a basic form of respect, although he reserves the term *respect* or *veneration* for our response to other free beings that may do us either good or evil (1989, 109). In generosity, we recognize the worth of others, so that respect, veneration, and magnanimity follow wonder. In Descartes's view, having rightful self-esteem protects us from dependence on what others think of us, and prevents jealousy and envy, as what we think worth pursuing depends only on ourselves (1989, 105). Here, he is a little sanguine in believing that our sense of ourselves can and should be independent of others' views of us.

Furthermore, Descartes argues, generosity strengthens a healthier form of regard for others, and prevents hatred, because we regard them as equally capable of a virtuous will (1989, 104). The lack of virtue that the virtue of generosity and its virtuous humility can be contrasted with are improper pride on the one hand and vicious humility or servility on the other (1989, 105–107). The worst kind of pride is that which is baseless, and he notes that we are often led into this kind of pride by flatterers who praise us for worthless or even blameworthy actions. The person proud in this way focuses on worldly goods rather than their own virtue, and tends to be driven by anger, hatred, envy, and jealousy due to the scarcity of those goods. Although Descartes is not considering contexts of oppression where a severe lack of those goods could be an appropriate case for anger, his point about the way this kind of pride can distort passions is well taken. In contrast, unvirtuous humility or servility, he suggests, is usually due to a lack of resoluteness, weak will, and dependence on others for our survival and well-being. Such a person is servile to those they are afraid of or hope to gain something from, but arrogant to people they do not see as useful. Here Descartes neglects our important dependence on others, yet describes a very recognizable sycophantic character type.

In a more positive vein, Descartes is optimistic that everyone can attain the virtuous will no matter how weak they are, although ignorance is the greatest obstacle to doing that. Generous or noble-minded people find doing good to others important and disdain their own interests: "They are always perfectly courteous, affable, and of service to everyone" and "entirely masters of their Passions" (1989, 105). He sees this control of the passions emerging from our focus on whether we have acted rightly rather than on the things the unjustly proud is concerned with. If we have generosity or proper self-esteem, we respect other people appropriately, and have no remorse, he argues, for we know that we have done our best. Moreover, we have little cowardice or fear—we are self-assured due to our confidence in our own virtue (1989, 191). These points explain why Descartes believes generosity is the key to the virtuous life. One problem that arises for Descartes is whether acceptance of our will and a resolution to carry out the most ethical course of action is sufficient for a virtuous life. Some people may be in a better position to judge what the best alternative is, say, by having a better education, or by having more experience of the world. As Descartes expresses this point, "There are some people who possess far sharper intellectual vision than others" (1985, 191).[25] He believes that everyone can act virtuously, although the best way for some to act virtuously is to take cues about what is moral from those possessed of a sharper intellectual vision (1989, 49). Nevertheless, on his account, generosity is the key virtue even when we are being guided by others.

Despite coming from such a different perspective, Irigaray also suggests that self-respect is central to developing ethical relations with others. This aspect of her account can be seen if we go beyond her discussion of wonder and see that in the context of her project. She does not use the precise language of generosity as proper self-esteem or respect, but she does discuss autonomy, the development of a distinct identity, and human dignity (1996, 50).The development of self-respect is the corollary of not being appropriated by the other and having one's specificity acknowledged (for example, 1996, 48, 62). Her account of the history of male theorizing about women is one of women's assimilation to a distorted masculine experience, where women cannot articulate a distinct subjectivity. A wondering recognition by the other would be one aspect of human relations that would facilitate development of self-respect.The transformation in our cultural and political acknowledgment of women that Irigaray argues for would also be of great benefit.

The difference between Descartes and Irigaray here is that Descartes conceptualizes self-respect as something that we will easily feel and will easily extend to others whereas Irigaray sees self-respect, especially for women, as a self-relation we will have to struggle to attain. As she writes, "I search for myself, as if I had been assimilated into maleness. I ought to reconstitute myself on the basis of a disassimilation" (1993a, 9). One can see this as a woman finding respect for herself as different from men. Yet another perspective that makes more sense of Irigaray here is that one needs to respect what it is about oneself that makes one special—the possibility of change and choice that we share with others. In wonder the autonomy of the other is recognized and so each, both men and women, can have self-respect.

The other difference from Descartes here is that Irigaray is conscious of how we cannot unilaterally develop self-respect but self-respect is related to how others regard us and the social, political, and cultural context in which we live. Her view recognizes that self-respect is to a great extent reliant on the respect of others. Her approach to the question of self-respect, respect for the other, and love, is to consider the conditions that could bring that about, not just how the individual might by themselves develop self-respect. For Irigaray, self-respect comes both from the self and through relations with others. Her return to historical women figures can be understood as developing a connection that enables women to experience themselves as part of history and so as having a place from which to relate to others, or self-respect (1993a, 1993b). Self-respect is dependent on that recognition that there (at least) two sexes, that women's identity is not subsumed into men's. She notes that what men and women have in common is both the capacity "*To suffer and to be active. . . .* Becoming more open because of the freedom of each, male and female" (1993a, 93). Here, Irigaray stresses both freedom and necessity, with freedom for women being dependent on a conception of the feminine distinct from that of the masculine.

There must also be possibilities of a sense of self that is not simply relational, "as keepers of home and children, mothers, in the name of the property, the laws, the rights, and obligations of the other's State" (1993a, 109). This is not to deny the importance of those relations, but, again, to conceive women as not reducible to those relations.

Similarly, Irigaray's later concern with overcoming exploitation and advancing women's civil identities as "human persons" (1996, 21) is linked to developing women's self-respect. The love for self and other she describes, which I will discuss in the following chapter, is linked to going beyond self-effacement, self-sacrifice, erasure, and changing the dynamics of the couple and the mother-daughter relationship. I will argue that respect in general has a special relationship to love that is relevant to both self and other relations. Irigaray's work also delineates limits to esteem for the self that might prevent respect for the other, such as the "solipsistic, egocentric, and potentially imperialistic subject" (1996, 47). The self should have respect for self and respect for others, recognizing their existence, their needs, their desires and interests. She states quite explicitly that the truth of the self involves "fidelity to the being I am, being given to me by nature and which I must endorse, respect and cultivate as one half of human identity" (1996, 107). The respect for the self needs to be established and cannot be taken for granted. In recent work, Irigaray stresses the "shared world" that is created through respect for the other and their difference. But she also notes that this must be done "without forgetting to come back to oneself for a gathering of one's self" (2008a, 110), a way of referring to reflection on who we are as autonomous beings. Irigaray emphasizes cultivating our affects, especially the need for "mutual respect" and self-affection, a question I will discuss in the following chapter (2008a, 134–36).

In formulating what is central to generosity and respect for others, Descartes's reliance on the notion of free will, particularly understood as a capacity that we all possess equally, may give some reason for hesitation in accepting generosity as a useful passion. However, although this understanding of free will is central to his account, and I accept that free will is important, I do not believe that one must be committed to this specific characterization of the basis of similarity between human beings to find generosity central to developing an ethics of the passions. One might take the shared human condition as a starting point, for example, or one could include a rich notion of the human condition with a stress on freedom. Yet Irigaray's appropriation of Descartes may not be so far away from him in spirit in her stress on autonomy and the openness of wonder to difference and change in the other. For instance, she writes, "It is . . . incorrect to say that my will could be identical, equal or similar to that of everyone else. It must be distinguishable in order to be appropriate to myself and positive in relation to others while respecting their own identity" (1996, 52).[26] Here, Irigaray focuses on the way in which our differences will mean that we make different choices, choices that in general we should value. She also centers on freedom in recent work, contextualizing that freedom in relation to the freedom of others and nonhuman living nature: "Freedom must, at every moment, limit its expansion in order to respect other existing beings and, even more, to find ways of forming with them a world always in becoming where it is possible for each human or non-human living being to exist—or ex-ist" (2008a, xx). Respecting ourselves and others for our capacity for freedom—generosity—is another way of being open to difference. In the final section of this chapter, I consider the relation between wonder and generosity.

Wonder and Generosity Meet

Generosity appears to be the converse of wonder, in the sense that generosity implies regarding others as like us in some basic sense, in that the differences between people are recognized as an expression of our similar freedom. That recognition may be difficult in the case of distant others, when people find it hard to extend their self-respect in that way because they seem to be utterly different. In contrast, wonder involves regarding others as very different from ourselves in what they wish for and how they experience the world, in how they express that freedom. My argument here is that generosity and wonder are both needed in the development of a passional ethics of respect for difference. Generosity and wonder balance each other. First, generosity can both provide the basis for respect for others and the kind of limit wonder needs to prevent it becoming an investigative wonder. The notion of generosity provides a way to conceptualize the fundamental similarity between human beings in relation to their myriad differences, within the context of the passions.

Therefore, we should accept the importance of wonder, yet also realize that it cannot replace a respect for what we share with others. Similarities and commonalities form the background against which we can perceive differences, just as familiarity forms the background against which we can respond to objects of wonder. This contrast between familiarity and unfamiliarity can exist either between objects or within an object of wonder. As Young writes: "People who are different in such social positionings are not so totally other that they can see no similarities and overlaps in their lives, and they often stand in multivalent relations with one another" (1997, 45). We share a common humanity with all and we share many more specific characteristics with other groups. The idea of a wonder that lasts, suggested by Descartes and Irigaray, is one that we can still respond to someone who has become familiar to us with. This point is put very well by Dorottya Kaposi in the conclusion of her essay on *Admiration* in Descartes: "The *admiration* which can become habit as a disposition of the soul does not concern an unknown object which can become known, but an object which intrinsically has an extraordinary character" (2010, 118). That is how wonder can play a role in ethics at all.

Based on Descartes's warning that we should not wonder at everything, a note of caution can be applied to our attitude toward the other. This caution applies to Irigaray's views on sexual difference in general, and also to attempts to expand the ethics of wonder beyond sexual difference. As Young observes, we should beware of overemphasizing difference because it can lead to regarding the other as exotic or alien. Generosity can provide the limit that prevents wonder from falling over into exoticizing, crass curiosity, or contempt since generosity is an acceptance of a fundamental sense in which we are all of worth, regardless of the differences that may exist between us. Generosity involves a proper judgment of both self and other that forms the background against which we respond to others with wonder.[27] It also acknowledges that people are different because they have the freedom to become different, not because they are interesting objects to study and manipulate.

Conversely, wonder can prevent the presumption that others will think and act like oneself and desire the same kinds of things as oneself, such that one could make decisions and judgments on their behalf. It helps us to recognize the limitations on our own power and on our imaginations. Wonder allows for openness to difference and change in the other. The two passions of wonder and generosity have to work together in a complex way to provide the basis of an ethics of respect for difference.

Finally, it is important to consider how passions such as wonder and generosity can become more reliable responses or attitudes, because if they were only momentary or spontaneous reactions, they could hardly form the basis for an ethics. One way of describing them as attitudes is the idea that when we reflect on questions concerning ethical relations, it should be in terms of wonder and generosity. Another, closer to the spirit of both Descartes and Irigaray, is that we can cultivate wonder so that it becomes our response to others whenever we encounter them.

Descartes makes an important distinction between a habit or inclination and a passion (1989, 108–109). Virtuous habits bring together our bodily and mental being, as emotional responses are associated with appropriate objects. True generosity is a habit that disposes us to have certain types of thoughts, and also a virtue because it is based on and generates wise moral judgments and it is in this form that it can serve as the basis for an ethical life. We can cultivate generosity so that we have proper self-respect and respect for others.

Similarly, this distinction between a passion and a virtuous habit suggests how Irigaray's ideas about wonder could be extended by understanding how to cultivate wonder as a virtue. Immanuel Kant's distinction between astonishment, which decreases with the familiarity of the object, and wonder, which is stable, an "astonishment that does not cease when the novelty is lost," helps us to see how wonder could be continuous or long-standing in that sense (2000, 5: 272). The French term *admiration* expresses this sense well.[28] Descartes thought that astonishment is an excess of wonder, which prevents us finding out more about the object of wonder, since we are "frozen" with astonishment. However, Descartes characterizes generosity as continuous, and notes that when we consider the marvels of free will being present in such limited subjects, "they always give off a new Wonder" (1989, 108). This point deepens the initial idea of wonder as simply surprise at something rare, and has more of a sense of how wonder is an accepting, nonjudgmental response to that which we have not fully understood—in other words, the sense Irigaray was so insightful to focus on in Descartes's work, the sense that she calls "a wonder that lasts," which we would need to develop (1993a, 80).[29] In order to cultivate wonder as an attitude, we need to cultivate generosity as well, so that people respond to the differences between each other on the basis of respect and do not immediately move to fear, dread, contempt, awe, or any of the other contrary passions I described. As I noted above, Irigaray makes clear that passions have to be cultivated and developed, and her project is partly to outline the conditions under which that is possible, a focus in the following chapter.

A question suggested by my discussion of wonder and generosity is whether passions in general can provide a basis for an ethics. Some would say that ethics should be based on principles, or obligations, or consequences, and that any system based on passion is too private, and individual. Certainly, how one can deal with ethical conflict, how one can treat others justly, and how one should organize society cannot simply follow from an acceptance of the value of wonder.[30] Nevertheless, combined with generosity, it should be a central feature or basis for an ethics in conjunction with consideration of these other important questions. Generosity gives us the basis for a general respect, and wonder gives us the basis for an acceptance of the limitations of ethical generalizations. I will consider these questions of the nature of ethics and the relation between ethics and politics in chapter 4.

These two views about the kind of passions we should cultivate relate directly to questions about imagination in ethics. Responding to others in terms of generosity is to imagine others as like ourselves. Responding in terms of wonder is to accept the limits of our imagination and accept difference. In my view, we must understand the passions and our relation to others through both of these ways. Ethical thinkers such as Kantians, utilitarians, and contractarians still tend to focus on the way we project our lives onto others and finding others like ourselves rather than recognizing their difference, sexual, cultural, or otherwise. This consideration of difference, and the focus on the passions can enrich a number of ways of thinking about ethics. The view I develop through Descartes and Irigaray is closer to virtue ethics yet is connected to principles and actions, as will unfold through successive chapters. Irigaray's suggestion that we regard others with wonder can be implemented as an important counterpart to conventional ethical views. In wonder we do not project ourselves onto the object, but appreciate the object in its otherness. Generosity and wonder combined also speaks to the issue of the two sides of ethical relations: attitudes to others and attitudes to ourselves. Wonder is a response to others that accepts their differences and can be reflected back in an appreciation of oneself. Generosity involves a basic esteem or respect for oneself that is also extended to others.

We need both generosity and wonder: we need to regard others as both like ourselves and different; and we need self-respect as well as acceptance and appreciation of others. The passion of wonder should be cultivated and extended to differences beyond sexual difference, as I will explain in more detail in chapter 3. The range of differences between human beings should be recognized and accepted. While wonder and generosity are essential to ethics, by themselves they do not provide a comprehensive ethics. Judgments have to be combined with passions, and we need to understand the role of other passions, not just wonder and generosity. Furthermore, the ethics of wonder or generosity needs to be linked with considerations of the political context in which we live and specific actions, as I do in later chapters. Nevertheless, by combining the two different ways that we can respond— by acknowledging the way in which others are like us and acknowledging the way in which they are different, we can get a more complex understanding of the passions, ethics, and how we can be open to new experiences. Against the background of an enormous neglect of otherness and difference, it is important to emphasize attitudes such as wonder. At the same time, we must not lose sight of the way in which difference can only be appreciated in the context of recognition of similarity and commonality. In the next chapter, I will develop this ethics of the passions further by elucidating the relationship between respect and love for others.

2

Love and Respect

Respect is without doubt what is primary, because without it no true
love can occur, even though one can harbor great respect for a person
without love.

—Immanuel Kant, *Religion and Rational Theology*

D escartes's delineation of the nature of wonder and generosity and Irigaray's elaboration of the role of wonder in ethics provide an excellent
starting point for thinking about ethics. Furthermore, Descartes gives a very
useful account of how we should cultivate virtuous passions in ourselves.
Nevertheless, I find a turn to Immanuel Kant's work on ethics at this stage
important for a number of reasons. First, as becomes evident in Descartes's
sketch of generosity, the overall context of his ethics is a conformist one.
While *The Passions of the Soul* (1989) makes a major addition to the provisional ethics in the *Discourse on the Method* (1985), he does not alter their
conservative character.[1] In the *Discourse,* his concern is to remain resolute in
his actions, and to carry on life as happily as he can. To that end, he sketched
four maxims:

1. To obey the laws and customs of my country, adhering to religion, and having moderate opinions. This is best pursued by
   following the opinions of those with good judgment, based on
   their actions, and being prepared to change my own judgments.
2. To be as firm and resolute in my actions as I could be, and to
   follow even doubtful opinions, once my mind was made up. In
   action, it is best to follow the most probable opinions, because

there is no time for delay. If one acts this way, one will be delivered from penitence and remorse since it is possible to accept that one acted rightly.[2]

3. To try always to conquer myself rather than fortune, and to alter desires rather than try to change the world, since only our thoughts are entirely within our power. [Descartes gives the examples, "We shall not desire to be healthy when ill or free when imprisoned, any more than we now desire to have bodies of a material as indestructible as diamond or wings to fly like birds" (1985, 124) to explain what he means by conquering oneself rather than fortune. He notes that this course requires long exercise and meditation, and training of the mind.]

4. To occupy my life in advancing my reason through the method of doubt, and discovering the truth as much as possible. [Descartes notes that he is not saying anything about the occupations of others.[3] For him, our will tends to follow our judgments, so if we can judge well, we are likely to act in a virtuous way]. (1985, 122–25)

While Descartes's maxims give an excellent prescription for avoiding conflict with other individuals and the state, they do not incorporate a basis for criticism of existing political arrangements or strategies of resistance. The *Discourse* explicitly rejects social reform, stating that it is difficult to make even minor changes to public institutions: "Moreover, any imperfections they may possess . . . have doubtless been much smoothed over by custom" (1985, 117–18). In later correspondence with Princess Elizabeth, Descartes replaced the idea of obeying the laws and customs of his country with using his mind to discover what he should do, but his idea is still "to make himself content by himself without any external assistance" (1991, 257). Thus, for the kind of ethics I wish to develop, one that takes into account oppression and aims to overcome it, Descartes's ethics can only take us so far.

The second reason I turn to Kant is because his moral psychology develops in much more detail an account of love and the relationship between self-respect, respect for others, and love. For Descartes, love is "when a thing is represented to us as good from our point of view, that is, as being suitable for us" (1989, 53). Furthermore, he believes that only a father's love is "pure" and does not involve a desire for possession (1989, 63). As in the case of wonder, I wish to explore the possibility of love as a passion that goes beyond "what is suitable for us" partly through the work of Irigaray.

In contrast to Descartes, Kant articulates an account of love as a general ethical concept, at least in the sense of benevolence. He also introduces the idea that respect involves a certain "distance" from the other, which I argue is crucial to understanding both respect and love. One can see Descartes as anticipating elements of Kant's ethics in making free will the basis of our respect for others and Kant, conversely, as elaborating features in Descartes's thought in his ethics such as these concepts of freedom and of generosity as including self-respect and respect for others.[4]

In the previous chapter, I argued that wonder and generosity should play a fundamental role in an ethics that respects difference and similarity. I also noted that by themselves they were insufficient to develop an ethics. Generosity, or proper self-respect, provides the basis for our respect for similarity in others. Once we have recognized the other's difference, how should we regard them? In this chapter, I will develop an ethics of wonder and generosity in more detail by discussing Kant and Irigaray's work on the relation between respect and love. When we move beyond wonder to a more positive relation to the other, we are likely to feel respect or love for them. However, while respect is generally taken to be essential to the ethical life, love is often thought to be an optional extra, particular in relation to politics. What role should love play in ethical life? Those philosophers who believe that love is relevant to ethics are divided over its nature and how fundamental an ethical concept it is. Furthermore, many philosophical discussions of love, such as Descartes's, neglect the social and political context in which love is experienced.

In this chapter, I examine the work of Irigaray and Kant, who both show considerable insight into the role of love in ethics and politics.[5] Kant's discussion of respect for others as a basis for ethics is well known, as is Irigaray's treatment of love. There are a number of important similarities between their views. Both philosophers emphasize the importance of the relationship between love and respect for others and both accept (to different degrees) the importance of love of the self. Both are against the tradition that stresses the unity of love and the view that love is merely a means to other ends. Both philosophers are concerned with ethics in the very general sense of how we should live, as we have already seen in Irigaray's case.

We can also discern significant contrasts between them. Kant emphasizes love for others as a duty, whereas Irigaray focuses on love as a passion. For Kant, love involves charity and concern; for Irigaray, the openness of love is central. Kant argues that we have an ethical duty to friendship, not romantic love, whereas Irigaray argues that love and eroticism are not different kinds of love, contending that "no more dissociation of love and eroticism" is necessary for genuine love to flourish (1993a, 67). Irigaray also introduces the political to ethics, as she did in the case of wonder and generosity, by arguing that we need to have the right conditions for genuine love and respect to flourish and that love relations have political implications. Kant, while not concerned with sexual relations, concedes that there are important questions concerning the application of the metaphysics of morals and they could include issues about respect for particular individuals and groups, or what he calls "forms of respect." In chapter 4, I consider Kant's view of the kinds of restraints that ethics must have on politics. He does not consider this question in relation to love as he holds that love is a matter of virtue, rather than that of right or politics.

The pairing of Irigaray and Kant is probably more surprising that that of Irigaray and Descartes in the previous chapter, since she explicitly discusses Descartes's work. My reasons for doing so here include the interesting point that Kant is a major philosopher whom Irigaray has not really "romanced."[6] This space between the two allows an interpretation that Irigaray has not anticipated in detail. Second, by defining love and respect for others as ethical, Kant makes explicit what often remains implicit in Irigaray's work, and enables me to highlight the distinctiveness of her account. Third, Irigaray brings to the discussion a concern with love as a passion and with the specific relation between love and respect and politics lacking in Kant, although Kant has a developed political philosophy. My primary interest in the comparison in this chapter is the question of whether love is essential to an ethical life, rather than merely a supplement, or as Kant says, an indispensable supplement (1996c, 8: 338). This developed account of love and respect for others will be important in articulating the practical questions of later chapters.

Defining Love and Respect

Many ethical theories take respect, in some sense, to be the fundamental ethical concept. In Descartes's ethics, as we have seen, generosity, or proper self-respect and respect for others, is the key to living the good life (1989, 105). Kant follows Descartes in thinking that respect—self-respect and respect for others—is central to ethics and one can see Kant's work on respect as a development of Descartes's work on generosity. However, traditionally love as an ethical concept is neglected or only certain kinds of love are believed to be ethical. For example, Descartes takes the love between a parent and child to be the purest ideal of love (1989, 63) and the only love that is altruistic.[7] Kant takes friendship to be the ideal but in general believes that emotions such as love are too unreliable and ephemeral to be important to ethics. Irigaray's views stand in stark contrast to this tradition, as we shall see, for she takes love as a passion seriously, and she takes erotic love to be ethical.

Kant's work on ethics clarifies what is at stake in taking love as a passion to be fundamental to ethics because he distinguishes between love as duty and as passion, or feeling as he calls it, and argues that only love as a duty is ethically significant. Thus, a case for an ethics of love must be able to respond to his concerns. His most extensive discussion of love and respect is in *The Metaphysics of Morals* (1996a) in part two, concerning the doctrine of virtue. I will primarily focus on this text since it represents both his more considered and most promising views. Kant begins his discussion of ethical duties to others by distinguishing between two sorts of duties: one sort of duty, love, demands the gratitude of others, and the other, respect, does not since it is a duty that is owed (1996a, 6: 448).[8] The term *love* (*Liebe*) is not used here to refer to the feeling of pleasure or delight in, for example, the perfection of others (aesthetic love) or to the desire to benefit another (pathological love) but to the maxim of benevolence (practical love) that brings beneficence (1996a, 6: 449). Pathological love is distinct from practical love since it is benefiting another because one wants to rather than from obligation (1996a, 27: 417). Practical love is supposed to be independent of feelings and desires. Kant argues that love in the sense of feeling or delight in others cannot be a duty since "others cannot put one under obligation to have feelings" (1996a, 6:449).[9] Also, he says, "Love is a matter of *feeling,* not of willing, and I cannot love because I *will* to, still less because I *ought* to (I cannot be constrained to love); so a *duty to love* is an absurdity" (1996a, 6: 401). In contrast, he believes we can be under an obligation to act in particular ways toward others, so we can have a duty of practical love. This practical love involves benevolence toward other human beings.

According to Kant, respect (*Achtung*) is "the *maxim* of limiting our self-esteem by the dignity of humanity in another person" and so is also practical, not a matter of comparing our value with that of others (1996a, 6: 449). Esteem for others is the feeling of inferiority we have when we compare our worth to that of others, whereas respect involves the recognition of others' dignity as ends in themselves. This distinction is very similar to the distinction Descartes makes between generosity, which relates to us as human beings in virtue of our capacity for free will, and pride, which involves notions of comparison with others (1989, 105–106).[10] For Kant, the dignity of humanity is founded on our autonomy, which enables us to determine the laws of morality (1996a, 4: 436). Since humanity itself is an end, we are under obligations to recognize the dignity of every human being.

Respect is a narrow duty, love a wide duty. For Kant, a narrow duty is one that limits our actions or obligates us to refrain from doing something rather than one that commands us to positively do something (1996a, 6: 419), The duty of respect toward others is supposed to be only a negative one of not putting oneself above others, analogous to the duty of right not to impinge on other people's property. Respect for one's neighbor simply involves the maxim not to treat another person as a mere means to my ends. One can see this duty as not violating the other's self-respect. We should never deny respect, in this very basic sense, even to a vicious person.

In contrast, the duty of love for one's neighbor is broad or positive because it is the duty to make others' ends my own (if they are not immoral). "Making others' ends one's own" seems to mean that we should help others to bring about their ends and keep their ends in view. Doing this will involve both beneficence and sympathy.[11] Kant says that through the duty of love I put others under an obligation because I deserve something from them, such as gratitude. Together beneficence, gratitude, and sympathy comprise the duties of love for him.

Kant characterizes the relationship between love and respect in naturalistic terms. For him, the laws of duty are analogous to the laws of nature; in the moral world, as in the physical world, the forces of "*attraction* and *repulsion* bind together rational beings (on earth)" (1996a, 6: 449). Kant describes these forces in this way: "The principle of **mutual love** admonishes them constantly to *come closer* to one another; that of the **respect** they owe one another, to keep themselves *at a distance* from one another; and should one of these great forces fail, 'then nothingness (immorality), with gaping throat, would drink up the whole kingdom of (moral) beings like a drop of water'" (1996a, 6: 449).[12] In this image the forces of love and respect are like natural forces, as all ethics reflects the purpose of nature.

Considering what it would mean for one of these forces to fail underscores and illustrates the centrality of both forces to ethical life. Either ethical anarchy or the governance of the world by evil would constitute a failure of both love and respect. A failure of love only would mean we treated each other with respect but failed to exhibit sympathy, benevolence, and gratitude to each other; and a failure of respect alone would mean that we were generous and kind to others, but failed to allow them the proper distance we should: both situations would be utterly unethical, on Kant's account. Love as a duty, at least, is essential to ethics, more than a supplement to the ethical life.

The image appears to overemphasize the conflict between love and respect in representing love as coming closer and respect as drawing away.[13] What Kant has in mind is that respect enjoins us not to become too intimate with people either by telling them too much about ourselves or by expecting them to reveal too much of themselves to us. He claims that love, by contrast, is a force that moves us to become more intimate with people, partly through shared confidences.

However, repulsion does not seem like the best way to describe respect, as Marcia Baron notes (1997, 29). We are not repulsed or repelled by others, but our respect for them means that we will treat them with consideration by both doing some things and not doing others. As in the case of love, where we find the object loveable, in respect we find the object worthy of respect. Hate, rather than respect, is a form of repulsion.[14] We can be respectful by being close and disrespectful by being distant. The idea of respect as only a negative duty and a drawing away from others limits our understanding of respect, which may involve coming closer to people and should be conceptualized as a positive demand.[15] While being disrespectful may sometimes involve an excess of familiarity, treating people coldly, distantly, and not wanting to know more about them may also be forms of disrespect. Equally, acting with respect involves taking an interest in the lives and problems of people we are close to. Not treating others as a mere means to my ends involves acknowledging they have their own ends (without necessarily making them my own). I see showing interest in others as a positive form of respect as it is a coming closer to others, involves actively doing something rather than refraining from doing something, and is not the same thing as love, as it is also distinct from arrogance and contempt. Conversely, as we shall see, Irigaray demonstrates to us how a certain kind of distance is essential to love.

Since Irigaray argues that we need to learn how to love ourselves, a brief look at Kant's view on the nature of self-love in *The Metaphysics of Morals* is instructive. Although Kant believes that you do not have a duty to love yourself, as that happens automatically or naturally, the universality of the duty permits you to be benevolent to yourself if you are benevolent to everyone else (1996a, 6: 451).[16] The maxim of benevolence, "Love your neighbor as yourself," is a duty of all human beings to others, whether or not one finds them worthy of love. Saying we should love our neighbors as ourselves seems inconsistent because on the one hand we are closest to ourselves and on the other hand the universality of love seems to allow no difference in degrees of love. Kant avoids this possible inconsistency by making a distinction between benevolence in wishes, which is just taking delight in the well-being of others, not contributing to it, and active, practical benevolence (beneficence), that is, "making the well being and happiness of others my *end*" (1996a, 6: 452). We can be equally benevolent to everyone in our wishes, but be partial in acting depending on the different objects of love, without disturbing the maxim's universality. Kant notes that "one human being is closer to me than another and in benevolence I am closest to myself" (1996a, 6: 451).

In *The Critique of Practical Reason,* Kant identifies self-love with making the seeking of one's own happiness (or prudence) into a principle and so sees self-love as directly opposed to morality (1996a, 5: 35–36). This sense of self-love is closer to the contemporary terms *self-interest* and *selfishness.* He also distinguishes between self-love understood as benevolence toward oneself and self-conceit, which is being satisfied with oneself (1996a, 5: 73). Self-love in the sense of benevolence is rational if it is constrained by the moral law. This restriction of the moral law both reduces self-conceit and increases our respect for the law. Kant does not change his mind concerning the immorality of self-love understood as selfishness or self-conceit, and self-love is always limited by our respect and love for others.

However, what is surprising about Kant's view in *The Metaphysics of Morals* is that he is taking for granted and accepting, from an ethical point of view, that we love ourselves and are allowed to be benevolent to ourselves. Proper beneficence to ourselves is very like an Aristotelian ethical mean, where we should look after ourselves but not to the point of "effeminacy" or indulgence, on the one hand, or depriving oneself of enjoyment due to avarice or excessive discipline, on the other hand (1996a, 6: 452). Thus, Kant accords self-love a significant place in ethics without believing that there is any difficulty in relation to it, whereas Irigaray sees lack of self-love, especially for women, as an ethical problem that needs to be overcome.

Beneficence to others will involve helping others in need depending on one's means to do so. While when expressed as "loving your neighbor as yourself," practical love sounds like an impossible ideal, Kant's notion of benevolence or love for all humanity is quite minimalist. As he says, the love for all human beings is great in extent, but small in degree—all he means is that we should not be indifferent to them (1996a, 6: 451). The question that comes to me is whether even a minimal degree of love for all is sometimes too much. Indifference could be, on occasion, an appropriate ethical attitude. I argue that it can be arrogant and presumptuous of us to bestow our benevolence on people we have never met. It could be offensive not to be indifferent to others, either because they would resent our interest or since we can know and understand nothing of their lives. It is not paradoxical to suggest that the most ethical way we could relate to some others would be to be utterly indifferent to them. Yet Kant's formulation makes this universal love so slight that he is probably only suggesting that if something terrible happened to a stranger and there was nothing we could do, we should still care that it happened. Baron notes that it is puzzling that only some violations of duties of love are vices. Indifference is a lack of virtue rather than a vice, for Kant (1997, 31). The vices that are breaches of the duty of love are vices of hatred: envy, ingratitude, and malice (1996a, 6: 458). She believes that a lack of love or utter indifference to others is a vice. However, a more nuanced account than both Kant's and Baron's is needed, where indifference is accepted as appropriate in some circumstances but deplorable in others, for example, where the person concerned is close to us. I focus on this point to demonstrate that a concern with an ethics of love does not entail the view that we must love everyone. In that sense love differs from respect for others.

Clearly, Kant sees *practical* love, or love as duty, as essential to the ethical life. He considers the possibility that benevolence could be considered morally indifferent, provided everyone was conscientious about duties of right. However, he says, benevolence, that "moral adornment," is needed "to present the world as a beautiful moral whole in its full perfection" (1996a, 6: 458). Kant's views about love changed over his writing life, becoming more open to love's importance for ethics. In the *Groundwork,* Kant dismisses the role that love (as an inclination) might play in ethics, saying, "Love as an inclination cannot be commanded" (1996a, 4: 399). Wood says this dismissal is due to Kant seeing empirical love's "selection of its objects [as] an indirect expression of self-conceit" (1999, 272). In other words, this condemnation of love is based on a view of love as flattering to us since we love those who look up to us, in addition to Kant's idea that inclinations are not subject to the will. In *The Metaphysics of Morals,* he notes that cultivating our natural sympathetic feeling is an indirect duty, so for example, we should not avoid places where we may be affected by the suffering of others (1996a, 6: 457), although he also says, "I cannot love because I *will* to" (1996a, 6: 401). Later, he notes the importance of love as inclination in general. For example, in

"The End of All things," published in 1794, Kant wrote that when we consider whether people *will* live ethically rather than how they *should* live, love is an "indispensable" supplement to human imperfection—without love, people will have little incentive to act well (1996c, 8: 337–38).[17] He argues that "what one does not do with liking he does in such a niggardly fashion—also probably with sophistical evasions from the command of duty—that the latter as an incentive, without the contribution of the former, is not very much to be counted on" (1996c, 8: 338). This point is an important admission from Kant that genuinely emotional love is essential for the realization of ethics and brings his views closer in spirit to those of Irigaray. However, it is on the question of understanding and creating the political and social conditions under which an ethics can thrive and the centrality of love to that project that Irigaray's work is particularly important.

Irigaray on Love of Self and Others

Irigaray's concerns demonstrate fascinating connections and disconnections with those of Kant, and her distinctive views enable a reworking of his account, which takes seriously the reality of sexual oppression and has the potential to help us respond to other forms of oppression.[18] On the one hand, I demonstrate, in addition to respect for the self I discussed in the previous chapter, that respect for others plays an important role in her conception of ethics. This role tends to be neglected in accounts of her work, and is a role I argue must be central to any ethics. On the other hand, Irigaray conceives love as a passion as well as a duty and considers the significance of love for both ethics and politics. As we saw in chapter 1, Irigaray examines wonder in Descartes's work; she also considers texts in the history of philosophy concerning joy and love, in Spinoza, Hegel, Freud, and Levinas, with her most extensive and developed discussions focusing on love. She does not explicitly discuss Kant's work on love and respect; however, her thought is clearly informed by the tradition that Kant belongs to.

Irigaray is concerned with love as a passion, not only a duty, or rather, she does not distinguish affect and reason in the way that Kant does. She describes her idea of love in *democracy begins between two*: "This is not, then, an affection which seduces the other into renouncing the intellect and the spirit, falling back into unmediated sensibility, but instead a determination to lead the lived experience of the sensibility towards coexisting with the other, thanks to a measure of respect, rationality, and thought" (2000b, 117).

I interpret her understanding of love as one that incorporates both feeling and inclination (as "affection") and reason (as "the intellect"). She also notes that respect is something I feel for the other (2000b, 112). Where Kant insists that love, like other feelings, cannot be commanded, Irigaray argues that love can be cultivated or is "governable" (1996, 129). The difference, however, is one of emphasis. Kant acknowledges that natural sympathy can be cultivated and that a habit of acting well toward others can lead to good wishes toward them.[19] Irigaray sees love as a passion but for her that does not mean love is unreliable or irrational, a "mere" inclination. Since love, like other passions, involves understanding, it can be cultivated or educated. She writes, "We should not renounce love but educate it so that we can be faithful, even in passion, to our highest ideal" (2000b, 108). By "our ideal" she means the ideal of recognition of sexual difference in citizenship and the new culture she envisages.

While, as Kant says, we cannot *will* love in the sense of deciding that we will love someone and then expecting a sudden change in our feelings, we can bring about the conditions for loving relations, we can educate people to be loving, and we can nurture loving feelings in ourselves. Again, we cannot have a duty to feel love for particular people, but we can have a duty to be loving and an obligation to cultivate love in our lives. As she maintains in the case of wonder, Irigaray says that love is not comparative; love is neither based on the model of smaller and larger, nor of part and whole (1993a, 61). As we have seen, wonder is a nonjudgmental response to the difference of the other, and love for others is based on wonder as well as respect.

Self-love can also be understood as based on wonder if we see that an accepting, nonjudgmental response to difference is a relation that we can have to ourselves. Just as we cannot fully understand others, we cannot fully understand ourselves. Comparison can have no role in a nonhierarchical ethics of the passions. Love in this sense is aesthetic, in Kant's terms, or is delight in another, rather than a desire or obligation to do good for another. Love of this kind allows the other to be and appreciates them in their uniqueness. According to Irigaray, there must be a profound change in social and political conditions for love of self for men and women, love between men and women, and love between women to be genuine. Such a change is one aspect of creating an ethics of love. Love cannot take place within a hierarchical division of society between women and men where women have no specificity or identity.

Whereas Kant believes that we love ourselves as a matter of course, Irigaray believes it is important to love the self—indeed it is essential in order to genuinely love others—and that is something we need to learn to do. Kant is focused on love as a duty but in my view, Irigaray's concerns with love as affection toward oneself is close enough to the Kantian idea of benevolence to make the comparison worthwhile. Both are forms of care for the self, quite distinct from the self-respect of generosity. She defines self-love as "that which can be given-returned as affection for self *through the other here and now*" (1993a, 61),[20] For Irigaray, love of self poses particular problems because of the complications in how subject and object relate. According to her, in self-love there is a play between active and passive as we affect ourselves (1993a, 60). By this point she means that we are both the actors or agents of love and the ones who experience that love in this case.

According to Irigaray, male and female versions of love of self differ, and self-love for women in current circumstances is difficult and complex. A whole history separates women from self-love. As an example of the problem in traditional thinking about women and self-love, Irigaray cites Freud's view that women have to give up love of self and mother to love men (1993a, 66). Instead, she argues, women must not depend on "man's return" or the love of a man for self-love, but be able to be autonomous or independent. Love of self involves a two that is not really a two—as self and I are both separate and not separate (1993a, 62). Love of self, for the female, requires a change from the situation in which women are tradition-ally placed. Irigaray argues that women need love for the child they once were, a shared enveloping of mother and child, and in addition to that mutual love, openness that allows access to difference.[21] This love of self is necessary in order to achieve genuine love of the other.

Irigaray writes that "[w]omen can no longer love or desire the other man if they cannot love themselves" (1993a, 66). Masochism is one extreme example of the dangers of the lack of self-love. Another more prosaic exam-ple is the need to learn to forgive ourselves; I discuss the question of for-giveness in detail in chapter 6. Irigaray focuses on the dangers for women of trying to found their own self-love through the love of a man. Her view is that women and men need to establish self-love as a basis for the openness of love to others; without that basis, love involves "a loss of self or of the other in the bottomlessness of an abyss" (1993a, 69). Her work makes a signifi-cant contribution to ethical understanding of love by demonstrating how lack of self-love can be a problem and that we do not "unavoidably" love ourselves, as Kant believes. Instead, self-love has to be learned or practiced.[22] Irigaray's account of the positive contribution of self-love to love of others also contrasts with Kant's claim that self-love needs to be limited by our respect and love for others. Clearly, she does not see self-love as self-interest or selfishness. More importantly, Irigaray does not conceptualize self-love as something that needs to be limited, but as a rich source that contributes to our love for others. Such self-love enables the openness essential to love, and means that love of the other is not designed to fill a void or provide all of life's meaning. In *Sharing the World,* a text Irigaray has translated herself, she uses the term *self-affection,* a concept that includes self-respect and is linked to wonder. She writes, "Self-affection is the real dwelling to which we must always return with a view to faithfulness to ourselves and an ability to welcome the other as different" (2008a, 136). I take the reference to welcoming the other as different as concerning wonder.

Although much of Irigaray's focus is on love between men and women, she also considers that love between women requires ethical and political transformation. As we saw in the previous chapter, Irigaray contends that love between women is "one of the most essential places for an ethics of the passions: *no love of other without love of same*" (1993a, 104). She also concedes that the Other can exist only if it can draw on a well of sameness for its matter—otherwise we could not conceive the other (1993a, 97). The danger of love between women, she points out, is the confusion of identities, the lack of respect for or perception of differences. This is a state of abandonment or dereliction where women do not love themselves or each other (1993a, 67, 126). One can see a similarity here with Kant's view that we should not disclose everything to the other, as we shall see. Irigaray observes that women have been and still tend to be instrumental in their own oppression, by making comparisons or fusing identities with other women. In such cases, she says, it is not another woman who is loved and respected but the place or role she occupies (1993a, 104). So, respect for others is essential to loving them, for Irigaray. Equally, love of the same is based on acceptance of sexual difference (1993a, 99). One could say that love of self and the same and love of the Other are co-conditions for each other.

Irigaray's main point concerning love for others, against many traditional views, is that it takes two to love, that we must not consider love to involve the formation of a unity. Descartes, for instance, says that in love there is a "consent by which we consider ourselves from the present as joined with what we love, in such a way that we imagine a whole of which we think ourselves to be only one part and the thing loved another" (1989, 62).[23] Irigaray's point may seem obvious, but she stresses it to emphasize the contrast between her view and the view that lovers become one or must be similar in their tastes, for example, to each other. For love to exist between two people, both must be independent beings who are not subsumed in love. Love must accept difference and specificity in the other.

In *I love to you: Sketch of a Possible Felicity in History* (1996), Irigaray states explicitly that love allows for respect, and "attracts while maintaining distance" (1996, 150).[24] She diagnoses one of women's problems as being too close both to each other and to men. She says, "What women need most are mediations and means of distancing. Immediacy is their traditional task—associated with a purely abstract duty—but it puts them back under the spiritual authority of men" (1996, 5). The self-respect that is needed is one aspect of preventing excessive closeness. Respect for the other is also necessary. In describing the ideal relation of love, Irigaray uses the grammatical form "I love to you" (*j'aime à toi*) rather than "I love you" (*je t'aime*) (1996, 109–13). This change of form is intended to express the distance or gap between the lover and the beloved and the idea that it is being offered to the other rather than assumed. Implicit in Irigaray's account, in her noting of the need for mediation and the dangers of fusion of identities, is the view that love must be based on respect to be genuine. Otherwise, the lover can even justify a suffocating and restrictive relationship on the grounds of the strength of their love, whereas a basis of respect will always limit such claims.[25] On her account, the self has to be autonomous or independent enough to respond to the other and approachable enough for passion to be possible. Another way of seeing this point is that there must be a basis of generosity—self-respect and respect for the other—and then the potential for the openness of love exists.

Richard White, focusing primarily on *Elemental Passions* (1992), describes Irigaray's view in this way: "Love and proper autonomy are not mutually exclusive, and [that] love as a principle of individual development and growth actually requires something like the projected sovereignty of each individual as the condition for its fulfillment" (1999, 47). In Irigaray we can see a counter to Kant's view in *The Metaphysics of Morals* that love always involves a coming close that is dangerous and likely to violate respect for the other because genuine love is not opposed to respect and thus also involves an acceptance of limits for her. Her view is an improvement on Kant's idea that love and respect are in conflict since it gives a richer picture of respect and shows how love and friendship are possible ideals rather than impossible ones. Interestingly, in "The End of All Things," Kant appears to share this view, writing: "Respect is without doubt what is primary, because without it no true love can occur, even though one can harbor great respect for a person without love" (1996c, 8: 337). So, respect is a condition for love, but love is not a condition for respect.

Irigaray says that two have to know how to separate and come back together (1993a, 71). One can read her as saying that in accepting the limits of our knowledge of the other we are distancing ourselves in respect. A limit to knowledge is involved in not presuming to understand everything about the other and also in respecting the privacy of the other in intimate relationships. Her view allows for openness and vulnerability, but takes the point that love does not involve the complete assimilation or appropriation of the other.[26] Irigaray's discussion of wonder explains how such openness might be possible—wonder is the basis of all our ethical attitudes, naturally including love. Wonder provides a kind of framework in which all our relations to others, including love, should be experienced. While love, for Irigaray, is experienced in the context of particular relationships, taking love as central to ethics has implications for all our relationships. Love does not have to be for all of humanity to be relevant to all of humanity. Conjoined with respect, taking love as an ethical ideal could transform our entire outlook on the world because love is significant for intimate relations, friendships, and also how we view less intimate others. Irigaray's particular conceptualization of love as involving wonder or acceptance of the difference of the other enables us to rework the relationship between friendship and love.

Friendship and Love

In her account of love, Irigaray addresses a number of lacunae and distortions that exist in many discussions of friendship and love, including Kant's. As Jacques Derrida notes in *The Politics of Friendship*, there is a "*double exclusion* we can see at work in all the great ethico-politico-philosophical discourses on friendship: on the one hand, the exclusion of friendship between women; on the other, the exclusion of friendship between a man and a woman" (1997, 278–79).[27] Kant is clearly thinking of friendship between men in his discussion of friendship. He defines friendship as "the union of two persons through equal mutual love and respect" (1996a, 6: 469). On Kant's account, the love in friendship must be "moral" friendship, not just an affect or feeling (1996a, 6: 470). In other words, friendship must involve beneficence toward the friend. Furthermore, for Kant, human beings have an ethical duty of friendship as it makes friends deserving of happiness. Friendship is an ideal that can hardly be achieved in practice, due to the opposition, as he sees it, between love and respect. Kant mentions a saying attributed to Aristotle: "My dear friends, there is no such thing as a friend" (1996a, 6: 470).[28]

This saying reflects an important feature of Kant's view of the difficulties inherent in friendship. He argues that in friendship, love and respect come into conflict since they involve such different obligations, or, to return to his metaphor, as forces they pull in such different directions: "The principle of love bids friends to draw closer, the principle of respect requires them to stay at a proper distance from each other" (1996a, 6: 470). Kant believes that in making others ends one's own in friendship, one is likely to be interfering, pointing out flaws in the friend's character and burdening them with disclosures and revelations that violate respect for the friend (1996a, 6: 470).[29] Then the friend will be offended by the criticism. Another problem, he claims, is that if one does a favor for a friend, they will feel inferior in terms of respect. On this understanding of the difficulties of friendship, friendship should involve some reserve, due to the burden one's own disclosures place on others and the risks of indiscretion on the part of one's friends.[30] Since Kant sees love and respect as opposing forces, this reserve limits love.

Kant is talking about practical love here, and he says explicitly that the love in friendship cannot be an affect as "emotion is blind in its choice, and after a while it goes up in smoke" (1996a, 6: 471). In spite of his clearly stated position that the emotion of love is not the proper basis for ethical friendship, Kant hints that it could indirectly contribute to the ethical life. He argues in the section entitled "On the virtues of social intercourse" that being agreeable, tolerant, and showing mutual love and respect, has value, as it leads indirectly to what is best for the world (1996a, 6: 473).

Irigaray and Kant are in agreement on the point that love and friendship should not be directed toward some other end. Irigaray argues that love among men is, traditionally, teleological—it aims for a goal outside them— and this directedness would change in a future where the autonomy and specificity of both men and women was recognized.[31] Kant remarks that "friendship cannot be a union aimed at mutual advantage but must rather be a purely moral one," because we would lose respect for our friend if we were only concerned with the help they could give us (1996a, 6: 470). He is quite concerned that friendship is between equals who regard each other as equals.

However, Irigaray advances the discussion of friendship by theorizing friendship between men and women and among women. She argues for the importance of friendship between women and sees friendship between men and women as necessary to sexual love. *Eros, philia,* and *agape* (erotic love, friendship, and love of humanity) are often taken to delineate completely different *kinds* of love. For example, Emmanuel Levinas says in *Totality and Infinity,* "Love accordingly does not represent a particular case of friendship. Love and friendship are not only felt differently; their correlative differs: friendship goes unto the Other; love seeks what does not have the structure of an existent, the infinitely future, what is to be engendered" (1991, 266).[32] On his account, love and friendship are different because they have different goals. Friendship is an offering to the other, whereas love is aimed at future productivity. Irigaray's notion of "I love to you" precisely contradicts Levinas's idea by making love a "going unto the Other" or an offering to the Other that is also fruitful. Her aim in not dissociating love and eroticism (1993a, 67) is to move away from what she calls "technocratic sexuality," so the move is to bring love into sexuality rather than to bring sexuality into all love.[33] If there was such a shift in sensibility, it would have profound effects on the way sexuality is manifested in society.

Furthermore, all relationships involve a balance between respect and love for the other, whether they are friendship or erotic love, even though there is greater intimacy in erotic love. Irigaray implicitly agrees with Kant on the point that in friendship and in erotic love, we must respect the other, and accept the limits to our knowledge. This point—reversed—could imply a limit to our disclosures. However, a challenge to Kant's injunctions against disclosures being a problematic feature of love is the idea that genuine love, since it is based on wonder and respect, will entail an understanding of the limits to interference, knowing when it is important for a person to help themself, and when disclosures are inappropriate. In his account of love as a moral emotion, J. David Velleman argues that respect is the minimal response to the incomparable value of a person, love the maximal (1999, 366). He sees love as making us vulnerable to the other, but does not theorize the check that respect places on love. Nevertheless, Velleman's idea of love and respect as both responses to the value of a person, with love being the 'maximal' response, implies that love includes respect in the way that Irigaray contends. The importance of respect to love implies a rejection of the commodification of other human beings in all its forms.

Perhaps Kant is right that friendship is an ideal that can never be fully reached; however, the conflict between love and respect may not be as great as he imagines, because they do not always draw us in different directions. Taking Irigaray's idea that love and respect for the other both involve a certain distancing that militates against presumption and excessive disclosure, we can see that the two are not necessarily in opposition. If both love and respect involve an acceptance of the difference of the other, love does not threaten either ourselves or the other with secrets. Love and respect should accept difference, on Irigaray's account, since neither involves incorporation or assimilation of the other to ourselves. Her primary concern here is sexual difference and the difference of the other as individual. The relationship of sexual difference to other differences will be explored in the next chapter. Such acceptance keeps love from becoming a dominating or homogenizing project. An advantage of Irigaray's account is that love can continue to grow and deepen without that threatening self-respect, respect for others, or wonder.

Irigaray's idea of "the two" of love can be contrasted with many traditional discussions of friendship and love as reflecting similarities between the friends. Aristotle's classic discussion of friendship in the *Nichomachean Ethics* sees friends as mirrors of each other: "Perfect friendship is the friendship of men who are good, and alike in excellence" (1984, 1156b5–10); the friend is "another self" (1984, 1166a32).[34] Kant's ideal of friendship as the perfect balance between love and respect that is equal and mutual between two people seems to suggest a similar mirroring of positions and ethical views. Irigaray's ethics of sexual difference is premised on an understanding of difference that must be recognized in relations between women and men. Irigaray's theorization of sexual difference makes self-love and love of the other very different. However, does that mean that same-sex friendship must be a "mirroring" love?

As I discussed in chapter 1, there are difficulties in Irigaray's construction of an opposition between sameness and difference and her attribution of difference to women and men and heterosexuality in particular. These difficulties arise again in relation to friendship. For instance, Penelope Deutscher argues that while Irigaray criticizes the ideal of sameness between women and men, she does not challenge the sameness or mirroring ideal—found in Aristotle (1984) and Montaigne (1976, 135–44)[35]—of same-sex friendship: "The relentless heterosociality of Irigaray's evocations of friendship and love can offer no counter to this suppression of alterity in same-oriented representations of homosociality" (1998, 179).[36] This problem arises because Irigaray contrasts same-sex relations of all kinds with the unique ontological status of sexual difference. On her view, while there may be differences between same-sex friends, they are different in kind from sexual difference, and are ontic or empirical rather than ontological. Irigaray's logic leads her to think of homosexuality as inherently conservative in contrast to heterosexuality. For example, in *I love to you,* she says that a real change will not come for women through other women, for homosexuals, "being closer to the tendencies of our tradition concerning relations between women and men, . . . actually do far less to upset existing institutions and dogmas than would a real change in the respective status of the female and male genders" (1996, 5). Irigaray's suggestion is that there is something conservative about homosexual (and homosocial) relationships in a world where women are oppressed.

However, Ewa Ziarek reasons that Irigaray can be understood as respecting the alterity of the other in both heterosexual and homosexual relationships because she does not theorize the Other as "the complement of the subject" (2001, 165). The best way to resolve the question, as I suggested in the previous chapter, is to develop concepts such as wonder, generosity, and love in ways that relate to all kinds of differences.[37] Although it is Irigaray's view that sexual difference is more fundamental than all other differences, in developing an ethics that takes cultural difference, for example, seriously, it is possible to incorporate the idea of respect for difference in that context. I examine this question in more detail in the following chapter, by considering the way in which sex and race, and sexism and racism, are compared and analogized. One has to conceptualize both love and friendship, whether among the same sex or different sexes, in parameters that take it that there is sameness and difference in friendship and love whether within or between the sexes. There has to be recognition of diversity among all others and an acceptance of the particularity of loves. How such recognition could be realized becomes clearer through a consideration of political context.

Ethics and Politics

In chapter 4, I will discuss in detail the relation between ethics and politics. At this stage, I focus only on love and show how Irigaray conceives the role of love in ethics and politics in a way that improves on and goes beyond Kant's account. Kant makes the interesting point that although the respect that we owe others is universal and unconditional, the *forms* of respect that we should show others varies greatly, according to "differences of age, sex, birth, strength, or weakness, or even rank and dignity" (1996a, 6: 468). Kant's point appears to imply that he accepts these conventional and "arbitrary arrangements" as reasonably dictating how much and what forms of respect we should show to others. So, if someone has a higher status than another, we should show them more respect or a different form of respect. And it would seem to follow that if women are held to be weaker than men or to have a lower status, then women should be shown less respect or a different form of respect.

Kant's claim that he cannot go into these matters in a book on *metaphysical* first principles of virtues is reasonable. However, questions remain as to whether Kant believes that we should show forms of respect according to the political contingencies of the age or according to ethical principles. Does Kant contend that we should show deep respect to a powerful person if they are extremely unethical? For Kant, these are questions of application, not obligation, although they are part of a complete setting out of the ethical system.[38]

Irigaray, in contrast, although she may sound as if she is establishing an impossible ideal, is describing how things are and then setting out the conditions we would need to bring about in order to genuinely love and respect each other, and articulating how this love and respect are themselves transformative. Her project is to demonstrate how her ethical ideals could be applied. In several essays in *An Ethics of Sexual Difference* (1993a) and in her later work, Irigaray introduces the political dimension to the discussion of respect and love. One could say that she is interested in the contingent, not the metaphysical, in Kant's sense, because she believes that what he calls arbitrary arrangements (1996a, 583) have deep effects on our capacity for feeling and expression of love and respect, both for self and other. On the one hand, politics should make a space for love, taking into account the importance of love to human lives, and on the other hand, Irigaray suggests that loving ethically or genuine love could make a difference to how political culture, particularly democracy, develops.[39] To understand how politics is relevant to love, a theory of love and its role in ethics must acknowledge how political circumstances affect the possibility of genuine love. Like Simone de Beauvoir (1997, 652–79), Irigaray argues that women and men cannot truly love where women are oppressed. In *Sexes and Genealogies,* she makes this point very clearly: "But love is only possible when there are two parties and in a relationship that is not submissive to one gender, not subject to reproduction. It requires that the rights of both male and female be written into the legal code" (1993b, 4). If women are thought of as inferiors, or as the reflections of men, there is no basis for the recognition of difference through wonder or respect for the autonomy of the other that love must involve to be genuine. In pointing out the effects of oppression on relationships, she shows how we cannot describe an ethics without taking this political problem into account.

Thus, in order to overcome the oppression of women and for the ideal conditions for the couples Irigaray envisages to thrive, there must be wide-ranging changes in social practices and law. [40] Love involves these conditions, which are both ethical and political: the first is a breakdown of the traditional division of labor between women and men; second, a bringing together of love and eroticism; third, that women form a social group, and have access to society and culture in a way that enables women to genuinely respect each other; and fourth, an articulation of a genealogy of a female divine (1993a, 67). By breaking down the traditional division of labor she means the division between maternal and paternal roles, and their association with private and public, respectively. Irigaray sees this division of labor and association of women with the private sphere, exemplified in Hegel's work in particular, as perpetuating women's experience of only occupying the role of wife (and mother) rather than as individuals with their own interests and needs. [41] Irigaray notes that without access to culture, women cannot know or love each other or themselves, women cannot sublimate, and love remains impossible (1993a, 67). Women have to establish new values that correspond to their creative capacities, in a sexuate culture, or one that acknowledges sexual difference.

For women to have access to society and culture, women must have full citizenship as independent and concrete human beings (1996, 53). These changes will enable the "culture of difference" to emerge (1996, 5). Irigaray's view is that rights cannot belong to abstract individuals, as none of us are abstract individuals. Rather, there must be *sexuate* rights for men and women, or rights particular to each sex: "The law has to be changed for love" (1996, 133). [42] In this context, the particular laws Irigaray sets out do not need to be analyzed, but her main point—that the law can both hinder love and allow love to flourish—is essential. [43] I will discuss these in the following chapter. Voluntary motherhood, for example, affects the love between parents and children and between women and men by ensuring that women's autonomy is respected and that children are wanted. Irigaray delineates the conditions for love to flourish and envisages that love relations can serve as a model for ethical relations in general.

As Irigaray believes, in love we love particular or singular people. [44] Therefore, an ethics of love cannot be an ethics exhorting us to "love everyone." Although she focuses on the couple, I believe her conception of love is relevant for all loving relationships. Irigaray's argument is that everyone is linked through particular relationships and if these relationships are distorted that has a deleterious affect on political relations more generally (2000b, 118). Conversely, changing these relationships is central to wider political change. Every person is linked to others through love relationships that influence our character and our conceptions of how to treat others, so positive transformations within those relationships must have positive ramifications for relationships in general.

I argue that "aesthetic" love, or love as delight in others, should be taken seriously as part of ethics because it is central to living a full human life and has great potential as an ethically motivating and transforming force. This love is one that involves understanding, as Irigaray conceives of love, and can be cultivated, in a similar way to how Descartes believes we can cultivate generosity, or respect for ourselves and others. She does not develop the arguments that demonstrate exactly how love can act transformatively, but it is possible to suggest the direction these arguments should take. While we cannot *will* emotional love as an instant decision, we are able to cultivate the possibility of love. Although no individual can fairly demand that you feel love for them, each person can be expected to love others. Thus, love can be subject to moral obligation. In addition, if political understanding were to acknowledge the importance of love, rather than positing conditions where people are primarily regarded as rivals, as Irigaray notes, the ethical value of love would be reinforced.

A world without love would be a deeply impoverished place from an ethical point of view. Irigaray contends that "[d]etermining and practicing relations of indirection between us, which enable us to respect ourselves and each other, form alliances, love ourselves and each other—as two or in the community—opens up the possibility for a fairer and better future" (1996, 148). Rather than being a private benefit that we may or may not choose to pursue, loving is an important contribution to the good or ethical life for everyone. Both self-love and love of others enable human beings to reach their full potential because, combined with generosity, they affirm and nurture us. One can see the ethical importance of love from the perspective of the individual, where the passion of love provides the motivation to genuinely take an interest in others.[45] Love is the impulse behind much of our practical care for others, as even Kant himself admits at one point. A duty to practical benevolence does not provide sufficient motivation for the care of particular others. While respect ensures that we treat others ethically in a basic sense, experience of love, and a loving outlook, provides the basis for partic-ular acts of caring for others.[46] Furthermore, love makes an essential contri-bution to ethical life in a community by ensuring that individuals genuinely engage with other. Being loved inspires us to be worthy of that love in both moral and nonmoral ways. Experiencing loving relationships makes it more likely that we will recognize the importance of love in the lives of others and make provision for it. So, love and the encouragement of love through political conditions and through moral education are essential to ethics.

Love as a passion can be essential to ethics even if Kant is right to say that "others cannot put one under obligation to have feelings" (1996a, 6: 449). My argument is that while Kant's distinction between respect and love is invaluable, his ethics is incomplete because it does not adequately account for the importance of love as a passion and he overemphasizes the conflict between love and respect for others. Love should be understood as a feeling as well as a duty or responsibility (and in certain cases not as a duty at all) but this does not make love an accident. In an ethics of love, love must be understood as cultivatable. Although I believe Kant should have taken the feelings of love more seriously, there is something valuable in his idea that love must not be an abandonment of self to another and this idea has resonances in Irigaray's account of how women's relationships to each other and to men need to change. Kant makes more precise the self-respect and respect for others of generosity that Descartes recommended. Irigaray articulates the important ways in which *both* love and respect must involve a type of distancing from others. Wonder plays a role here in that responding with wonder allows the other to be themself in love, rather than forcing a kind of mirroring or unity in love. Irigaray also demonstrates how love and generous respect for others are not opposing forces but interlocking ones, which make love and friendship realistic possibilities not necessarily fraught with conflict. Love not premised on generous respect for others will in some sense be stunted and impoverished. This generous respect for the other is more important than love for ethics in a basic sense, as it is a condition for genuine love but love is not a condition for respect. However, love as a feeling, as delight in others, is central to an ethical life. On the one hand, the possibilities of ethical love depend on political conditions that enable love to flourish, conditions that Irigaray sketches for us. On the other hand, ethical love will also facilitate a transformation of those oppres-sive conditions.

Love has a complicated interaction with generosity, as we have seen through this discussion of the role of self-respect and respect for the other, and with wonder, as wonder is a step on the way to love. Wonder and generosity are relevant to our most intimate relations and yet they are also capable of development as responses in more political circumstances. In the following chapter, I consider in detail the structure of prejudices and oppression that can prevent wonder, generosity, and love for others from being developed and examine the relation between sexual difference and other differences in the work of Irigaray, Beauvoir, and other feminist philosophers. I also show how central the responses of wonder and generosity are to understanding those prejudicial attitudes and to working out a nuanced response to the structures and experiences of different oppressions.

3

Responding to Difference
and Similarity

She refuses to confine herself to her role as female, because she will not
accept mutilation; but it would also be a mutilation to repudiate her sex.
. . . To renounce her femininity is to renounce a part of her humanity.
—Simone de Beauvoir, *The Second Sex*

In this chapter, I would like to elaborate on the question touched on in
earlier chapters concerning the relation between sexual differences and
other kinds of differences between human beings. I argue that both wonder and generosity are needed in our responses to oppression in relation to
these differences and that as concepts, they enable us to understand oppression, the inadequacy or incompleteness of analyses of oppression, and how
we can overcome oppression. As I remarked in the introduction, debates
about women's liberation tend to polarize between equality and difference
approaches, as do arguments about racism. While I obviously sympathize
with Irigaray's sexual difference approach and find her work greatly fruitful for developing the concepts of wonder, generosity, and love, there is a
tendency to neglect the importance of conceptions of equality, even the
extent to which they exist in her own views. She also overlooks in some
respects the relations between sexist oppression and other forms of oppression. Reflection on the relationship between sexist, racist, and other forms
of oppression can generate insights into the structure and experience of
both oppressions and ideas concerning how a new ethics and politics can
develop. Furthermore, my understanding of wonder and generosity enables
us to see how equality and difference approaches should interact. In this

chapter, I reflect on the relationship between different forms of oppression and how we can promote an ethics and politics of wonder, generosity, and love to prevail over them.

In recent years, white feminist philosophers, including Irigaray, have been criticized for elements of racism and for ignoring class in their works, for example, by bell hooks (1987), Elizabeth Spelman (1988), and Melissa Lucashenko (1994). The most powerful critiques have shown that some feminists, in their attempts to demonstrate that sexism is more fundamental than racism, have made black women's and men's experience invisible and have disregarded the specificity of oppressions and the problem of understanding simultaneous oppressions. One lesson that can be drawn from these discussions is that we should be vigilant in relation to discussions of racism versus sexism and not *assume* that one is more fundamental than the other.

Nevertheless, I argue that we can learn a great deal from examining the ways in which racism and sexism are compared. Even those feminist philosophers who most forcefully criticize analogies between the two observe a number of significant similarities. Spelman, for example, in criticizing the notion that there are no positive features of a black identity, notes that blackness is not only about pain and suffering and one can identify as a black woman in ways that are not racist, just as one can identify as a woman in ways that are not sexist (1988: 125).[1] Problems with comparisons between racism and sexism arise if the analogy is constructed asymmetrically—for instance, if the theory of racism is modeled on an understanding of sexism.

A more promising approach is to use an explanatory analogy, where two things are compared in order to shed light on both. Such a comparison might lead to helpful arguments by analogy, such as when similarities between racism and sexism suggest a similar way to overcome these forms of domination. If sex, race, and class are used as points of comparison with each other, if their relation is analytically reciprocal, there are insights into the general structure and the experience of oppression to be gained from the approach, insights I will explore in this chapter. These insights enable the clarification of the role of wonder and generosity in defeating oppression.

Here, I wish to take the feminist arguments of earlier chapters farther by linking them to concern for other forms of oppression. In my view, a consistent feminism is antiracist as well. As Linda Martín Alcoff expresses it, "The problem of racial difference and racism operates increasingly as a crucial condition of adequacy for acceptable feminist theory" (1998, 477). Furthermore, as Michèle Le Dœuff observes, "It is not a pure coincidence that many feminists are also active in anti-racist movements" (1991, 281).

The connection is both conceptual and empirical in that the particular ideas and issues feminists consider and the kind of reflection, concern, and imagination that is involved in analyzing the problem of sexism is linked with and likely to lead to intellectual and practical concern with other forms of oppression. Antiracist feminist philosophy can take into consideration the problems that arise in constructing analogies between racism and sexism and present an account sensitive to the specificity of race, sex, and class and the interaction between them and so incorporate wonder. Generosity will also be essential in the development of self-respect and mutual respect for these groups. Then, in later chapters I demonstrate the sense in which different oppressions interact in specific contexts.

My argument is that while forms of oppression are distinctive, they share a general structure, which emerges in personal experiences of oppression and in both ethical and political approaches to overcoming oppression. First, I will briefly sketch the central analogies between *analyses* of racism and sexism in feminist philosophical work. This sketch is intended to act as a background against which I offer a critical reassessment of the usefulness of the analogy, one that takes into account Spelman's articulation of the risks involved. Then I will examine Irigaray's work to see how she understands the relation between sexual difference and other kinds of difference, such as race, culture, and class. As we saw in previous chapters, Irigaray claims that sex is the most fundamental difference because it is ontological (1985a, 145), whereas other sorts of differences are empirical differences. However, as I noted, it is possible to develop an ethics and politics that takes cultural and other differences seriously, in addition to sexual difference. We need to go beyond Irigaray at the same time as utilizing her understanding of wonder, generosity, and love, as well as the contributions of Descartes and Kant. I find Simone de Beauvoir's work constructive in seeing how we can develop Irigaray's work and give a complex account of the structure and experience of different oppressions, their interaction, and assess strategies for resisting oppression. Beauvoir's analysis demonstrates how one can combine equality and difference approaches to these questions and suggests how wonder and generosity are essential to overcoming forms of oppression.

Similarities in Feminist and Antiracist Discourse

Many analogies between racism and sexism emerge at the level of analysis. By this I mean that theorizing *about* racism and sexism is similar, rather than (necessarily) racism and sexism themselves. There are parallels in the status attributed to race and sex. It has been noted in numerous discussions of racism that the idea of race as biologically based is a fiction, even if race is important socially (Frye 1983; Zack 1998; Haslanger 2000). Marilyn Frye, in *The Politics of Reality*, argues that the criteria that are supposed to distinguish one race from another are chimerical (1983, 113–18). First, it has no serious biological basis, in the sense that it is not possible to distinguish between races genetically, and second, other commonplace attempts at characterizing race, such as by using skin color, are inadequate. It is sometimes thought to follow from the fact that race does not have a secure biological basis and the fact that racist oppression involves biological categories that the concept of race cannot be part of a nonracist future (Zack 1998), although Frye does not hold this view. The parallel argument with regard to gender goes like this: gender difference is a fiction and has been used to oppress women, so we should abandon such categories in favor of androgyny (Jaggar 1979; Okin 1998). What this would mean in practice is that there is no public recognition or acknowledgment of gender differences between men and women, although there might be private recognition of sex differences.

Judith Butler takes things one step farther by arguing that "sex" is also a political construction or fiction rather than a biological basis on which or in relation to which gender is constructed (1990, 147). She argues that the category of sex is itself gendered, and so cannot act as the basis on which gender is constructed or performed (1993, xi). On this view, we are socially and politically categorized as sexed, as either "male" or "female," subjected to the norms of heterosexuality, and we perform gendered identities as "man" or "woman" that make it appear that there is a basis or substance behind these performances. Butler concludes that we should give up the norms of sex and gender to allow gender to proliferate and thus undermine the limitations and restrictions of current gendered and sexed identities.[2]

In her more recent book *Undoing Gender,* Butler reaffirms her performative account of gender (2004, 218), although she is more flexible about the issue of sexual difference. There, Butler suggests that we keep using the terms *sex* and *gender* and "make no decision on what sexual difference is but leave that question open, troubling, unresolved, propitious" (2004, 192). In that sense, Butler sees her work as compatible with Irigaray's because she sees Irigaray as also concerned with sexual difference as a question, rather than a foundation. While Butler's primary focus is on gender and sexuality, she sees the parallels with critiques of racism, such as those of Frantz Fanon

(1967), in that both discourses concern themselves with those excluded from the human.

Another interesting similarity between theories about racism and sexism is the idea that race and sex both involve two explanatory levels: one level that is cultural or socially constructed, and the other that is more basic, natural, harder to change, or even more valuable. First, many feminists are committed to the view that sex can be distinguished from gender, a distinction that is understood in a variety of different ways. Second, the cultural and social aspects of race and racism are distinguished from deeper and more personal experiences of race. One example of the different explanatory levels is Adrienne Rich's distinction between institution and embodiment, which she uses to explain how although motherhood as an institution is composed of damaging myths it may be a freely chosen experience (1976, 273–80). Spelman uses this idea to distinguish between the devastating effects of racism and the importance of pride in one's race (1988, 129). Again, the concept of "Whiteness," used to refer to a racist construction of white identity that whites can challenge, has the cultural and social characteristics gender is thought to have. Frye argues that "Whiteness" is the socially constructed idea of the entitlement and superiority of whites (1983, 114–18).[3] However, feminist antiracist theorists differ over whether they take race and sex or gender to be valuable concepts for analytic purposes in current circumstances *and* whether these concepts will be valuable in circumstances where there is no racist and sexist oppression.

Another important analogy between feminist and antiracist discourse is the stark choice often presented between equality feminism and difference feminism and between what we can call equality antiracism and difference antiracism. This is where the concepts of wonder and generosity can take us beyond that forced choice. Very roughly, the "difference" position, such as Irigaray's, is often supposed to be based on essentialist views of sex or race, and the "equality" position is purportedly based on the idea that sex and race are socially constructed and therefore of no ethical or political importance. However, there are a range of difference positions, which share the view that race and sex are significant features of our identity that should be recognized even when there is no racist and sexist oppression. Difference positions are those that implicitly suggest that wonder is the appropriate response to difference in the other. Equality positions are those which imply that generosity in the form of respect for what we share with others is paramount.

The parallels between the analyses that are given of race and sex, or race and gender, are closer than the parallels of either with class. Nancy Fraser, who highlights the distinctions between different forms of oppression, sees race and sex as forms of identity that we might wish to claim something from, even if we were no longer oppressed, but sees class as something that has to disappear with oppression, or, as she says, "The logic of the remedy is to put the group out of business as a group" (1997, 19). In that sense, class differences are thought not to be worthy of wonder; we should just work to eliminate them along with the oppression they signify. Race and sex are theorized as at least more salient than class to our sense of self. However, there may be working-class cultural features, for example, that we wish to retain even when class oppression no longer exists.

There is also a range of "equality" views, some of which also take race and sex as significant features of identity, but have as either a near or ulti-mate goal that there will be no public recognition of race and sex.[4] One of the benefits of examining the analogies between antiracist and feminist theories is finding a view that refuses that choice, and combines generosity and wonder, as I will discuss after considering Irigaray's views on the rela-tion between sexual difference and other kinds of differences. Both equality and difference strategies alone are flawed, I argue, because they do not take into account either the complexity of our experience of our identity or the complexity of racism and sexism. Furthermore, neither properly acknowl-edges the importance of both wonder *and* generosity.

Irigaray's Understanding of Race, Culture, and Class Differences

What is needed is an approach that takes into account the insights of both equality and difference feminism and equality and difference antiracism. Such an approach can also overcome the limitations of both. As I noted in earlier chapters, while a number of commentators have criticized Irigaray for privileging patriarchal oppressions over other forms,[5] others have sug-gested that Irigaray's work can be *extended* to questions concerning race, class, and sexuality, beyond the work that she does in her writings.[6] She discusses both race and class explicitly in a number of texts. Before turning to this aspect of Irigaray's discussions, I would like to consider the question of sexual difference as ontological difference, as Irigaray argues.

Irigaray calls sexual difference "ontico-ontological difference" in *Specu-lum of the Other Woman* (1985a, 145). She believes that the two sexes are different in kind, or genre, as she expresses it. In *I Love to you,* Irigaray writes that "it is evident that female and male corporeal morphology are not the same and it therefore follows that their way of experiencing the sensible and of constructing the spiritual is not the same. Moreover, women and men have different positions in relation to genealogy" (1996, 38). In an interview she is even more specific about the distinctness of sexual difference: "Let's say between a man and a woman the negativity is, dare I say it, of an ontological, irreducible type. Between a woman and another woman it's of a much more empirical type, and, furthermore can only be understood and can only live in the ontological difference between man and woman" (1995a, 110). This claim is one of the most controversial in Irigaray's account and is not accepted by many feminists, although it is defended by, for example, Rachel Jones (2011) and Alison Stone (2006).

Beauvoir, for example, anticipating the idea of sexual difference as ontological, rejects this view. While she accepts that mortality and the need to be reproduced are part of what it means to be human, she does not believe that sexual differentiation follows from the ontological necessity of perpetuation of the species. She states that we can imagine "a parthenogenetic or hermaphroditic society" (1997a, 39). Nevertheless, Beauvoir argues that sexual differentiation is part of any *realistic* definition of human being (1997a, 39). Elizabeth Grosz argues that sexual difference is pre-ontological in the sense that "it makes possible what things or entities, what beings exist (the ontological question) and insofar as it must preexist and condition what we can know (the epistemological question)" (1994a, 209). Stella Sandford, in a thorough discussion of what Irigaray could mean by "ontological sexual difference," concludes that what she means is the "difference between incommensurable masculine and feminine beings" (2001, 12). In my judgment, Irigaray alerts us to something significant, in that sexual difference is different from other kind of differences in being irreducible and ineliminable in ways that other differences, such as race and class, are not. The points she makes about different morphologies and a different relation to genealogy are well taken.

However, I do not believe that it follows from these points that sexual difference must be conceived as ontological or that in order to take, for example, ethnic and class differences seriously, we need to think of them as ontologically different. What is important in each case is the shared history that we now face. That is why in this chapter I stress the different forms of prejudice, some that involve overemphasizing difference, or neglecting generosity, and some that involve refusing to recognize difference *properly,* or not responding with wonder, as Irigaray theorizes in the case of women and men. The existence of sexual difference and other kinds of differences call for an ethics and a politics. At the same time, as I argued in the first chapter, the differences have to be recognized in the right way, with wonder and generosity. So the ethics and politics is one that develops in relation to differences and we need to reflect on where we may be exaggerating difference—neglecting generosity—and where we may be neglecting difference—excluding wonder. At this point, given Irigaray sees race and class as different in kind from sexual difference, I will discuss how she elaborates these "empirical" differences.

In her book *Between East and West: From Singularity to Community* (2002a), Irigaray discusses what she learned from study of Buddhism and the practice of yoga about living and thinking in a way different from Western tradition. While she is critical of the fact her yoga teachers did not explore questions of sexual difference, she observes that the Gods of India tend to appear as a couple, thus implying that Indian culture is imbued with the ideal of the couple she recommends. Irigaray also seems to gesture toward a notion of pre-patriarchal cultures she calls "feminine aboriginal cultures," which will enable better relations between the sexes (2002a, 15). This is evident in her comment about Indian women:

> At the time of a trip to India in January 1984, I was happily surprised to see that the majority of women there, even poor ones, keep a great dignity, an attitude foreign to that of humiliated, submissive, or arrogant women that Western women often have. I am not ignoring what happens in India concerning prostitution, violent acts, and even the murders perpetrated against women. But the one does not prevent the other. There exists there a cohabitation between at least two epochs of History: the one in which women are goddesses, the other in which men exercise a blind power over them. (2002a, 65)

In this passage, Irigaray concedes that having a fundamental dignity within oneself does not alone prevent violence. Yet her final comment that there is an epoch in history where women were goddesses implies that such a state is desirable and in opposition to a reality of male dominance over women. That way of expressing a vision of dignity seems unlike wonder and more like a response, such as awe, that I take to be undermining of a true ethics, as I argued in the first chapter. Elsewhere, Irigaray suggests that European and Eastern traditions need to be united, a view that does not properly acknowledge the oppressive features of Eastern traditions (2002a, 70).[7]

Irigaray affirms the acceptance of the limits to our understanding of the other, which I explored in the preceding chapters, in relation to race. Yet she still insists that sexual difference is "the foundation of alterity" because it is universal, because responses to sexual difference are the basis of traditional, cultural, and legal differences, and sexual difference "can bring together the most natural with the most cultural" (2002a, 127–28). Although she believes that "mixed" couples—a black man and a white woman, or a Catholic woman and a Muslim man, for example—have the potential to become "a site of civic education," they risk regressing to "instinctuality" unless they begin with recognition of sexual difference (2002a, 135–37). Irigaray maintains that such couples could increase tolerance toward others and acceptance of diversity. *East and West* thus points in the direction of cultural and racial difference but does not develop the concepts of wonder or generosity in relation to them. The relations of wonder and generosity Irigaray envisages are between heterosexual couples that are the fundamental origin of ethical and political change. Her argument for this point is that "it is often the manner of treating this difference—in the sexual relation or in the genealogical relation—that is at the origin of differences of tradition of culture, manifesting itself notably in common law" (2002a. 128). In *Conversations,* Irigaray reaffirms her focus on this difference, saying that "[s]exuate difference can serve as the foundation of . . . a conception of alterity, because it is the most basic and universal difference of those which exist in all humanity" (2008b, 132). Here, she is according significance to other differences while reasserting the fundamental nature of sexuate difference. The difficulty with her argument is that while a great many differences between cultures and traditions may be elaborations of sexual difference and many cultures may have sexually differentiated customs and laws, that does not show that all differences have that as their origin.[8] We also have to understand the history of cultural and racial relations and how they have developed over centuries.

Here, I will also consider the sources for understanding class relations in Irigaray's work. Her most detailed discussion of this aspect of oppression is in her essay "Women on the Market" (1985b, 170–91). There, Irigaray begins by saying, "The Society we know, our own culture, is based upon the exchange of women" (1985b, 170). She argues that only men's work is valued as real work, and women are seen as objects to exchange between men. She characterizes this system as one of "hom(m)o-sexuality," a system of relations between men that does not recognize or acknowledge women as true partners. As we saw in earlier chapters, this is the system that needs to be replaced by one where men and women recognize each other as autonomous individuals with their own desires, in other words, with wonder and generosity.

Irigaray criticizes Lévi-Strauss for theorizing women as scarce commodities, and understands Marx's analysis of commodities in *Capital* (1967) as "an interpretation of the status of women in so-called patriarchal societies" (1985b, 172). She does this by analogy, taking many of his points about objects to be relevant to understanding women's place in society. For instance, she sees women in patriarchy as valued in terms of use, and in terms of men's desires rather than their own; and she interprets the phallus as the equivalent that expresses women's value as money does for objects.

Furthermore, Irigaray connects the commodification of women with the valuing of imaginary and symbolic relations over natural and corporeal (re)production, or in other words, women's capacity for maternity. Her analysis takes women to be the exploited class throughout history, or at least this exploitation arises with private property and patriarchy (1985b, 173).[9] Irigaray is also critical of Marx for not thinking about the mystery of the role of the body in exchange relations: "The material contribution and support of bodies in societal operations pose no problems for him, except as production and expenditure of energy" (1985b, 182). While she sees this economic system as based on men's needs and desires, she does not mean that these are natural needs or desires but that they too are also created culturally, through religion, law, and custom.

However, can one understand Irigaray's reading of Marx as a reduction of class relations to relations between the sexes? Is she not taking class seriously as a kind of oppression? Much of the essay encourages such an interpretation, although close to its end Irigaray suggests otherwise: "Women are the symptom of the exploitation of individuals by a society that remunerates them only partially, or even not at all, for their 'work'" (1985b, 190). This point implies that while one can analyze capitalism in terms of women as commodities, women are not the only group oppressed in this way by the system. Men are also limited in their relation to nature, the body, and desire. Her alternative to capitalism and patriarchy is what she calls "a double system of exchange," "a shattering of the monopolization of the proper name (and of what it signifies as appropriative power) by father-men" (1985b, 173). Nevertheless, like Fraser, Irigaray takes class to be less fundamental than sexual difference and although she sees the exploitation of women as beginning with private property, for her the solution to economic exploitation is based on recognition of sexual difference. Her analysis may prove to be accurate, but she does not delineate the specific features of economic exploitation and disadvantage or show how these problems may distinguish between different women, some of whom are economically privileged. Why Irigaray remains a vital source for thinking about these questions is that we can take her work farther in thinking about a range of difference between human beings. Her thoroughgoing approach to the question of sexual difference is one that suggests the potential of trying to think of what could happen in a world where all kinds of oppression were overcome.

As I argued in chapter 2, part of Irigaray's concern is with enabling women to be free and autonomous, regarded with respect and so self-respecting and generous, in order that more loving relations can become possible. Her positive political program includes concrete suggestions for reform of the law.[10] It is worthwhile revisiting these suggestions to see if they take into account different forms of oppression. In her outline of sexuate rights, Irigaray makes some very important proposals, such as the right to human dignity for women, which involves "a) Stopping the commercial use of their bodies and images b) Valid representations of themselves in actions, words, and images in all public places c) Stopping the exploitation of motherhood, a functional part of women, by civil and religious powers" (1993b, 86).[11]

While there is a great deal of value in Irigaray's approach, such complex problems, as I will argue, cannot be solved by an exclusive focus on celebrating sexed, or indeed raced, identity. Some of her further recommendations, such as "the legal encodification of *virginity* (or physical and moral integrity) as a component of female identity that is not reducible to money" (1993b, 86), tend toward an overemphasis on sexual difference and could have an effect opposite to the one she intends. Although her concern is with the treatment of virginity as a commodity, having a particular law about virginity appears to reinforce that perception. Irigaray says she's thinking of "rape and incest cases, for example, or cases against forced prostitution, pornography, etc." (1993b, 88), all serious concerns for women, but not exclusively related to virginity or to women. In her discussion of Irigaray's sexuate rights, Deutscher says we should interpret Irigaray's concept of virginity as invoking "psychological and moral ideas of inviolability" (2002, 51). While this interpretation has the advantage of making a focus on "virginity" sound less conservative and connects the thought with a self-respecting integrity, it has the disadvantage of making it too abstract to be the subject of law. That said, Irigaray's idea that these rights to physical and moral integrity should be conceived as positive and that the whole of society would be concerned in such cases, rather than the woman left as the accuser, is a fruitful way of thinking about these questions.

One of the interesting aspects of Irigaray's thought in general, and her conception of sexuate rights in particular, is that in spite of her stress on difference, several kinds of equality are essential to her view. As I argued in chapter 2, a basic equal respect for both the sexes is fundamental. Furthermore, in point 7 of her list of sexuate rights, she recommends that "[w]omen shall be represented in equal numbers in all civil and religious decision-making bodies, given that religion also represents civil authority" (1993b, 89).[12] Thus, Irigaray believes that equal representation of women in decision-making bodies is essential for sexuate rights, a representation that Le Dœuff, for example, calls *mixité,* although she, for her part, is very critical of difference feminism, and more specifically Irigaray's work (2003, 65).[13] Feminists with very different emphases can come together on this question.

In an early interview, Irigaray states how important it is to focus on the struggle that is most immediately important, saying, "I think the most important thing to do is to expose the exploitation that is common to all women and to find the struggles that are appropriate for each woman, right where she is, depending upon her nationality, her job, her social class, her sexual experience, that is, upon the form of oppression that is for her the most immediately unbearable" (1985b, 167). But this comment about political practice is at odds with her theorization of sexual difference as most fundamental. Thus, while Irigaray is aware that there are other dimensions of oppression such as class, culture, and race and refers to them, she does not explore them in a great deal of detail, even in their interaction with sexism. That task must be taken up by other authors.

In relation to Irigaray's analysis of women as commodities, Ellen Armour makes the point that not all women are *legitimate* objects of sexual exchange between men, because race relations often make white women taboo for black men (1998, 221). She also notes that Irigaray's image of women as passive objects of contemplation (1985b, 221) does not resonate with many African American women at all, although it is an image whose effects are expanding. Armour concludes that Irigaray's work needs to be supplemented by an analysis that pays closer attention to the realities of a number of forms of oppression, a view I support. What makes Irigaray's view so useful is that she has articulated what is central to wonder, its being open to the difference of the other, in a way that includes sexual difference, thus making her view distinct from a general focus on alterity or a view that did not recognize the importance of wonder. She also expresses the need for self and mutual respect of generosity first foregrounded by Descartes. In the next section, I will sketch an analysis that shows how the passions and the virtues that develop from them I have been discussing are related to developing responses to a range of forms of oppression.

Wonder and Generosity, Equality and Difference

Following on from my argument that there is a need for both wonder and generosity, and both equality and difference, we can examine how these possibilities relate to each other in the context of intersecting oppressions. Equality and difference strategies are often understood as the twin horns of a dilemma between overcoming oppression by abandoning one's group and accepting that one belongs to an oppressed group, but thereby implying there is an essential or natural identity that forms the basis of group membership. Simone de Beauvoir, in *The Second Sex* (1997a), shows an awareness of the pitfalls of both the approach of rejecting the idea of membership of a group and essentializing members of it, views that she calls nominalism (or constructionism) and conceptualism (or essentialism) respectively. Her understanding of the relation between sexual difference and other differences can provide a framework through which we can elaborate on Irigaray's work and understand the role of wonder, generosity, and love in these varying contexts.

Beauvoir discusses the relevance of racist oppression to understanding the oppression of women, and argues that there are "deep similarities between the situation of woman and that of the Negro. Both are being emancipated today from a like paternalism, and the former master class wishes to 'keep them in their place'—that is, the place chosen for them" (1997a, 23).[14] In her search for a solution to oppression, Beauvoir does not take the path of rejecting the concepts of race or sex, and I contend that is because she could foresee the problems that arise from this approach.[15] Her solution is to argue that women should assert themselves as *both* human and women. Like Irigaray, Beauvoir believes that sexual identity is important to one's sense of self. As she remarks: "She refuses to confine herself to her role as female, because she will not accept mutilation; but it would also be a mutilation to repudiate her sex. . . . To renounce her femininity is to renounce a part of her humanity" (1997a, 691–92).[16] Both denying one's sex and denying one's humanity are forms of mutilation. On this issue, Hannah Arendt also argues that it is debilitating to be forced to choose between one's identity and one's humanity. She writes of the forced choice between being a pariah, outside politics and society, and a parvenu, accepted as an exception by the dominant group: "Jews felt simultaneously the pariah's regret at not having become a parvenu and the parvenu's bad conscience at having betrayed his people and exchanged equal rights for personal privileges" (1976, 66–67). This forced choice makes it difficult to feel comfortable with one's place in both society and political life.

However, unlike Irigaray, Beauvoir does not hold that sexual difference is the only ontological difference whereas other differences are merely empirical, as I noted. She believes that we should reject the myth of the "eternal feminine," but at the same time she argues that it would be bad faith to deny one's race or sex, as they are features of our facticity. Toril Moi, in her essay "What is a Woman?" (1999) highlights this aspect of Beauvoir's work and allows the complexity of her account to be elucidated. Taking a position between the two extremes of nominalism and conceptualism enables Beauvoir to describe how race and sex are of varying salience. While race and sex are features of our embodiment, they are not *always* the most significant things about us, in terms of how we think about ourselves, nor can they be used to justify oppressive treatment by others.

Beauvoir writes in the introduction to Volume Two of *The Second Sex*: "The point here is not to proclaim eternal truths, but rather to describe the common background from which every particular female existence stands out" (1997a, 31; Moi's translation, 1999, 198). Moi's interpretation of this statement is that one's body is a potential source of meaning, and, "It follows from Beauvoir's analysis that in some situations the fact of sex will be less important than the fact of class or race; in other situations it will not" (1999, 201). Moi points out that sometimes there will be a hierarchy of these features of our identity and sometimes they will be equally salient. This is the most plausible interpretation of Beauvoir's views, as she says unequivocally that many women experience race or class as more important to their sense of self than sex.[17] This view makes sense of our experience, which depends on our particular situation. For example, for Jewish women living in Nazi Germany, their Jewishness was likely to be experienced as more central to their identity than their sex. But for a woman working in an institution dominated by men, many of them aggressive and sexist, her sex will be experienced as most significant.

In the early pages of *The Second Sex,* Beauvoir tells an anecdote about herself. I find this anecdote, and Moi's reading of it, particularly useful for explaining Beauvoir's position regarding sexism and for developing and extending her insights into the nature of the experience of oppression in general. She describes the situation like this: "In the midst of an abstract discussion it is vexing to hear a man say: 'You think thus and so because you are a woman,'" and she points out the difficulty of responding to such a remark (1997a, 15). It appears that Beauvoir's only defense is to say, "No, I think it because it is true," but doing so removes her embodied subjectivity from the argument. Beauvoir argues that it would be out of the question to say, "'And you think what you do because you are a man,' for it is understood that the fact of being a man is no peculiarity" (1997a, 15). The reason Moi believes the second response is out of the question is that such a reply just would not be understood or would be seen as a sign of abandoning the abstract discussion. Furthermore, in such a case of *ad feminam* attack, as Moi calls it, there is little point in stooping to the same level. The moral of this story is that Beauvoir is being forced to a choice that is oppressive: between accepting that her views are determined by her sex or removing her embodied self from the context.

An alternative response Moi suggests is using a defiant silence (distinct from the silence that is being forced on Beauvoir), turning on one's heels, and walking away. However, this strategy can only work if it is clear that this silence is different from the silence that is being imposed by the man's remark. Although Moi does not recommend that Beauvoir say, "Yes, I do think that because I am a woman," many of Moi's students claim they would. However, this response is also problematic because again there is unlikely to be any "uptake" of such a response. It could not be understood or taken seriously by her interlocutor. Moi's students provide different contexts, where it might be held as a claim to expertise: "I think this because of my special insight as a woman." However, none of the suggested responses seem to affirm both one's humanity and one's sex. Moi notes that Beauvoir is not *denying* that her being a woman may be relevant by referring to the truth of her views. Moi's point is that if one tries to separate one's sex from one's thought, one will not have access to all one's own experiences. It is not possible to distinguish the experiences that we have *just as human beings* from those we have as raced and sexed beings.

Moi draws a valuable conclusion from her discussion of Beauvoir's anecdote. She says that women's oppression is "the compulsory foregrounding of the female body at all times" as well as "preventing women from foregrounding the female body when they want it to be significant" (1999, 202).[18] The example Moi gives from Beauvoir is a personal one, from the point of view of the oppressed. The insight highlighted in the anecdote can be usefully developed by reflecting on what it demonstrates about the nature of racism and sexism, and it is relevant more broadly to developing an ethics and politics of wonder and generosity.[19] Because sexism and racism have a dual structure, our response must also have a dual structure. Examples of the compulsory foregrounding of women's sex are discrimination and sexual harassment, laws against women working or driving, insisting women change their names on marriage, and compulsory wearing of the chador, which covers women's body and may cover the face almost entirely. Examples of attempts to background women's sex are reactions against affirmative action, women's groups and shelters, and maternity leave. In both sets of cases, others decide whether women's sex is relevant or not. The first set shows a lack of generosity or respect for the other, the second a lack of wonder.

Moi argues that the same logic works in racism, where on the one hand, people are made conscious of their race when they would prefer to be forgetful of it. As Frantz Fanon, in *Black Skin, White Masks,* says: "All I wanted was to be a man among other men" (1967, 112–13). All he wanted was for generosity to be extended to him. On the other hand, there could be reasons for highlighting one's group membership, and expecting a response of wonder, even if one believes that race is a fiction. If Beauvoir's example is read in terms of race, readers may not feel that she gives the best possible interpretation of this situation. Perhaps if someone was accused of holding a particular view because of their race they might be able to say proudly, "Of course I think that because of my race." However, the question still remains as to whether such a response will have "uptake," since racism also involves the determination of when race is relevant by the privileged group. As an example of how the appropriateness of race is determined by the privileged group, Linda Alcoff describes the experience of an Asian lecturer teaching introductory philosophy to a primarily white class in upstate New York. The students were comfortable with him as a teacher until he started to discuss cognitive aspects of racism. Then some of the students refused to look at or speak to him (Bernasconi 2001, 280). In that case, the lecturer is introducing the idea that race is relevant to the philosophy course, and this is what the white students would not accept.

Beauvoir's notion of lived experience is a valuable one for thinking about the intersection of sex and other features of identity, because the way the body is lived is important to one's sense of identity and consequently to how others should respond to oppressed groups.[20] It can allow that indigenous women, for example, may sometimes find that being Aboriginal is more important for them than being women or that the two aspects of identity interact in such a complex way that they cannot be separated.[21] Beauvoir's analysis shows that we need to be aware that both extremes of thought—of denying one's membership of a group and highlighting it at all times—contribute to the oppressiveness of racism and sexism. A more complex account is one that recognizes that the significance of sex, race, culture, and sexuality will differ according to context. Sometimes what is lacking is appropriate wonder; sometimes it is generosity.

Nevertheless, there needs to be more discussion concerning in which contexts gender and race should be recognized or responded to with wonder and in which it should not, and when generosity is the stronger need. I argue that oppressed people should be able to determine those contexts.[22] The connection I see between the phenomenology of oppressed people's experience and ethics and politics is that both must involve generosity or respect for oppressed people's experience and sense of their own identity. This can be contrasted with a view of politics in particular that involves oppressed people sooner or later denying their own sense of themselves as members of a group or that involves recognition or acknowledgment of group membership in all contexts. An important point is that no one should have to deny their identity in order to be part of the public and political sphere. I believe Irigaray and Beauvoir would agree on this point. Irigaray's sexuate rights are a way of making women's status as members of the public sphere, or citizens, evident. Beauvoir, as I noted, believes that to have to deny one's femininity is a mutilation.

As I mentioned earlier in the chapter, some feminist and antiracist theorists argue that the concepts of race and gender should be abandoned because they are fictions, and damaging fictions at that. However, I argue that we need these concepts, used nonhierarchically, for the foreseeable future and may do so even in a just political future because they are central to people's identity and may remain so even if they are not oppressed.[23] Although there are damaging racist ways to think about race, the idea of race per se is not the problem. A better response is to avoid using these concepts in particular ways, ways that do not accept racist identifications and descriptions. The concept of race needs to be interrogated and reworked, rather than rejected. Nor is the idea of sexual difference damaging in itself. On the contrary, respect for differences between men and women are central to ethics, as I have argued. Instead, all kinds of differences should be responded to in ways that accept the specificity and autonomy of the other. The concepts of wonder as a response to the difference of the other and generosity as response to human commonality capture this point well.

In my interpretations of both Irigaray and Beauvoir I have concentrated on the similarities in the general structure of racist and sexist oppression. Irigaray, while finding sexual difference to be the most fundamental difference and the most basic oppression, does not elucidate the specific character of racist oppression. In contrast, Beauvoir claims that there are important disanalogies between racist and sexist oppression. She argues that the othering of women is different from that of other oppressed groups because women internalize the view others have of them. Although African Americans feel they are othered, Beauvoir says, "the Negroes submit with a feeling of revolt, no privileges compensating for their hard lot, whereas woman is offered inducements to complicity" (1997a, 325).[24] However, this claim is problematic since those oppressed by racism also internalize the view that the oppressor takes of them, at least to a certain extent, as is made clear by the notion of "double consciousness." Although this notion can be understood in a number of different ways, as either a negation of black consciousness or as a conflict between black and white ideals, double consciousness implies that blacks find it difficult not to be seen through white eyes, or to put it another way, not to be affected by white's perceptions, just as women are affected by men's perceptions.[25] The reciprocity of generosity between the racist and the one who has to live with racism scarcely exists, at least not the kind of reciprocity one finds between people who regard each other as equals. There are "inducements to complicity" for racially oppressed groups as well as women.

However, antiracist theorists argue that a way of escaping double consciousness is possible in the case of racist oppression that is not possible in the case of sexist oppression. Ernest Allen says, "It was not necessary to the healthy psychological edification of the black individual that African-American self-recognition be tied absolutely to recognition by whites; for there was always the *mutual recognition* which black folk bestowed on one another, an acknowledgement which, under prevailing conditions, served as a bulwark against the possibility of absolute black self-deprecation" (1997, 54). In other words, this mutual recognition enabled African Americans to maintain a fundamental level of self-respect. It is precisely this mutual recognition and support that enables the development of generosity which Beauvoir argues does not exist between women. She raises the problem of the lack of solidarity among women compared to other oppressed groups. Her point is that women form a group, just as Jewish people and black people do, but do not have the solidarity of those groups because women's lives are bound up with the lives of individual oppressors, women lack the means to be independent, and some women are "very well pleased with her role as the other" (1997a, 21), a difficulty Irigaray also notes. Another sign of the lack of solidarity among women is the racism some white women express toward black women (Simons 1999, 180; Beauvoir 1998, 231). However, Beauvoir's claims need some qualification. Oppression is a matter of degree; as women escape from oppression, women can provide mutual support, recognition, and solidarity to encourage generosity.

Although there are similar structures involved in racism and sexism, indigenous women, nonindigenous women, poor women, and women of different religions and ethnicities experience sexism in very different contexts, so different women may need to explore different forms of liberation, some where the focus is generosity, others where the focus is the need for wonder. Racism and sexism interact, but they also function independently in some contexts. For example, some aspects of racism may disappear sooner than sexism as when sexism can become more obvious in salaries and positions, and some aspects of sexism may disappear faster than racism, as when equal rights legislation affects middle-class women first (Spelman 1988, 131). The forms of liberation of oppressed races of both sexes may come into conflict with the forms of liberation of some women. How wonder and generosity should interact will also vary according to context, in that there are different forms of racist and sexist oppression. I will show that in more detail in the next section.

The Dual Nature of Racism and Sexism

Racist attitudes involve both the view that race is irrelevant and that it is overwhelmingly significant and so are linked to lack of both wonder and generosity. This dual nature can be seen in the attitudes of white Australians to indigenous people, for example. In the "Report of the National Inquiry into the Separation of Aboriginal and Torres Strait Islander Children" (1997) (known as the "Bringing Them Home Report"), an aboriginal woman observes that children were taken from their families to be brought up as whites, but at the same time they were expected to defer to whites: "They tried to make us act like white kids but at the same time we had to give up our seat for a whitefella because an Aboriginal never sits down when a white person is present" (1997, Submission 640). Aboriginal identity was taken to be of no cultural relevance in a positive, wondering, sense so that aboriginal families could stay together, but to be a marker of lesser privilege that was supposed to justify the denial of opportunities and the extension of generosity.[26]

Moreover, aboriginal people had no say in whether or when their aboriginality mattered. The poor thinking and irrationalism conveyed in both racism and sexism is a sign of the exercise of the power to judge when these features of identity are pertinent, in that they shift between saying there are no differences to saying that there's all the difference in the world. These shifts are linked to impoverished emotional responses to the oppressed, or failures of wonder and generosity. Those who are particularly racist tend not to be disturbed by their own inconsistency because they are not inclined to assess their views or their passions.[27] Jean-Paul Sartre, in *Anti-Semite and Jew*, shows the sloppiness and bad faith of anti-Semitic thinking, where the same vice or virtue is interpreted differently, depending on whether they are discussing a Jewish person or a Christian. He says that the anti-Semite "can agree without embarrassment that it is possible for certain Christians to be avaricious, for to him Christian avarice and Jewish avarice are not the same" (1995, 56). In the case of sexism, Le Dœuff demonstrates how male philosophers, in particular, do not live up to their own standards of reasoning when they write about women (1991, 70). Instead, they tend to echo contemporary prejudices or their own unreflective view of women. Differences, in these cases, are overstressed.

In addition, political and institutional structures mirror the view that one's "particularity" (of sex, race, class, or culture, for example) must be foregrounded or not foregrounded in the situations those in power believe are appropriate. These structures can produce racist actions and attitudes by individuals, as well as mirroring them. In the "Bringing Them Home Report," the documents testify to the way successive governments denied aboriginal humanity, for example, by claiming that aboriginal mothers soon forgot their children. A protector in Western Australia boasted, "I would not hesitate for one moment to separate any half-caste from its aboriginal mother, no matter how frantic her momentary grief might be at the time. They soon forget their offspring" (1997, Submission 385). Of course the subtext here is that aboriginal mothers' feeling for their children is completely distinct from and lesser than that of white mothers and thus exhibits a lack of generosity or respect for the other.

At the same time, government officials failed to cultivate wonder at a rich, distinct culture in denying the importance of aboriginality and claiming that aboriginal children would be perfectly happy with a white family. In the Australian context, the view that race is irrelevant can be seen in the demand for sameness of treatment of white and indigenous Australians, and a failure to recognize the unique historical and cultural background or the present implications of those differences. The question of how we can make up for these historical injustices is considered in detail in chapter 7. Some political currents in Australia, for example, involve the desire to reduce difference. The claim that indigenous people are gaining "special treatment" is based on the idea that we are all the same and no one should be treated differently.[28] In the general refusal to countenance reserved seats in parliament for indigenous people, their unique position is not recognized; in the former government's refusal to apologize for past injustices, their unique history is not acknowledged; and in the attacks on Mabo and Wik (court judgments acknowledging aboriginal land rights), aboriginal people's unique connection to the land is ignored.[29] Furthermore, claims by whites to be aboriginal involve taking the power of self-definition away from aboriginal people.[30] In these cases, there is no wonder at cultural difference or acceptance of the limits of non-aboriginal understanding.

Yet this is only half the story. There are deficiencies of generosity, in not regarding indigenous people as worthy of respect, as well. In racist claims about crime, for example, aboriginality is often treated as most salient. Basic human rights are neglected in relation to problems that affect aboriginal people. For instance, violence against aboriginal women is not adequately addressed, which betokens a lack of generous respect. A specific example of this need for respect can be found in views about sexual violence toward aboriginal women. In the Northern territory, a fifty-five-year-old aboriginal man who sexually abused a fourteen-year-old aboriginal girl was originally sentenced to only one month in prison because she had been promised to him in marriage under traditional law. Fortunately, this verdict was later overturned on appeal. (ABC online, http://www.abc.net.au/pm 2005) There are a number of different aspects to this case, since one could suspect the judge of sexism in his interpretation of the law, as well as not taking an aboriginal girl's rights seriously. Claims concerning asylum seekers and refugees in Australia involve highlighting the differences of refugees by describing them as the sort of people who would throw their children into the water, for example.[31] In such cases, there is no generosity or respect for others as deserving of basic human rights or concern.

One caveat to my analysis is that probably the most extreme forms of racism and sexism involve the highlighting of one's race or sex at all times, or a complete lack of generosity, which Jewish people suffered during the Nazi period and women did under the Taliban in Afghanistan. In chapter 6, I will consider how we should respond to these very worst cases of abuse and violence. Second, the cases I have given may also suggest that what is really involved in racism and sexism is foregrounding or not foregrounding race and sex to the material detriment of the oppressed. If this were the correct interpretation of my account, then people's sex or race or sexuality being highlighted to their benefit or advantage would be a sign of antiracism or antisexism. One example is the idea that people would like to have women bosses, or women colleagues. Yet this example is also a sign of an assumption of the power to determine when sex is relevant, and in what way. This way of thinking can create oppressive situations through expectations of a certain style or character, such as the "motherly" boss, even if, arguably, individuals sometimes benefit from such stereotypes. Women should be accepted in workplaces without such limiting conditions. My point is rather that oppressed groups should be able to determine when certain features of their identity are significant and have that taken seriously. What this means in practice is that appropriate strategies for bringing about a more ethical world may vary, that wonder and generosity do not have a fixed relation of proportion, but are responsive to specific situations.

Wonder and Generosity in Overcoming Racism

My analysis suggests why some antiracist and feminist strategies are more problematic than others, because they fail to take into account the dual nature of racist oppression and focus on only one aspect. Correspondingly, it is usually thought that only either wonder or generosity is needed as a reaction to oppression. One sort of response, that people want the distinctiveness of their race or sex to be recognized or acknowledged, or others to respond with wonder, is at the basis of identity politics or politics of difference. The idea that race and sex are irrelevant, at least in ethical and political terms, is behind equality views, sometimes called liberalism or humanism, and focus on the need for generosity.

In the previous section I contended that to be forced to choose between denying one's race or sex and affirming it at all times is oppressive. What is relevant to the current social and political construction of "race," as Frye notes, is that it is generally whites who decide who is white, thereby controlling membership of that privileged group (1983, 115). Similarly, in the case of sex, it is predominantly men who are able to decide when sex matters—when women should be thought of as specifically women and when sex is irrelevant. Moi sees the debate between equality and difference feminism as a reflection of this oppressive structure, and Beauvoir's project as an attempt to think beyond that forced choice, beyond essentialism and nominalism or constructionism.[32] The debate between "equality antiracism" and "difference antiracism" also reflects this oppressive structure. These debates also reflect a stress on *either* wonder or generosity as a response to the other.

As I have argued, we have to both accept humanity or sameness and accept difference, and respond with both generosity and wonder. However, many antiracists believe we must either reject commonalities between human beings or reject the notion of identity, whether it is black identity or whiteness, for example. Approaches that only focus on either affirming difference or denying difference will lead to difficulties. A particular approach that is increasing in popularity (in the United States) is the notion of the "white traitor." I will briefly consider this strategy as it illustrates in a more complex way the risks of denying group membership, and of extolling fixed identities for others in a way that lacks the generosity of respect and the openness of appropriate wonder. For example, Frye (1983) and Alison Bailey (1998) argue that it is possible to disaffiliate from the group of whites. Frye maintains that white women should reject their attachment to white men, because the desire for equality with white men involves a share in racial domination. Examples of limited forms of white treachery are protests against the benefits of being white, or Frye's idea that we should not promote "whiteliness," which she sees as the display of certain characteristics, such as assuming authority in relation to people of color.

Bailey argues that it is possible for white people to become aware of their privileges and to act in ways that disrupt racist expectations. This behavior could take the form of "choosing to stop racist jokes, paying attention to body language and conversation patterns, and cultivating awareness of how stereotypes shape perceptions of people of color" (1998, 36). Another case she cites is of a white couple assisting a black couple to buy a house in a white neighborhood. However, occasional acts of this kind are not sufficient, says Bailey; we should cultivate a traitorous character, as we would cultivate a virtuous character, in Aristotelian or Cartesian terms.

These strategies can seem to be an appealing way to reject one's role as oppressor. However, as Linda Alcoff points out in "The Whiteness

Question," in *Visible Identities* (2006), there are problems with notions of white treachery that involve a rejection of white identity. Her chapter is not a direct response to Bailey's article, but to the phenomenon of white treachery generally. The risk in white treachery is like the risk of exotification of women that I discussed in the first chapter, a kind of improper, excess wonder rather than a genuine openness. White treachery can be as simple as denying being white to shopkeepers, or moving to predominantly black neighborhoods. However, some of these practices can themselves exacerbate perilous situations. In one series of incidents in Morocco, Indiana, the behavior of so-called white traitors who dressed in styles judged "black" by other whites made life dangerous for themselves and very dangerous for their African American neighbors, who had not been consulted (2006, 213–15). Alcoff is critical of these types of actions because, outside the clear-cut political context of strikes, boycotts, and protests, such as existed in the civil rights movement, their meaning is unpredictable and potentially hazardous. Furthermore, even white traitors benefit from being white. To be fair to Bailey's understanding of white treachery, she acknowledges that acts of white treachery can be dangerous for people of color (1998, 40), that we need to develop practical wisdom in relation to such practices, and she would accept that white traitors still enjoy privileges.

However, Alcoff is attempting to develop a different model for dominant groups to respond to racism, rather than individual acts of defiance. In her view, crossover culture is an attempt to appropriate black subjectivity that does not allow recognition of difference, or as I would say, wonder (2006, 217). It focuses on a fixed sense of identity of the other, and usurps the oppressed groups' prerogative to self-define, rather than being properly open in a wondering way to oppressed groups' self-definition. The crossover approach also denies the membership of one's own group. Alcoff argues that instead whites need to develop a "double consciousness" that accepts both a connection of responsibility to the racist past and present *and* recognizes the ways in which whites have challenged racism. For Alcoff, it is important that white antiracists can keep their self-respect: "For whites, double consciousness requires an ever-present acknowledgement of the historical legacy of white identity constructions in the persistent structures of inequality and exploitation, as well as a newly awakened memory of the many white traitors to white privilege who have struggled to contribute to the building of an inclusive human community" (2006, 223). This is a different and positive use of the notion of double consciousness, which involves accepting both the painful and triumphant aspects of the past. One could see this double consciousness as an acceptance of facticity or identity combined with a realization that it is possible to change, to become antiracist. It also involves generosity in Descartes's sense, rather than self-loathing.

Alcoff provides a good example of dealing with racism without acting in bad faith, which is how I believe Beauvoir would understand the thinking behind forms of white treachery that seek to deny white identity. Alcoff's double consciousness is parallel to the avoidance of bad faith by members of oppressed groups who, while not denying their identity as members of the group, deny that they are determined to live in a particular way. Although being white might not be the most salient feature of a person at every moment, a political strategy based on the denial of one's own culture and history is likely to be disempowering and risky for oppressed groups and antiracist activists. Another way of understanding the problem with some forms of white treachery is that people act in their own self-interest in the case of crossover culture, and in some spontaneous acts the concern is to provoke social and political change without ethical consideration for others. They do not wonder at the difference of others and they do not properly respect themselves and others.

This chapter has shown how wonder and generosity can enable understanding of a range of oppressions and how we should respond to them. What emerges from my consideration of feminist and antiracist strategies is that racism is not paying attention to race, but paying attention to it in the wrong way at the wrong time in the wrong context. And the same is true of sexism. Our response to all forms of oppression must be one that respects the humanity of all, or is generous, while at the same time responding with wonder to difference. Love can also play a role in ethical and political life and defeating oppression in a number of ways, as I argued in the previous chapter and as I will show in later chapters. "Color-blindness" or equality approaches alone are flawed: they institute the values of the dominant group, fail to allow self-definition of oppressed peoples of different races, and overlook the reality of day-to-day discrimination. The strategy of sex-blindness cannot be successful because it too imposes the dominant values and fails to recognize the value in being a woman or a man.[33] This strategy shows generosity toward the other but fails to express wonder at differences. Similarly, pure difference strategies that involve highlighting a person's race and sex in all circumstances are also flawed, since they refuse to allow oppressed people's self-definition and impose demanding and constricting expectations. In that case, wonder becomes all-consuming, like the attitude of wondering at everything Descartes warns against, and regards others as exotic and strange. This idea is lacking in generosity or in extending respect for self to the other.

While Irigaray does not suggest that wonder take this excessive role, her emphasis on sexual difference does not give sufficient significance to other differences between human beings. We can, however, extend her work with the help of Beauvoir's more flexible view about differences, and take specific identities and oppressions into account. If we think of Irigaray's call for the recognition of specificity and autonomy as one that can apply more generally, we can see that all oppressed groups should have such recognition. Racism is constituted by the assumption of the power to determine when oppressed people's race is relevant and when not, a structure similarly constitutive of sexism. Thus, the intricate response of wonder and generosity must be one that comes from the authority of oppressed people to determine in which contexts their identity is significant.

In the following chapters I will further explore how an ethics and politics of wonder and generosity can help us both to understand and to respond to difficult issues affecting oppressed groups, including the inhospitable treatment of asylum seekers and refugees, the extremes of abuse and violence against women and Jewish people, and a history of injustice against indigenous and other racialized groups. These questions will be addressed on both an ethical and political level. In order to do so, I need to address the question of the complex relation between ethics and politics, through an examination of the way they are conceived by three very different thinkers: Kant, Derrida, and Arendt.

4

The Relation between
Ethics and Politics

Politics says, "*Be ye wise as serpents*"; morals adds (as a limiting condition) "*and guileless as doves.*"
                                        —Immanuel Kant, "Toward Perpetual Peace"

It is necessary to deduce a politics and a law from ethics.
                                        —Jacques Derrida, *Adieu to Emmanuel Levinas*

In the center of moral considerations of human conduct stands the self; in the center of political considerations of conduct stands the world.
                                        —Hannah Arendt, *Responsibility and Judgment*

In the previous chapters, we saw that many important issues straddle the divide between ethics and politics and that many ethical matters can be resolved depending on political circumstances. Furthermore, our ability to feel wonder, generosity, and love is co-implicated with political circumstances. For these reasons, it is essential to consider the question of how we should conceive the proper relation between ethics and politics. One well-known and important position is that of Immanuel Kant, who argues that ethics and politics do not come into conflict because ethics places limits on what can be done in politics, or indeed that politics is a part of ethics. I focus on his work as it represents a kind of ethical limit-point for taking ethics in politics seriously. However, it is often contended, both by philosophers and in everyday life, that politics raises particular problems independent of ethical considerations. In this chapter, I introduce the work of Jacques Derrida and Hannah Arendt as they challenge Kant's views and center on significant contemporary and recent political questions. Is the answer, as

Derrida argues, that we must negotiate between ethics and politics? There are a number of significant differences between Derrida and Kant on this question that help me to clarify and develop my argument concerning the role of the passions of wonder and generosity in ethics and politics.

For Kant, ethics is based on the possible, and for Derrida ethics is necessarily guided by the impossible. Derrida goes beyond Kant in seeing ethical virtues as being part of politics, a view that is central to how I see the relation between ethics and politics working. Against a prevalent interpretation of both Kant and Derrida, I contend that we should not understand ethical and political decisions in aesthetic terms. In examining Derrida's answer to this question of ethics and politics, I take Arendt's point that we must be wary of the danger of moralism in politics seriously. Nevertheless, I argue that in order to expand the realm of ethics into politics, politics should create the best conditions for ethical relations to ourselves and to others, in addition to the constraints or limits that ethics should place on politics. While we should acknowledge the special circumstances of politics, politics should be ethical in more than one sense. An understanding of this fundamental relation between ethics and politics will enable a clearer conception of wonder and generosity in relation to hospitality, forgiveness, and apology in later chapters.

Kant on Ethical Politics: A Proper Politics

I begin with Kant's discussion of the relation between ethics and politics because he states what is at stake in their relation very clearly. Derrida's moves beyond Kant will then stand in sharp relief, and I can develop my own argument, which borrows insights from both. On Kant's account, morals has two divisions: right, those duties that can be enforced, and virtue, those duties that cannot be enforced. His most extensive discussion of the relation between ethics and politics occurs in "Toward Perpetual Peace," which I also discuss in the following chapter. In this essay Kant argues that ethics should be taken much more seriously in political decisions; in fact, it should be the overriding consideration, rather than what he calls "expedience." As he writes, "[A]ll politics must bend its knee before right" (1996a, 8: 380). Kant claims that only the enforceable aspect of ethics, or right, is relevant to politics. But what does it mean for politics to bend its knee here?

In an appendix to "Toward Perpetual Peace," Kant examines this question. The first section is entitled "On the disagreement between morals and politics in relation to perpetual peace." Here, he considers the common view that in politics circumstances sometimes dictate that we must act against morals or right. I should note that Kant thinks of morals as comprising both right or law and virtue or ethics and these are both expounded in the *Metaphysics of Morals* (1996a). He begins by saying that because morals give us the laws by which we ought to act it is absurd to say that we cannot act on them. Kant contends that if it were so, morals could not have any authority. This position follows from his view that ought implies can, which he discusses in *The Critique of Practical Reason* (1996a).[1] There, Kant argues that our awareness of the moral law when we construct maxims of the will leads us to the concept of freedom. Furthermore, our experience confirms this concept of freedom when we remember that we can act against our strongest desires and even our love of life in order to act ethically (1996a, 5:30). Elsewhere, in a review of Schulz's "Attempt at an Introduction to a Doctrine of Morals," he asserts that without this possibility of freedom, any imperative is absurd and the only position we can adopt is fatalism (1996a, 8: 13). The view that we are always free to act morally is the first step in Kant's demonstration that there is no conflict between politics and ethics.

Kant's further argument is that there is

> no conflict of politics, as doctrine of right put into practice, with morals, as theoretical doctrine of right (hence no conflict of practice with theory); for if there were, one would have to understand by the latter a general *doctrine of prudence,* that is, a theory of maxims for choosing the most suitable means to one's purposes aimed at advantage, that is, to deny that there is a [doctrine of] morals at all. (1996a, 8: 370)

Kant defines right as "the sum of the conditions under which the choice of one can be united with the choice of another in accordance with a universal law of freedom" (1996a, 6: 230). Right is distinguished from virtue because it is possible to give external laws to ensure these conditions are met, which is not the case for virtue.[2] Given that Kant sees politics as the application of morals (that aspect of morals described in the doctrine of right), it follows that any conflict or deviation from morals in their application would undermine the idealism of morals and make it egoistic or self-interested.[3] Thus, complaints of conflict between politics and morals are simply complaints of inconvenience. This is what Kant means by his claim that a moral politician, who makes political prudence conform to morals, is possible, but a political moralist, who makes morals conform to the political interest of a statesperson, is not possible (1996a, 8: 372). Any attempt to make morals conform to political interests, he argues, undermines the concept of right altogether and replaces it with force, so that it is no longer morals at all.

Kant expands upon the argument that politics and morality are compatible because of the existence of freedom and the moral law, and the necessity of joining politics with the concept of right, in the appendix of "Perpetual Peace." To support his conclusion, he argues that reason tells us sufficiently what our duty is, although we cannot predict all the consequences of our actions. The categorical imperative (in one formulation: so act that you can will that your maxim should become a universal law) should take precedence over the end you are trying to achieve, because the categorical imperative has "unconditional necessity." In a concession to the idea that obeying the categorical imperative may not be easy, Kant notes that such obedience should be combined with political wisdom or an understanding of how best to institute or work toward perpetual peace (1996a, 8: 377). This is what it means to be "as wise as a serpent," in the Biblical quotation Kant modifies and that I quote at the start of this chapter. Nevertheless, adherence to political maxims must derive from the concept of the duty of right.

As I have described it so far, Kant's clever dissolution of any conflict between morals and politics might suggest that he does not take the realities of politics seriously. However, he sees it as important to explain why there is a perceived conflict between morals and politics. Objectively, Kant says, there is not a conflict between morality and politics, but there is a conflict subjectively, in the self-regarding inclinations of people. According to him, the aims of moral evil are self-contradictory and self-destructive whereas those of moral goodness are consistent and conducive to happiness, so evil makes way for the moral principle of goodness (1996a, 8: 379).[4] Kant observes that the real danger to acting morally is self-deception that convinces us we are justified in following our own interests rather than duty. We have to assume that the principles of right can be carried out, and then, "True politics can therefore not take a step without having already paid homage to morals, and although politics by itself is a difficult art, its union with morals is no art at all; for as soon as the two conflict with each other morals cuts the knot that politics cannot untie" (1996a, 8: 380).[5] As I noted in chapter 2, Kant is of the view that following our own interests, like our inclinations, is an unreliable business as it is difficult to calculate whether our actions will have the right results, but in acting according to morals we have a dependable guide.

Again, this claim that morals can resolve its own conflict with politics may sound oversimplified. What does it mean to apply morals in the form of right? In a second appendix to "Toward Perpetual Peace," entitled "On the Agreement of Politics with Morals in Accord with the Transcendental Concept of Public Right," Kant maintains that rights must be able to be made public. His first transcendental formula of public right is, "All actions relating to the rights of others are wrong if their maxim is incompatible with publicity" (1996a, 8: 381). The key idea appears to be that actions that affect the *rights* of others are unacceptable if they need to be kept secret. However, the reverse is not held to be true—actions that are consistent with publicity are not necessarily right, as Kant observes, since a very powerful state can be quite open about its maxims even when they are immoral (1996a, 8: 385). The power of such a state means it does not have to be concerned about opposition or resistance to its maxims.

Kant argues for this principle of public right as follows:

> For a maxim that I cannot *divulge* without thereby defeating my own purpose, one that absolutely must *be kept secret* if it is to succeed and that I cannot *publicly acknowledge* without unavoidably arousing everyone's opposition to my project, can derive this necessary and universal, hence a priori foreseeable, resistance of everyone to me only from the injustice with which it threatens everyone. (1996a, 8: 381)[6]

This principle is both ethical (part of the doctrine of virtue) and juridical (related to right), and Kant shows how it is relevant to civil, international, and cosmopolitan right.

First, civil right concerns right within a state. Kant upholds the right of human beings to respect by the state, saying that "[t]he right of human beings must be held sacred, however great a sacrifice this may cost the ruling power" (1996a, 8: 380). Nevertheless, with regard to the rights of people against the state, Kant argues that rebellion is shown to be wrong by the fact that publicly revealing a maxim of rebellion would make it impossible, whereas a head of state can publicly declare their willingness to punish rebels.[7] Second, international right is the right of nations. This right, Kant says, must be an enduring free association between states. He examines three examples of apparent conflict between politics and morals in international right and presents their resolution. One case is where one nation promises to aid another nation but decides to release itself from the promise because it affects their state's own well-being. Such a maxim could not be made public, in Kant's view. Another case is where lesser nations could not make public the idea that they intend to attack a greater power preemptively. Finally, Kant notes that a large nation could not make known that it would absorb smaller nations if it thought that necessary to its preservation (1996a, 8: 383–84). Third, Kant, tantalizingly, says that cosmopolitan right's maxims work by analogy to those of international right.[8] Cosmopolitan right is the right to hospitality or the right to visit all the countries in the world.

Realizing that the first transcendental principle of public right only concerns what is unrightful, rather than what is right, Kant introduces a second. The second transcendental principle of public right is: "All maxims which *need* publicity (in order not to fail in their end) harmonize with right and politics combined" (1996a, 8: 386). Kant's argument for this principle is that if maxims can only be successful through publicity, they must correspond to the universal public end, which is happiness, and for him this is what politics must do. He adds, "But if this end is to be attainable *only* through publicity, that is, by the removal of all distrust toward the maxims of politics, such maxims must also be in accord with the right of the public, since only in this is the union of all ends possible" (1996a, 8: 386). In other words, these maxims are ones that people could have chosen for themselves, and reasonably would have. On Kant's account, the principle of public right is transcendental since it concerns only the form of universal lawfulness. Thus, Kant's ethical politics is primarily one where politics is restrained by right, or those duties that can be enforced externally. It does not center on internal duties to treat others in a virtuous way. such as to regard them with wonder and generosity. However, within states, these rights are to freedom, equality, and independence, which are the principles upon which states should be established.[9] In that sense, these rights can be considered as respect for the other in the political sphere.

"Toward Perpetual Peace" contains examples of what Kant thought of as the moral constraints on politics that will further peace between states in both its preliminary and definitive articles. The first comprise the exclusion of "secret reservation of material" for another war from true peace treaties, the nonacquisition of existing states, the abolition of standing armies, no national debts with regard to external affairs, noninterference with the governments of other states, and not using duplicitous means in war, such as assassins, breaching surrender, or incitement to treason (1996a, 8: 344–47).[10] The definitive articles that recommend republicanism for all states, a federalism of free states, and the cosmopolitan right of hospitality represent the ideal moral conditions for international and cosmopolitan politics (1996a, 8: 350–60).

On Kant's account, politics can be made commensurable with morality only within a federative union of states that maintains peace. He concludes: "Thus the harmony of politics with morals is possible only within a federative union (which is therefore given a priori and is necessary by principles of right), and all political prudence has for its rightful basis the establishment of such a union in its greatest possible extent, without which end all its subtilizing is unwisdom and veiled injustice" (1996a, 8: 385). This point suggests, reasonably, that so long as states are at war or are not willing to pursue peace, politics and morality are likely to conflict.

Although Kant believes that politics can be made commensurable with morality, he concedes that practical circumstances or conditions can make it difficult to bring this ideal into effect and that it may be brought about gradually. For instance, states may have to wait to introduce reforms until it can be done peacefully. Another example Kant gives is that "it cannot be demanded of a state that it give up its constitution even though this is a despotic one (which is, for all that, the stronger kind in relation to external enemies), so long as it runs the risk of being at once devoured by other states; hence, as for that resolution, it must also be permitted to postpone putting it into effect until a more favorable time" (1996a, 8: 373). Thus, it is sensible to wait until the state is secure from invasion before rectifying injustice if that injustice is protecting the state.

There are also complicated exceptions to the agreement between politics and morality mentioned by Kant in his essay "On the common saying: that may be correct in theory but it is of no use in practice" (1996a). He observes that sometimes unconditional and conditional duties might conflict. Such duties may conflict

if it is a matter of preventing some catastrophe to the state by betraying a man who might stand in the relationship to another of father and son. This prevention of trouble to the former is an unconditional duty, whereas preventing misfortune to the latter is only a conditional duty (namely, insofar as he has not made himself guilty of a crime against the state). One of the relatives might report the other's plans to the authorities with the utmost reluctance, but he is compelled by necessity (namely, moral necessity). (1996a, 8: 301)

In this case, the duty to prevent catastrophe to the state clearly trumps the duty to prevent misfortune to a relative. However, Kant does not discuss a case where great misfortune to the state would conflict with a duty to prevent a violation of the rights of the relative or indeed any other person. Although it is a difficult practical problem that he does not examine in depth, he is quite clear that such rights should never be violated, and he does touch on the issue briefly.

In *The Metaphysics of Morals,* Kant says, "[T]here is a categorical imperative, *Obey the authority who has power over you* (in whatever does not conflict with inner morality)" (1996a, 6: 371). Morals, then, can conflict with political practice if a leader demands we do something unethical, and when they do, we must obey morals. However, here and elsewhere, as I have noted, Kant condemns revolutions, a condemnation that seems counterintuitive according to his own theory. If a leader is trampling on human rights, wouldn't it be our duty to overthrow them? In Kant's notes concerning the "Doctrine of Right," he comments, "Force, which does not presuppose a judgment having the validity of law is against the law; consequently the people cannot rebel except in the cases which cannot at all come forward in a civil union, e.g., the enforcement of a religion, compulsion to unnatural crimes, assassination, etc." (XIX, 594–95, quoted in Dostal 1984, 732). The implication appears to be that if such acts were forced the state concerned could not properly be a civil union. Therefore, tyranny and totalitarian regimes may well not count as civil unions for Kant. Then revolution could be moral in the sense that such a revolution would be creating a civil union.[11] Thus, such examples of conflict between duties to the state and other duties that could be brought against Kant would be accounted for by this caveat. However, revolutions for such reasons as poor government or inequity would still be excluded as they could occur in a civil union.

Cases where the state tried to prevent philanthropy provide other examples of conflict between politics and morality, this time relevant to the doctrine of virtue. Kant also believes that politics and virtue should agree, but notes that philanthropy is an imperfect duty, or in other words, that how it is fulfilled is to a great extent a matter of discretion.[12] In any case, his view is that politics easily agrees with this sense of morality "in order to surrender the rights of human beings to their superiors" (1996a, 8: 386). What he has in mind here is that "politics," or rather those in power, like to pretend that perfect duties of right, which do not allow for latitude or exceptions, are imperfect duties that they bestow only as benevolence and so are very ready to claim that they are moral in that sense.

Kant's argument provides an important step toward an ethical politics, in spite of his unappealing condemnation of revolutions and lack of consideration of conflicts between human rights and duties to the state. Such a politics is one where at the very least *certain* human rights are respected. It might be thought at this point either that Kant says too much or that he says too little. Aren't there extreme cases where politics demands that we override the rights of individuals? And should not there be an argument that politics should be virtuous or rather that state decision makers should make virtuous decisions in relation to other countries, where imperfect duties to others such as philanthropy or hospitality are made an essential part of politics?[13] I will discuss the first question in relation to Arendt's objections to ethics in politics. For now, I will examine the second. This question is one that Derrida focuses on and this focus highlights the difficulties of a virtuous politics in a very interesting way, and shows how wonder, generosity, and love can have a place in an ethical politics.

Derrida on Negotiating between Ethics and Politics

In recent years, Derrida has referred more and more to Kant's ethics and his political philosophy, for example in *The Politics of Friendship* (1997) and *On Cosmopolitanism and Forgiveness* (2001a). On the one hand, Derrida is influenced by Kant's approach to ethics and politics, and on the other hand he wants to go farther than Kant in stressing the unconditional nature of a range of ethical concepts. Derrida's hyperbolic ethics goes beyond political considerations and yet Derrida accepts that we must act according to political concerns. In *Adieu to Emmanuel Levinas*, Derrida's position is that "it is necessary to deduce a politics and a law from ethics" (1999, 115).[14] Like Kant, Derrida concerns himself with questions of ethics and politics within the state, between states and between individuals and states. He does so in a series of writings on justice and law, on democracy, on cosmopolitanism and refugees, on terrorism, and many other subjects.

Derrida famously claims in "Force of Law" that "[j]ustice in itself, if such a thing exists, outside or beyond law, is not deconstructible" (1992,

14). Justice is contrasted with law or right, a concept he believes is deconstructible. Furthermore, Derrida's promotion of respect for international law
(as well as reflection on its foundations) parallels Kant's concern with establishing a cosmopolitan world order (Borradori 2003, 114–15). He accepts
with Kant and Arendt that a world government is not desirable, and believes
we need to go beyond their views to think of a "democracy to come" (*la
démocratie à venir*) that will unite law and justice (Borradori 2003, 120).
The reason Derrida is so positive concerning the concept of democracy is
that it "is the only one that welcomes the possibility of being contested, of
contesting itself, of criticizing and indefinitely improving itself" (Borradori
2003, 121). This democracy to come is not intended to refer to a future
state of democracy but to a call for "a militant and interminable political
critique" (Derrida 2005, 86).[15] On an international scale, this democracy is
envisioned by Derrida to challenge the authority of the state and to emerge
in new institutions such as the International Criminal Court.

In later chapters I examine closely Derrida's work on hospitality and
on forgiveness in relation to wonder, generosity, and love. In this chapter, I
focus on his more general remarks concerning ethics and politics. In *Adieu
to Emmanuel Levinas*, Derrida treats the Torah (representing justice) in Jerusalem (representing political realities) as an exemplification of the problem
of ethics and politics. He sees the problem as fundamentally one of negotiation between the demands of ethics and the realities of politics. The Torah
is read by Levinas in "Cities of Refuge" as justice: "The Torah is justice, a
complete justice . . . because, in its expressions and contents, it is a call for
absolute vigilance" (1994, 46). Derrida says that the Torah in Jerusalem
"must still inscribe the promises *in* the earthly Jerusalem. And henceforth
command the comparison of incomparables (the definition of justice, of the
concession made, out of duty, to synchrony, co-presence, the system, and
finally, the State). It must enjoin a negotiation with the non-negotiable so
as to find the 'better' or the least bad" (1999, 112). It is important to note
that Levinas's idea of justice appears to be very different from Derrida's. For
Derrida, justice is the ultimate ethical ideal, the undeconstructible, that goes
beyond particular laws (1992, 14); for Levinas, justice is the political necessity of weighing different competing claims, contrasted with the infinite
responsibility for the particular other that is the ethical relation. In Derrida's
outlook, justice takes this concern with singularity.[16] The complete justice
of ethics must be inscribed in concrete politics and law.

Derrida's view that we must negotiate between ethics and politics
leaves us with the question of how far toward each we should tend in

our negotiations. Ethics with its unconditional demands is impossible to satisfy for Derrida, and politics must be limited by ethics. They seem to act as constraints on each other such that the decision, the action, will always lie somewhere between the two. There is an in-between position or many in-between positions that Levinas gestures toward in "Politics After!": "So there would be no alternative between recourse to unscrupulous methods whose model is furnished by *Realpolitik* and the irritating rhetoric of a careless idealism, lost in utopian dreams but crumbling into dust on contact with reality or turning into a dangerous, impudent and facile frenzy which professes to be taking up the prophetic discourse" (1994, 194). Levinas's presentation of a case against ethics in politics often put explicitly or implicitly highlights its absurdity and the need to sketch out alternative in-between positions. This is what Derrida attempts to do.

However, Derrida claims that there are no rules to determine what would be the better or least bad alternatives (1999, 114).[17] Nevertheless, politics and law must be deduced from ethics, so we can determine that "democracy is 'better' than tyranny" and "'political civilization' remains 'better' than barbarism" (1999, 115). I interpret him as suggesting that democracy is better than tyranny, for example, because democracy is open to criticism and perfectibility in a way that other political forms are not. He distinguishes between the formal injunction to deduce politics from ethics, which is absolute and unconditional, and the question of content that is conditional on circumstances and that we have a responsibility to determine for ourselves in each particular case.

One of the criticisms of Derrida's deconstructive ethics is that it does not give us any guidance as to how to make decisions. For example, Simon Critchley writes, "I would claim, with Laclau, that an adequate account of the decision is essential to the possibility of politics, and that it is precisely this that deconstruction does not provide" (1999a, 200).[18] However, Derrida's position is developed in more detail in "Ethics and Politics Today" (2002) in a way that addresses Critchley's concerns, at least to an extent. He says that all ethical and political decisions are structured by urgency, precisely because we have to make decisions and without any certainty about the rightness of what we do, just as Descartes believes. Derrida writes that in ethics and politics this structure of urgency "is simultaneously the condition of possibility and the condition of impossibility of all responsibility" (2002, 298). For him, ethics and politics also have in common that they are answering the question "What should I do?" and that we should give thoughtful and responsible answers to the question. Nevertheless, ethics and politics appear, at least, to be very different. Derrida characterizes these perceived differences between ethics and politics:

> Because ethical responsibility appeals to an unconditional that is ruled by pure and universal principles already formalized, this ethical responsibility, this ethical response can and should be immediate, in short, rather simple, it should make straight for the goal all at once, straight to its end, without getting caught up in an analysis of hypothetical imperatives, in calculations, in evaluations of interests and powers.... Whereas, on the contrary, still according to the same appearance, political responsibility, because it takes into account a large number of relations, of relations of power, of actual laws, of possible causes and effects, of hypothetical imperatives, requires a time for analysis, requires a gamble, that is, a calculation that is never sure and that requires strategy. (2002, 301)

This rich description of the fundamental difference between ethics and politics develops the account of *Adieu* and also reflects Kant's distinction between the dependability of ethics and the unreliability of mere hypothetical imperatives. Ethics is seen as occupying a higher and more impractical realm whose unconditional principles mean that one can respond immediately, whereas politics is seen as concerned with day-to-day practical strategies that need to be carefully planned out and are uncertain.

However, Derrida immediately notes that these differences are only apparent, and that politics can be understood as more urgent than ethics. He argues that there must be a negotiation of the nonnegotiable, so in that sense the political is always inscribed in the ethical.[19] For example, when hostages are taken, a refusal to negotiate is an acceptance of the risk to the hostages on the basis that it will save others in the future. Similarly, a decision to negotiate with the hostage takers is a decision to try to save the hostages in the hope that it will not be detrimental to others' lives. These different approaches have been used in response to the taking of foreign hostages in Iraq. "In both cases," Derrida writes, "the political imperative and the ethical imperative are indissociable" (2002, 305). Beauvoir makes a similar point when she says, "It is for us to decide whether one man must be killed in order to save ten, or to let ten die so as not to betray one" (2005, 190). Thus, political decisions inevitably involve ethical considerations.

Furthermore, like Kant, Derrida sees autonomy as the foundation of ethics, but believes that this autonomy will always be imposed on by heteronomy or the imperative of the other, of politics, of the conditional (Borradori 2003, 131–32). The unconditional imperative demands that we go beyond duty. The unconditional imperative of justice contrasts with law, as unconditional hospitality and forgiveness contrast with their conditional pairs, as we shall see in later chapters (2001). In every case, the unconditional tempers the conditional and must be taken into account when making decisions. Derrida presents his understanding as an analysis of the "logic" of these concepts, which, when deconstructed, split into these doubles.[20] The result is that Kant's imperfect duties, which allow some latitude in how we fulfill them, become perfect duties on Derrida's account. Of course, they are perfect duties in a paradoxical sense, in that although their demands are unconditional, Derrida does not believe, as Kant does, that we can actually fulfill them. Instead, we find ourselves always falling short, compromising, and negotiating with these demands.

The central features of Derrida's ethics, namely, the linking of ethics with politics, the concern with autonomy, and the setting up of unconditional ideals, make him sound very Kantian. He has both encouraged and resisted this interpretation. For instance, in *Limited, Inc.,* Derrida says that he uses the term *unconditionality* "not by accident to recall the character of the categorical imperative in its Kantian form" and "it is independent of every determinate context, even of the determination of a context in general" (1988, 152). However, Derrida does not characterize the injunction that recommends deconstruction in Kantian terms "because such characterizations seemed to me essentially associated with philosophemes that themselves call for deconstructive questions" (1988, 153), and has reservations about thinking of the unconditional as a regulative idea or ideal.

A problem with Derrida's disclaimer here is that a regulative ideal in Kant's sense does not appear to be the concept Derrida has in mind. As he notes, this term is used too loosely in philosophical discourse (2005, 83). Kant discusses the notion of regulative ideas in the *Critique of Pure Reason,* in "The Final Purpose of the Natural Dialectic of Human Reason" (1986, A669–704, B697–732). These regulative ideas are that of the existence of the human soul, an independent world, and God. These ideas are beyond the limits of experience and cannot be proven; nevertheless, we should posit them as they play an important role in our thinking by directing our studies of psychology and physics, in the case of our ideas of the soul and the world respectively. The idea of God provides the sense that everything in the world is part of an organized unity—"*as if* all such connection had its source in one single all-embracing being, as the supreme and all-sufficient cause" (1986, A686, B714). In contrast, Derrida's unconditional concepts are not something we posit as beyond the limits of experience and useful for theorizing but something we take seriously as action-guiding.

In a detailed discussion of justice and duties in *Philosophy in a Time of Terror*, Derrida outlines three reservations about aligning what he calls his "impossible reals" with Kant's possible ideals. First, he says, his impossible is "what is most undeniably *real*" in its urgency and its demands (Borradori 2003, 134).[21] This can be seen as in contrast to a possible ideal that we work toward, such as Kant's cosmopolitan ideal. Unlike Kant's dictum that ought implies can, Derrida's dictum is that "ought implies *cannot.*" This is an important difference between the two. On Derrida's account, one can take imperatives to be real even if one does not think they can be reached or satisfied. I would note that ideals can also be real in the sense of being urgent and making demands. At one point, Kant says that virtue "is an ideal and unattainable, while yet constant approximation to it is a duty" (1996a, 6: 409). The fundamental difference is that Kant believes that we can fulfill our duty in this approximation, but Derrida holds that such approximation is in no sense a fulfillment of duty.

Second, Derrida says that his notion of responsibility is one of going beyond any rule that determines my actions. Here, Derrida seems to be shifting from Kant's metaphysics, where the regulative ideas or postulates of world, God, and the soul play a role, to his ethics, where the categorical imperative and maxims play the central role. Kant's description of moral ideas in the *Critique of Practical Reason* also seems helpful. In a note, he writes,

> [I]f I understand by an *idea* a perfection to which nothing ade-quate can be given in experience, the moral ideas, are not, on that account, something transcendent, that is, something of which we cannot even determine the concept sufficiently or of which it is uncertain whether there is any object corresponding to it at all, as is the case with the ideas of speculative reason; instead, the moral ideas, as archetypes of practical perfection, serve as the indispens-able rule of moral conduct and also as the *standard of comparison.* (1996a, 5: 127)

Here, Kant is referring to moral virtues such as wisdom and holiness. This idea seems quite close to Derrida's in the fact that they are impossible—nothing in experience can match them—but are not transcendent, and can be used as a standard. Existing law can be compared to infinite justice, and as we will see, conditional hospitality and forgiveness can be compared to unconditional hospitality and forgiveness. Derrida also says that "as a quasi-synonym for 'unconditional,' the Kantian expression of 'categorical impera-tive' is not unproblematic; we will keep it with some reservations" (2000, 81). The problem here of needing to go beyond a rule that determines actions is one that requires some discussion, and I will return to this issue after briefly considering Derrida's third reservation.

In his third reservation, Derrida returns to Kant's metaphysics, saying that if we were to take up the term *regulative idea,* we would "have to subscribe to the entire Kantian and architectonic and critique" (Borradori 2003, 135). This last point seems rather an exaggeration, yet I believe he is right to reject the notion that he understands unconditional demands as regulative ideas. As I have pointed out, the concepts function very differ-ently. Justice is not necessarily destructive in the same way as hospitality is, as we will see, and justice is not deconstructible (1992). Thus, the answer to the question of whether Derrida's unconditional ethical concepts are like those of Kant's ethical imperatives can only be answered by looking at particular examples.[22] So Derrida is going beyond Kant in making conditional and imperfect duties into unconditional and perfect ones, albeit duties that have to be negotiated with their conditional equivalents.

What Derrida does not say is *how* we can or should negotiate between ethics and politics, between unconditionality and conditionality. A con-sideration of the issue of rule following mentioned above provides some indications. He hints that there is a connection with Kant's ethics when he notes that if we simply apply a rule when acting, "I would act, as Kant would say, *in conformity* with duty, but not *through* duty or *out of respect* for the law" (1992, 17). Thus, the problem of negotiation appears to become a question of how to make a decision or reach a judgment. Before examin-ing Arendt's views of how ethics and politics should relate to each other, I need to consider how ethical and political judgment should be understood.

Are Ethical and Political Decisions like Aesthetic Judgments?

A number of commentators on both Kant and Derrida have suggested that the answer to the problem of judgment in general can be found in Kant's aesthetics, a suggestion I will argue should be resisted. For example, in Olivia Custer's reading of Derrida's ethics, she finds that Kant's aesthet-ics provides the kind of judgment or decision without rules that Derrida is looking for.[23] Similarly, as I will discuss in the next section, Arendt finds the answer to the problem of political judgment in Kant's aesthetics. So could the solution to Derrida's reservations about Kant as well as an account of ethical and political judgment be found in the *Critique of Judgment*?

Derrida's claim is that "[w]ithout silence, without the hiatus, which is not the absence of rules but the necessity of a leap at the moment of ethical, political, or juridical decision, we could simply unfold knowledge into a program or course of action. Nothing could make us more irresponsible; nothing could be more totalitarian" (1999, 117). Derrida sees Kant as both irresponsible and totalitarian in prescribing rules for action through the categorical imperative as if we were nothing more than calculating machines.

Custer's defense of Kant against Derrida can be better understood if we realize that Derrida criticizes Kant for conflating right and virtue or assuming that politics *can* be deduced from ethics. As she observes, Kant made a fundamental distinction between morality and mere legality or right, but Derrida finds that Kant, "insofar as he suggests that it is possible to find an adequate passage between virtue and right, insofar as it is for him to deduce politics from ethics . . . in some sense effaces the distinction, or at least is not willing to take on the consequences of radical heterogeneity" (Rothfield 2003, 175). Custer sees this reading of Kant as emerging most clearly in Derrida's discussion of hospitality, where Derrida criticizes Kant for imposing restrictions on hospitality, thereby turning an ethical concept into a juridical one (2001a, 21–22). However, as we have seen, for Kant virtue is that part of ethics that cannot be enforced or made part of politics. In the case of hospitality, Kant is treating hospitality as a juridical concept, as he is focusing of what can be enforced. Custer notes, "All the progress Kant foretells for humanity is progress of *legality*, not morality proper" (Rothfield 2003, 182). Kant did not think that virtue and right would necessarily coexist but instead had a hope that people would live according to the virtues of love and respect once right was the principle under which politics was carried out. He considered that virtue would develop from having the right political structure and the right principles in place. He says at one point that "[t]he problem of establishing a state, no matter how hard it may sound, is *soluble* even for a nation of devils (if only they have understanding)" (1996a, 8: 366).[24] We also saw in chapter 2 that Kant has a sense that feelings of love, for example, can reinforce and promote ethical action. It could be said that it is Derrida who brings virtue into politics by emphasizing the importance of ethical concepts such as hospitality and forgiveness to politics, as we shall see in more detail in the following chapters. What Derrida really seems to be objecting to is the idea that ethics could give us *rules* for political life.

The distinction Kant makes between perfect and imperfect duties demonstrates the contrast here. While perfect duties may seem to provide a rule for action, imperfect duties leave leeway as to what it means to act out of duty. When I attempt to act from the duty of beneficence, for example, I need to consider the time, the context, those who would benefit and the appropriateness of my action (Kant, 1996a, 6: 452–55).[25] Thus, Derrida's criticism of Kant's notion of duty could only apply to the perfect duties of respect. As we saw, the duties of love do not follow determinate rules. There could also be conflicts between our imperfect conditional duties that we would have to resolve for ourselves in the absence of rules. It is Derrida's transformation of imperfect duties into perfect ones, in some sense, that makes duties of love seem as if they could involve rule following.

In her defense of Kant, Custer begins by showing that Kant did not claim that duties were immutable. Quoting from "What Is Enlightenment?" she argues that "the possibility of progress must remain open and this is as true for rules of conduct as it is for knowledge" (Rothfield 2003, 181). Nevertheless, as Custer writes, allowing for future correction is not the same as Derrida's contention that it is impossible to formulate rules for ethics. Furthermore, while we can know if we are conforming to the moral law, we can never know if we have acted out of duty (1996a, 4: 407). Kant understood that we cannot be entirely certain of our motives. Custer also notes that Kant does not believe that we can be virtuous by imitating others, unlike Descartes (1996a, 4: 409). Furthermore, as I noted above, Derrida acknowledges that according to Kant we must act *out of* respect for the law, not just in accordance with it, in "Force of Law" (1992, 17). Custer argues that what makes the crucial difference from Kant for Derrida is that thought of duty must "'endure' the impossibility of having rules for duty even as it accepts their necessity" (Rothfield 2003, 185; Derrida 1992, 24). Ultimately, Derrida blames Kant for not thinking of the impossibility of deducing rules for ethics at the same time as the necessity of it.

In order to show that Kant does in fact think through this tension, Custer turns to Kant's *Critique of Judgment* and his account of genius. The genius must understand and not break established rules at the same time as going beyond them, and will inspire their successor who will go beyond them and establish a new set of rules (2000, 5: 318). She argues that there is a parallel between the relation of Kant's theory of genius and the relation of morality to rules: "The act must follow rules and the act must be different in kind from anything rules can dictate" (Rothfield 2003, 190). For her, this account is one that can apply to acting from duty. To sum up her interpretation: "The act of duty, as the work of genius, can only be an event which invents a new response to an impossible challenge, the challenge of a choice in the strong sense of choosing where there are no criteria for choice, of deciding where no rules can help" (Rothfield 2003, 192). Custer believes that if we read Kant's ethics in the light of his aesthetics, we will find that Derrida does not really need to go beyond Kant.

I find Custer's interpretation appealing yet ultimately unconvincing due to the nature of ethics. One problem with these uses of Kant's aesthetics for ethics is the exceptional status of geniuses in the artistic context. How can a model that is intended to apply to rare and exceptional cases be adapted to ethical decisions generally? In his essay on theory and practice, Kant observed that even experts could lack judgment: "There can be theoreticians who can never in their lives become practical because they are lacking in judgment, for example, physicians or jurists who did well in their schooling but who are at a loss when they have to give an expert opinion" (1996a, 8: 275). He thinks that this is due to a lack of the "natural talent" of judgment. But as Kant makes clear, this difficulty in judgment applies to certain professional fields, not to ethics. For him, we are able to formulate moral laws for ourselves and act on them. Kant says it takes only "common human reason" to work out our duty, and "I do not . . . need any penetrating acuteness to see what I have to do in order that my volition be morally good" (1996a, 4: 403). Kant notes, however, that we can never be completely sure that our motives are pure (1996a, 4: 407–408). Thus, an aesthetic account of Kantian ethics is not true to Kant.

Furthermore, an aesthetic interpretation of Derrida in terms of a genius's invention is not true to Derrida since his account of judgment is explicitly not concerned with invention. While in judging, one must reinterpret and reaffirm existing rules, the judge is not just, as Derrida expresses it, if he or she "doesn't refer to any law, to any rule or if, because he doesn't take any rule for granted beyond his own interpretation, he suspends his decision, stops short before the undecidable or if he improvises and leaves aside all rules, all principles" (1992, 23). Such a process of judgment is not a process of artistic creation or invention. It involves the recognition of the specificity of particular cases, something like Kant's notion of a reflective judgment that begins with the particular, but it does not require the creation of new principles. Particular judgments, for Derrida, are always made in relation to an unconditional injunction such as justice, forgiveness, or hospitality. Derrida acknowledges that new judgments can conform to existing laws but they must reaffirm them. How I understand this point is as the need to consider each situation afresh even when applying a law or principle. Thus, I argue that we should not attempt to transfer an analysis of judgment from the aesthetic realm to the ethical realm. Aesthetic judgments could apply to very particular situations where we needed to invent a new maxim, but usually this is not necessary. We can rely on our responses of wonder and generosity linked to a consideration of the principles appropriate to the situation. I would suggest that most moral choices are not impossible, although political life tends to provide more of such dramatic choices than private life. Custer's interpretation helps to demonstrate how close Derrida's conception of the relation between ethics and politics is to Kant's. However, he does go beyond Kant, as Irigaray does, in raising the importance of virtue as well as right to politics. His account demonstrates the importance of ethics to politics although it does not give us a way of thinking about how important ethics should be. Before I return to this question of the role of virtue in politics in more detail, I wish to confront Arendt's criticism of ethics in politics.

Arendt and the Danger of Righteousness

One of the difficulties in considering the relation between ethics and politics is that how one sees their relationship depends on how one defines both. Thus, for example, a committed utilitarian is not going to see a great deal of difficulty in bringing them together, because the aims of ethics and politics can be defined in the same way. On Arendt's view, however, morality and politics are simply two completely different realms. Her position on morality and politics provides a strong counterpoint to both Kant and Derrida. While Arendt's adoption of Kant's aesthetic critique of judgment as a model for politics might suggest that she sees politics in a Kantian light, it is in fact indicative of her suspicion of morals in politics. Arendt is wary of morality's role in politics because she believes there is a danger of righteousness, or imposing moral standards that are considered by her to be inappropriate in that context.

One commentator, George Kateb, sums up her view as: "In a word, even a normal amount of moral concern, not just Socratic moral strictness, disfigures political action, by Arendt's reckoning" (2001, 123).[26] Arendt distinguishes between ethics, or as she says, morality, and politics in this way: "In the center of moral considerations of human conduct stands the self; in the center of political considerations of conduct stands the world" (2003, 153). Furthermore, because she sees morality as the individual understanding truths for themselves according to their own conscience, morality seems out of place in politics, where a plurality of actors argue concerning what is to be done. Politics is usually also thought to take into account the consequences of actions, although Kateb notes that Arendt's conception of politics is one where instrumental and practical concerns are not important (2001, 128).

The difficulty in seeing how Arendt's criticisms of morality in politics are relevant to Kant's and Derrida's views lies in the circumstance that Arendt is trying to develop a new or different conception of political philosophy from that of the tradition. She sees Plato as shaping that tradition through his identification of knowing with ruling and acting with obeying (Arendt 1998, 225). Her conception of politics is one where action is understood as beginning something new in the public sphere. Arendt writes that "[t]here are many ways in which political and moral standards of conduct can come into conflict with each other, and in political theory they are usually dealt with in connection with reason-of-state doctrine and its so-called double standard of morality" (2003, 154). The idea is that reasons of state, such as security, can override morality. This view is in direct conflict with Kant's view that politics must conform to morality, although as I noted he makes some concession toward reasons of state in relation to tolerating injustice temporarily for the safety of the state. Arendt believes that the only case where morals are absolute and one can have an excuse for not participating in politics is in extreme situations where one is asked to do something that one simply cannot live with (2003, 156). In totalitarian regimes, for example, people have to rely on their own conscience or sense of morality rather than the beliefs and actions of their community. Arendt believes that if one lives in a reasonable society we can rely on our community standards as guides for moral living (2003, 104). However, when moral standards are turned upside down, for example, when killing innocents becomes acceptable, then we have few moral guideposts beyond our own conscience.

Arendt's rejection of morals in politics has been tied to her concern with a general collapse of morals in totalitarian regimes. Kimberley Hutchings, for example, argues that Arendt has a "conviction of the uselessness of truth, morality or law as adequate protection against totalitarian development"

(1996a, 83). However, I think that this is an overinterpretation of what Arendt says in *The Origins of Totalitarianism*. Arendt writes that totalitarian governments "started to operate according to a system of values so radically different from all others, that none of our traditional legal, moral, or common sense utilitarian values could any longer help us to come to terms with, or judge, or predict their course of action" (1976, 460). What she is saying here is that none of our *traditional* moral values enable people to prevent the onslaught of totalitarianism. That problem leaves open the possibility that a new conception of ethics as well as politics could help us to do so. Hutchings writes further that morality cannot be part of politics for Arendt because it involves "the coercion of particulars by universal determinations . . . the commands of practical reason" (1996, 94).[27] Again, it is Kant's conception of morality that is being excluded here, rather than morality or ethics per se. This criticism appears to oppose Arendt's view, stated elsewhere, that the problem with morality is that it is concerned with the self. Nevertheless, I must concede that both points are different ways of expressing Arendt's conception of politics as an arena of opinion, discussion, and judgment not determined by categorical imperatives of any kind.

Arendt means to exclude morals from politics because she holds that morals become untrue when they enter politics. For her, morals generally concern the capacity for the individual to be at one with themselves, to not be willing to live with a thief or a murderer, whereas in politics the concerns are with "the world and with public welfare" (1968, 245). Arendt writes, "The disastrous consequences for any community that began in all earnest to follow ethical precepts derived from man in the singular—be they Socratic or Platonic or Christian—have been frequently pointed out," citing Machiavelli and Aristotle.[28] The only way, she argues, for ethical principles to be verified, is through particular individuals, such as Socrates, or fictional examples, like King Lear (1968, 248). When we are deprived of such examples we tend to be deprived of our moral sense, Arendt believes. She sees morals or ethics as quite distinct from the political realm because they do not concern what we share we others but our dialogue with ourselves in thought. Her essay "Truth and Politics" might be taken to constitute a concern with morals in politics. However, she is not concerned about the question of *particular* lies in politics, such as those diplomats might tell to an enemy, but with large-scale deception and self-deception that can affect a political community (1968, 256). For her, such deception is more serious than a deliberate lie because the distinction between truth and falsity is abandoned. The problem with such abandonment is that it undermines the conditions for politics, where opinions are debated in a context of facts that are generally accepted.

To see how Arendt's conception of politics might be taken as a challenge to Kant, it is important to note that Arendt does not take Kant's "Doctrine of Right" to constitute his account of politics. She dismisses it as a rather inferior philosophy of law and instead turns to the *Critique of Judgment* and his essays on politics (1982, 8). In this way, politics itself becomes aestheticized, so that it is the new and unprecedented that is conceived as profoundly political. Arendt believes that Kant's account of aesthetic judgment describes the process of forming political judgment, through the process of enlarging our mentality by imagining how I might think and feel if I was in others' places (1968, 241).[29] This conception raises the question of how Arendt understood the Shoah, as it too, was new and unprecedented. Kateb's interpretation is that the Shoah, and indeed the systems of Nazism and Stalinism, are perversions of the unexpected. Yet, conscience or morality was needed to see wrong in a situation where others saw normality. Kateb claims that this moral judgment is supported by the aesthetic judgment that refuses to subsume the new and evil into a judgment of acceptance (2001, 136).

There seems to be a real problem here, however, when one sees the importance of moral judgment in this extreme moral situation and considers how important such judgment is to everyday politics. Making the right judgment is not always to notice the novel or new when no one else does but also to see the similarity that one situation or action bears to another, perhaps when no one else can. Kateb's account focuses only on the negative moral judgments that are made in extreme situations. What Arendt says about conscience is that it does not provide an infallible guide, because we may feel guilty when we should not and feel innocent when we should feel guilty (2003, 107). Arendt's characterization of positive moral judgments (contrasted with moral decisions not to do something) is in terms of examples. Taking Kant's notion of a schema, she says that an example that is between a general rule and an individual case allows us to judge right and wrong. Achilles stands for her as an exemplar of courage (2003, 143). Thus, such exemplars may help us to make ethical and political judgments without giving ethics any precedence over politics.

Seyla Benhabib's interpretation of Arendt's conception of the relation between ethics and politics is that although her concept of politics could only make sense within a normative framework of universal human rights, equality, and respect, Arendt did not believe that such considerations could restrain politics and did not justify them in her work. While one could try to extrapolate such a justification, Benhabib writes, "[i]t is the step leading from the constituents of a philosophical anthropology (natality, worldliness, plurality, and forms of human activity) to this attitude of respect for the other that is missing in Arendt's thought" (Villa 2000, 81).

Benhabib is right to suggest respect as an ethical concept playing a role in Arendt's ethics and politics. Unlike love, which she considers unworldly and apolitical, Arendt's brief mention of respect in *The Human Condition* takes respect to be worldly and therefore relevant to politics: "Respect, not unlike the Aristotelian *philia politikē,* is a kind of 'friendship' without intimacy and without closeness; it is a regard for the person from the distance which the space of the world put between us, and this regard is independent of qualities which we may admire or of achievements which we may highly esteem" (1998, 243). This account of respect is very similar to that of both Descartes and Kant, who make the same distinction between respect and esteem. However, as Benhabib notes, apart from seeming disappointed by the replacement of respect by esteem in the modern world, Arendt does not give any justification for attitudes of respect, although the materials for such a justification exist in her work.[30] Thus, Benhabib argues against Arendt that "there is a normative foundation to politics insofar as any political system embodies principles of justice. In Kantian theory this domain covers the *Rechtslehre,* namely those human rights and public principles of legislation that embody respect for the moral worth and dignity of another" (1992, 139). The problem with Arendt's conception of morality, diagnoses Benhabib, is that she focuses on virtue or good rather than right, which can be incorporated into politics without distortion of politics' qualities, just as Kant argues. Yet my purpose here is to show how virtue in the form of cultivated wonder, generosity, and love, can also play a role in politics.

While there is much that is appealing in Arendt's conception of politics, it does not undermine the cases put forward by Kant and Derrida. Arendt's distancing of politics from ethics is a result of her aestheticized view of politics and her narrow view of ethics, and as such does not constitute a strong alternative to a politics that at the very least tries to take ethics into account. Although I disagree with her on this fundamental point, I find many of her comments about specific political issues, such as the nature of rights, kinds of evil, and responsibility for past actions, insightful, and I return to her work in later chapters.

A Proper and Generous Politics

My discussion of Kant, Derrida, and Arendt is intended to open the space for a conception of ethical politics that can deal with the difficulties they raise, and include wonder and generosity in political life. Derrida's setting up of unconditional ethics brings the imperfect duties of Kant to the forefront of politics, and this is a significant improvement, as I argued in relation to Irigaray's view of love, in chapter 2. At the same time, I want to take seriously the difficulties of moralism and the problems of the urgency of political conflict. While I do not believe that politics should interfere in the private or ethical relations to the self, as Arendt and Michel Foucault fear, nevertheless politics could, without such interference, make more ethical lives more probable.[31] Arendt blames ethics for being too superficial, so that under the Nazi regime people could change their ethics like table manners (2003, 50). However, I believe a better explanation is that ethics was not deeply rooted enough due to a political situation where ethics had no role. Thus, the challenge for politics is not to dispense with ethics but to be thought with the possibility of providing ethics with a deeper basis. One central feature of that ethics is the responses of wonder and generosity.

I do not accept Arendt's view of politics as a public realm quite separate from the realm of morality or ethics. Rather, I believe that every aspect of our lives is imbued with politics and what is needed is a conception of the political life that enables that life to be ethical. Thus, ethical considerations need to be incorporated in politics at the most fundamental level in the case of wonder, generosity, and love. In Norberto Bobbio's discussion of ethics and politics, he says that the concern with ethics is exclusively in terms of our duties to others (2000, 42). I would say that is correct if we are only thinking of the duties of politicians. However, if we consider that politics affects all individuals' lives, then politics could play a role in ensuring that we are able or more likely to carry out duties to ourselves, such as the duty to perfect ourselves.

The conception of the relation between ethics and politics I am aiming it is one that is both proper and generous—that conforms to norms of right, as Kant outlines, and is generous or virtuous, in Levinas's and Derrida's sense. In my judgment, Kant's view is an essential step toward an ethical politics, despite his condemnation of rebellion and minimal concern with conflicts between human rights and duties to the state, since this politics involves respect for some basic human rights. It should be noted that Derrida refers to the Declaration of Human Rights as a means of challenging the sovereignty of states (2005, 88). However, even these rights, according to Derrida, must be subject to negotiation or transaction with the conditional and must be questioned (2003, 133).

While Derrida goes beyond Kant in emphasizing the importance of virtue or imperfect duties, he does not advance beyond Kant by suggesting what kind of political structures would enable the flourishing of those virtues. His idea of democracy to come is inspiring, yet it leaves quite open how it could relate to unconditional ethics. His transformation of Kant's imperfect duties into perfect duties (in some sense) also makes the development of such enabling structures even more unlikely, and this is why I find Kant's position on this matter more compelling overall. Thinking of the virtues as perfect duties sets us on a path of construing ethical politics as a utopian dream and could justify the careless idealism Levinas fears or quietism in the face of impossibility. The ethics that is relevant to politics is both the "right" delineated by Kant and the unconditional demands put forward by Derrida. Kant's ethics is lacking in taking no account for the need for wonder or recognition of our difference from others. In that sense, Derrida is much more aware of the need to recognize difference. Nevertheless, the freedom implied by Kant's notion of an imperfect duty should be retained, as I will show in the following chapters. Between Kant's possible ideals and Derrida's impossible reals there is a possibility of ethical and political action that is not simply ameliorative, and that will encourage the development of wonder and generosity. Politics has to be conceived in a way that makes the negotiation between politics and ethics a more promising affair.

Derrida's insistence on the importance of unconditional ethical demands to politics forces us to think more carefully about that role and about the responsibility of both ethics and politics to each other. Despite his concern with democracy and fear of totalitarianism that prevents him from articulating any principles for negotiating between ethics and politics, Derrida's position neglects the question of how politics needs to be configured to make ethical living more likely. Kant expresses a vision where one focuses on enforcing what needs to be enforced while, in the main, leaving the other aspects of ethics to look after themselves. Derrida's vision reminds us how significant ethical virtues are to public life but does not suggest what political conditions could promote those virtues. His emphasis on unconditional ethical concepts such as forgiveness and hospitality places the onus on the individual to try to live up to unconditional demands. The idea of a "democracy to come" involves some important suggestions for international institutions but does not articulate changes that would be needed to assist individuals to live up to those demands.

Kant's account of these principles of right leaves much to be desired, particularly of independence as a citizen. He was no feminist, as he excludes women and non-property owners from the role of active citizens (1996a, 8: 295). Kant makes a distinction between active citizens, who are independent and can vote, and passive ones, who he argues are dependent on the will of others. Nevertheless, one could extend this principle, in other words extend generosity, in an inclusive way. Others argue that Kant was also a racist, and differ as to whether this prejudice is essential to his work.[32] Another problem I see in Kant's account of right is his acceptance of capital punishment for the crimes of high treason and murder (1996a, 6:320, 6:333). This acceptance appears to be in conflict with the categorical imperative to treat everyone as ends in themselves and with the whole tenor of the Kantian view that we should treat others with respect. However, as Nelson Potter argues, in the cases of his notion of passive citizens and his support for the death penalty Kant can be revised in a manner that makes his view more consistent, particularly since Kant himself was offering a critique of the contemporary cruel punishments often carried out as well as a limitation on the crimes capital punishment should be applied to (2002, 267–82).[33] These are reconstructions that would be necessary for genuine compatibility between ethics and politics, in my view. Kant's ideas of rights need to be reconstructed in a number of ways, some of which they already have been in practice (at least widely), to include women as active citizens, and some of which they have not, to exclude capital punishment, for example. The rights of members of all racial and ethnic groups should also be explicitly upheld. An ethical politics should make an explicit commitment to certain rights and work out how they can be established and maintained. This is generosity exemplified at a political level.

Benhabib's adjustment to Arendt's view of politics is to incorporate right into politics in the form of just institutions, and to add the notion of encouraging civic virtues of friendship and solidarity through democratic participation (1992, 140). I believe that Benhabib's approach to politics is a worthwhile extension of Arendt's, yet I would argue that it does not go far enough, and that other kinds of virtues, such as those of wonder and love, also need to be encouraged, cultivated, and form the basis of politics, as I argued in the earlier chapters in relation to both Descartes and Irigaray.

Working through the relation between ethics and politics requires a sense of what it is to act with respect for others, with wonder and with love, so that all our particular decisions, on an individual, national, and international level, have these ethical standards as touchstones to judgment. A generous and welcoming approach to asylum seekers, openness to the possibility of forgiveness, and collective apologies for past injustices are ethical political gestures. In the following chapters, I will show how the conception of the relation between ethics and politics and a framework of wonder and generosity as responses to difference and similarity helps to us to think about contemporary ethical and political issues, as responses both to injustice and to evil. The next chapter is concerned with the question of hospitality for asylum seekers and refugees.

5

Cosmopolitanism, Hospitality, and Refugees

> Yet this possible abuse cannot annul the right of citizens of the world
> *to try to* establish community with all and, to this end, to *visit* all regions
> of the earth.
>
> —Immanuel Kant, "Toward Perpetual Peace"

Hospitality is an act or set of acts, rather than a passion or attitude like wonder or generosity, yet both passions and attitudes are important to understanding hospitality. In this chapter, I discuss the concept of hospitality in the context of the moral and political philosophy of cosmopolitanism. Recent philosophers, political scientists, and cultural theorists have suggested that the concept of cosmopolitanism is useful to theorize an ideal relationship between different nations, and to confront the problems faced by asylum seekers and refugees.[1] Hospitality involves the openness of wonder to the difference of the arriving other, and generosity is also needed in terms of respect for asylum seekers and their rights as human beings. Immanuel Kant's view of cosmopolitanism, especially as rendered in his essay "Toward Perpetual Peace" (1996a), discussed in the previous chapter, is one of the most significant and influential in the debate concerning the treatment of asylum seekers. In a number of works, including *On Cosmopolitanism and Forgiveness* (2001) and *Of Hospitality* (2000), as I have noted, Jacques Derrida takes up Kant's cosmopolitanism, in particular his notion of the right to universal hospitality as a useful way of thinking through these questions. As Derrida says, "It is not for speculative or ethical reasons that I am interested in unconditional hospitality, but in order to transform what is going on today in our world" (Kearney and Dooley 1999, 70). Arendt's discussion of the "right to have rights" is also relevant here and I will show how this should be understood as extending generosity to asylum seekers. The problems faced by those fleeing persecution and hardship are among the most significant occurring in our world today, and these problems have only been increased by recent concerns about terrorism, and continuing violence in Iraq, Afghanistan, and elsewhere. Can the concepts of cosmopolitanism and hospitality help us think how to transform and overcome the difficulties asylum seekers and refugees face? Furthermore, what is the role of wonder and generosity here? The problem is one that cuts across ethics and politics and calls for both a personal response and a political framework that shapes and nurtures the appropriate personal responses. It is also concerns questions about how people interact with others of different races and cultures, and a problem that can affect women in ways that are not properly recognized in international law. Philosophical and theoretical reflection on these concepts can suggest that policies concerning asylum seekers and refugees need to be framed differently. Cosmopolitanism takes the idea of generosity or respect for all and gives it an international and political face. Hospitality exemplifies a genuine openness and welcoming of the other and can involve both wonder at difference and generosity. But this is to leap ahead. First, we need to be aware of the Kantian source of these concepts, which emerge from the ethical political framework I discussed in the last chapter.

Kant's Cosmopolitanism

A preliminary discussion of Kant's cosmopolitanism is necessary to situate these questions. In the broadest terms, cosmopolitanism refers to nations composed of people or elements from many different cultures or countries, or sometimes to individuals who are familiar with a variety of cultures— "citizens of the world." As mentioned briefly in the preceding chapter, Kant's philosophical idea is of a world cosmopolitanism rather than cosmopolitanism within countries and is compatible with, indeed in his view necessarily composed of, independent, autonomous nations. Kant's concept of cosmopolitanism occurs in the context of his teleological philosophy of history and his views on the politics of right. Kant set up the problem facing humanity in the fifth thesis of "Idea for a universal history with a cosmopolitan intent" in this way: "The greatest problem for the human species, whose solution nature compels it to seek, is to achieve a universal *civil society* administered in accord with the right" (1983, 8: 22).[2] According to Kant, we are continually progressing toward a more perfect state, a state in which we will all be perfectly moral, rational, and happy. Nature's purpose is to bring us to this ideal state but reason can also show us how this achievement is possible.

One can see Kant's essay "Toward Perpetual Peace" (1996a) as both a sketch of the answer to the problem of how to achieve a universal civil society and an account of reason's contribution to the progress toward perpetual peace. Cosmopolitanism, as Kant envisages it, is both the system whereby one ensures perpetual peace and institutes ethics or morals, at least the part of it concerned with right or law, in cooperative political relations between republican states, as we saw. Kant's version of cosmopolitanism should not be confused with multiculturalism. His cosmopolitanism is compatible, at least, with each nation being quite ethnically homogenous rather than multicultural, as long as all nations are on peaceful terms and allow visitation. However, his cosmopolitanism does not exclude multiculturalism, either.

The essay on perpetual peace is set out as a kind of political pamphlet but, as scholars have noted, it contains a complex and fascinating series of interrelated arguments (Beck 1957; Bohman and Lutz-Bachmann 1997; Covell 1998; Wood 1998). Perpetual peace, according to Kant, can be achieved through the institution of six preliminary articles for perpetual peace and three definitive articles. As I discussed in the previous chapter, the preliminary articles deal with practical matters that would need to be resolved to bring about the basis for the governance of right and the definitive articles concern the rights that would need to be in place for peace to exist.[3] The last of the three conditions or "Definitive Articles" of Kant's cosmopolitanism is a condition of universal hospitality.[4] I will concentrate on this article here. Kant says, "**Cosmopolitan right** shall be limited to conditions of universal *hospitality*" (1996a, 8: 357). Hospitality means "the right of an alien not to be treated as an enemy upon his arrival in another's country . . . as long as he behaves peaceably" (1996a, 8: 358). Another way to express the right of hospitality is to say that it allows freedom of movement to visit nations other than one's own.[5] Kant bases this right to visit on a claim that we all own the surface of the earth together because "originally, no-one had a greater right to any region of the earth than anyone else" (1996a, 8: 358). His idea is that we originally shared the earth with each other and so we should continue to acknowledge that sharing in this specific way.

The condition of universal hospitality can be violated either by a host country through denial of the right to visit, by robbery and enslavement of travelers or by a "visiting" country through invasion, settlement, political interference, and also by slavery. A number of Kant's remarks suggest that he believes that universal hospitality centrally involves reciprocal trading arrangements, rather than reflecting a concern with asylum seekers and refugees. In "Perpetual Peace," he claims that "[t]he *spirit of trade* cannot co-exist with war, and sooner or later this sprit dominates every people" (1996a, 8: 368). Kant clearly saw trade as a source for good, contributing to perpetual peace as it provides a reliable nonethical motivation to seek peace. While Kant notes that differences in language and religion create hostility and prevent people from melding into one whole, he also believes this hostility can be overcome through the spirit of trade and the progress of enlightenment. While Kant's views on race are mixed and controversial, in this context he clearly condemns the practices of colonialism, stating,

> If one compares with this the *inhospitable* behavior of civilized, especially commercial, states in our part of the world, the injustice they show in *visiting* foreign lands and peoples (which with them is tantamount to *conquering* them) goes to horrifying lengths. When America, the negro countries, the Spice Islands, the cape, and so forth were discovered, they were, to them, countries belonging to no one, since they counted the inhabitants as nothing. In the East Indies (Hindustan), they brought in foreign soldiers under the pretext of merely proposing to set up trading posts, but with them oppression of the inhabitants, incitement of the various Indian states to widespread wars, famine, rebellions, treachery, and the whole litany of troubles that oppress the human race. (1996a, 8: 358)

His comments show that the colonizing countries should have respected the inhabitants of these countries and not violated their trust and abused their hospitality through deception and oppression. Kant is comparing such practices to the true practices of hospitality, which involve trying to engage in trade and to visit peacefully.

As we saw in the last chapter, for Kant, politics can be made commensurable with morality only in a federative union. Thus, the vision of perpetual peace Kant would like to see established is also the place where it can be ensured that morality and politics coincide. Although Kant emphasizes political conditions in "Perpetual Peace," it is clear that he envisages ethical principles or "virtue" flourishing within the cosmopolitan state. However, as I explained in chapter 2, he claims that the love of humanity is a conditional duty, and respect for humanity is an unconditional duty (1996a, 8: 385). This universal respect would be manifest in the cosmopolitan world and we can hope that universal love would also be manifest and try to encourage it.

In his reading of Kant's essay, Allen Wood contrasts Kant's understanding of the ethical and the political through the distinction between the voluntary nature of the ethical or virtuous and the need for enforcement of the political, and argues that in "Perpetual Peace" "the international federation is quite evidently grounded in right rather than in morality," or in virtue (Cheah and Robbins 1998, 67–68). Wood's view is that Kant does not present either the practical means or the theoretical framework for the laws that would be needed. In contrast, Lewis White Beck claims that an implicit structure of argument that constitutes the theoretical framework can be found in "Perpetual Peace" if we look beyond the treaty-like order in which Kant presents his ideas. Beck argues that for Kant, principles of right and morality justify the ideal of perpetual peace (Kant 1957, ix–xiii). In other words, cosmopolitanism is both a political and an ethical ideal, in which we live according to the rule of right and we respect others, we treat them with generosity. This ideal state is also supposed to provide the conditions for love to flourish, although as I argued, it is not clear that Kant's account of political structure is sufficient to make that probable. There needs to be a role for wonder, too, in articulating a political framework that will recognize differences between the sexes and cultural and racial differences.

In the case of hospitality, Kant leaves unclear precisely what is included in the right to hospitality and cosmopolitan right. He distinguishes between civil right, international right, and cosmopolitan right: civil right concerns rights of individuals within nations, international right concerns relations between nations, and cosmopolitan right concerns relations between individuals and other nations. Kant says, cryptically, that cosmopolitan right's maxims work by analogy to those of international right, hence providing us with plenty of room for speculation as to what he has in mind. Cosmopolitanism for Kant does not appear to entail particular institutions to govern cosmopolitan rights, such as an international criminal court, in the way many contemporary cosmopolitans recommend. As Wood notes, "Kant proposes no specific mechanisms for determining or enforcing international rights" (Cheah and Robbins 1998, 67). It appears that membership in the federation must be voluntary and include all those states that wish to belong, even if they are not republican.[6]

What is interesting about Kant's model of cosmopolitanism is the way he *both* extends individual rights *and* supports the autonomy of states, rather than arguing that the world community should become one superstate. The extension of individual rights appears, for example, in his advocacy of a right to universal hospitality and his argument that individuals should not be used as means to fight wars, yet he defends the sovereignty of states, arguing that any interference is a violation of autonomy (1996a, 8: 346).

Contemporary cosmopolitans tend to believe in the first principle—the extension of individual rights—but not the second—the principle of the sovereignty of states. For example, David Chandler argues that "all cosmopolitan perspectives reflect the increasing prominence of individual rights claims in the international sphere," replacing principles of the sovereignty of states (2003, 25). As I noted, Kant's attitude to such rights is quite vague. However, his position may have some advantages. One of the dangers of cosmopolitan protection of individual rights is the possibility that it could be used to justify intervention in the affairs of nations, and it is inevitably the richer and more powerful nations that will be able to do so, as Chandler points out (2003, 30). Kant clearly envisaged such possibilities, as he makes clear in article five of the preliminary articles for perpetual peace: "No nation shall forcibly interfere with the constitution and government of another" (1996a, 8: 346). He allows the exception of civil wars, where two parts of one nation try to claim sovereignty over the whole nation, which naturally raises practical issues concerning how to determine when internal conflict becomes a civil war. More importantly, however, Kant's position on this question is based on his view that the autonomy of nations, like that of persons, must be respected (1996a, 8: 367). We should be generous to states as well as individuals.

Nevertheless, in relation to the question of individual rights, Kant argues that "a transgression of rights in *one* place in the world is felt *everywhere*" and sees the idea of cosmopolitan right as "an amendment to the unwritten code of national and international rights" (1996a, 8: 360). The complexity of Kant's position here is demonstrated by Katrin Flikschuh's reading. She notes that Kant wavered between conceiving cosmopolitan right in the context of a world state (1996a, 8: 357) and in the context of a federation of free republics (1996a, 8: 354), and that on the latter interpretation, fewer rights would belong to individuals. However, even on this latter interpretation, "refugee rights, including asylum rights and the right not to be imprisoned and/or tortured by the host state, would fall under cosmopolitan Right" (2000, 188). The former, stronger interpretation would allow intervention in nations' affairs to uphold individual human rights.

Thus, while Kant does not advocate forcibly interfering in the affairs of other nations in order to support individual rights, he assumes that citizens and states would use other means to persuade and encourage nations to uphold individual rights. Kant's essay is of continuing relevance and rereading it is a rewarding task, as we have already seen. Derrida's rereading develops and extends Kant's insights into the specific concept of hospitality, and I will address it in order to establish an understanding of hospitality in relation to wonder and generosity.

The Condition of Universal Hospitality

Derrida addresses the specific questions of cosmopolitanism, hospitality and refugees in a series of interconnected essays and interviews. His piece "On Cosmopolitanism" is a speech on the concept of cosmopolitan rights for asylum seekers, refugees, and immigrants. Derrida's reworking of Kant's cosmopolitanism involves a questioning of Kant's reliance on the idea of nation-states, a proposal for "refuge cities" in Europe, and a shift of hospitality to the ethical and political planes in addition to the juridical one, as one might expect.[7] He says we should distinguish between "the foreigner in general, the immigrant, the exiled, the deported, the stateless or the displaced person" (2001a, 4). While Derrida uses the concept of hospitality to apply to all these different groups, he is most interested in the difficulties of asylum seekers.

In this essay and his more detailed work *Of Hospitality*, Derrida considers the history of the concept of hospitality, which he sees as involving three traditions: the Hebraic tradition of cities of refuge described in the Bible, the medieval tradition of the laws of hospitality, and the cosmopolitan tradition the Enlightenment inherited from Stoicism, particularly from Cicero, and Pauline Christianity.[8] While there are conceptual connections between these traditions, his primary focus is Kant's formulation of the law of hospitality and the limitations Kant places on it.

As I noted in the previous chapter, Derrida finds in the concept of hospitality a distinction between unconditional and conditional hospitality. Unconditional hospitality requires that anyone be welcome regardless of whether they identify themselves and their origins. While Derrida does not use this language, this kind of hospitality involves wonder, a nonjudgmental acceptance of the difference of the other, who can surprise us in so many ways. Conditional hospitality is the hospitality determined and regulated by the state and its legal apparatus. This kind of hospitality might be thought to be linked to generosity and respect for the other, but that would inappropriately simplify matters, as regulated hospitality can also be lacking in a generous recognition of what the safe citizen or resident shares with those fleeing persecution. What is needed, rather, is a sense of how both wonder and generosity can contribute to a fuller hospitality. For Derrida, these two forms of hospitality correspond to a distinction between the Law of hospitality, or justice, and the laws of hospitality. The Law is the absolutely unconditional ideal of law, like the personified law in Plato's *Crito*, whereas the laws are the particular laws that are put into place in particular contexts (Plato 1999, 43a–54e).

Parallel to his discussion of the impossibility of the gift (1992) and forgiveness (2001a), as I detail in later chapters, in *Of Hospitality,* Derrida explores an antimony in hospitality. He argues that the Law of absolute, unconditional hospitality demands that we transgress all the laws of hospitality and the laws of hospitality transgress the Law of hospitality (2000, 75). However, Derrida also says that the Law of hospitality requires the laws, and that it would not be unconditional if it did not have to become effective, concrete. The justice of hospitality requires that there are means by which the other can enter our home, that relations to the foreigner are regulated by law (2000, 73). Conversely, Derrida claims that the conditional laws would not be laws of hospitality if they were not given aspiration by the Law of hospitality. He concludes that these two regimes of law are contradictory, antonymic, and inseparable. While a law cannot be both conditional and unconditional, both the Law and the laws depend on each other for their meaning. Another way Derrida expresses the distinction between unconditional and conditional hospitality is through the difference between hospitality and the concept of "invitation" An invitation involves preparation and expectation, but unconditional hospitality must be completely surprising (Kearney and Dooley 1999, 70). It must be rich with wonder, I would say. The complete surprise of the visitor and the lack of judgment of the host involve the response of wonder.

The distinction between conditional and unconditional hospitality can be traced to Kant's text. An important point Derrida makes is that Kant's description of the right to hospitality as a universal natural right generated by our shared inhabitance of the globe enables its separation from all that is cultural or institutional so that it becomes a conventional right that excludes the right of residence and is controlled by the state. Derrida argues that Kant's implicit distinction between the natural and the cultural allows him to support this understanding of hospitality:

1. Hospitality as a right of residence is excluded; hospitality is a right of visitation. The right of residence only arises through particular treaties. (For Derrida, this is a controversial point.)
2. The conditions of hospitality, particularly the question of a right of residence, are dependent on the sovereignty of the state, and are controlled by the law and state police. (2001a, 21–22)

In this way, the right to visit is sharply distinguished from the right to residence and the natural basis of the right shifts to a conventional one. In the *Metaphysics of Morals,* Kant clarifies what he means by distinguishing between having possession of the land and standing in a "community of possible physical *interaction*," which is how he sees the importance of our sharing of the earth (1996a, 6: 352). Kant bases the right of hospitality on that possible interaction, which allows the right to visit, but not to settle.

In this way, the contradictory logic of hospitality emerges again: first, it is unconditional, so that everyone should have the right of refuge, but second, there have to be some limits to the rights of residence. One way of reading this logic is to emphasize the very important difference between the right to refuge and the right to residence. So one could say that there is not really a contradiction at work, since the right to refuge can be unconditional whereas the right to residence is, perhaps rightly, conditional. John Caputo says, "Hospitality *is* impossible, what Derrida calls *the* impossible (the im-possibility of hostil-pitality), which is not the same as a simple logical contradiction. Hospitality really starts to happen when I push against this limit, this threshold, this paralysis, inviting hospitality to cross its own threshold and limit, its own self-limitation, to become a gift *beyond hospitality*" (1997, 111). Hospitality begins where I am open to the other in wonder. Within this paradoxical structure, Derrida is not suggesting that we try to achieve the impossible ideal of unconditional hospitality, or even to really uphold it as our ideal. Rather, his argument is that the law has to be transformed and improved by negotiating between the Law of hospitality and the laws of hospitality. This argument is analogous to his argument concerning negotiation between the ethical and political. The Law of hospitality *needs* the conditional laws to temper its irresponsibility, which would mean all kinds of dangers, as Kant foresaw, especially in his detailing of the horrors of colonialism. The visitor can always become an invader or colonist, so the host is at risk. We cannot wonder at everything, an issue I will focus on in the following chapter. It should be added that the laws of hospitality need the Law of hospitality to temper their frequent callousness. States regulating their affairs and asserting their sovereignty in the face of desperate people seeking refuge can lack both wonder and generosity. They fail to be open and welcoming and fail to admit that those searching for asylum also need and deserve a home.

While Derrida is critical of Kant's philosophy of history and the limitations of his political philosophy, as we saw earlier, he concedes that there is still a long way to go before reaching the fulfillment of Kant's views on the rights to universal hospitality: "A certain idea of cosmopolitanism, *an other*, has not yet arrived, *perhaps*" (2001a, 23). There is a large gap between the principles of the right to asylum of Enlightenment thinkers and the French Revolution and the implementation of these principles.[9] The right to asylum is constrained by juridical restrictions, and overseen by a "mean-minded" juridical tradition that serves the interests of the nation-state and that is far too conditional a form of hospitality. He notes that in France this tradition is becoming more restrictive, in its treatment of both refugees and those who help them. Derrida argues that immigration control often means that asylum is thought to be appropriate only for people who will not benefit economically from migration (2001a, 12). This skepticism and suspicion about motives for seeking asylum makes it difficult for political asylum to be gained. Furthermore, the police often enforce the orders for deportation, for example, and there is the problem of police powers continually increasing, particularly when they begin to make the law.[10] The notion of sanctuary was made a mockery of by French police in their storming of the Church of St. Bernard in Paris to apprehend immigrants *sans papiers* in 1996 (1999, 135). This kind of incident is a symbolic and practical breach of the tradition of hospitality and refuge.

However, it is not only economic interests that govern government policy; concern to be reelected can play a crucial role if a harsh stance against asylum seekers is seen to be popular. In Australia, asylum seekers arriving by boat are treated differently from those arriving by plane and granted fewer rights. The previous Australian government acted against economic interests in order to pursue political goals, as these actions aided them in winning an election and maintaining their popularity. It sought to overcome the traditions of rescue at sea and to avoid accepting asylum seekers by excising parts of its territory, offshore islands, for immigration purposes and "processing" refugees offshore. The successive government attempted to take this approach farther by sending asylum seekers to Malaysia in exchange for refugees there.[11] The so-called Pacific Solution was much more expensive than simply allowing asylum seekers ashore, as is prolonged detention (Marr and Wilkinson 2003, 160). Similarly, in the UK, many failed asylum seekers are held in detention indefinitely, sometimes for up to eight years, a process that has a deleterious effect on the mental health of those detained, and is also extremely expensive (Phelps et al., 2009). Arbitrary detention of asylum seekers in prison conditions is practiced in the United States, as is mandatory detention of asylum seekers who arrive there (Human Rights First 2009, 1). Canada is generally known as being more hospitable, encouraging refugees on a path to citizenship, and generally uses detention only in exceptional cases. However, recently the Canadian government has argued that tough laws and practices are needed as the system is being "abused" (Hayward 2011). Although most governments in the world do not live up to Kant's cosmopolitanism, Derrida rightly sees hospitality as demanding more from us than that. We should try to go beyond Kantian hospitality to a respectful and open treatment of asylum seekers.

Derrida interprets Kant's concept of hospitality as conditional, in requiring that the guest be a citizen of another country, and that they act peacefully in the foreign nation (Kearney and Dooley 1999, 70). The visitor has to be a good guest. However, conditionality is not the only problem he finds in Kant's condition of universal hospitality. Derrida makes an important distinction between the ethics and the politics of hospitality. As he observes, hospitality is a juridical notion for Kant, as he specifies in *Metaphysics of Morals* that making a settlement requires a specific contract (1996a, 6: 353). In contrast, Derrida argues for a different political notion of hospitality, a new cosmopolitics, and an ethics of hospitality. This broadening of cosmopolitanism to include rights for asylum seekers seems to me to be in a Kantian spirit. One could see Kant's claim that it is all right to turn away strangers as long as one does not harm them as the inverse of the rights of refugees to be accepted if they are genuinely fleeing persecution. Furthermore, although Kant does not consider that virtues can inform political structures, we should remember that Kant's vision of perpetual peace was one where ethical attitudes extend to all relations, where we live in a kingdom of ends of respect, and hopefully, love for others. This love is a duty of virtue for Kant, which goes beyond the right to hospitality and

promises a more complete ethics of hospitality. The inclusion of the ethics
of hospitality is designed by Derrida to make it a richer notion than the
mere legal allowance of visitation that can include our responses to others.

However, Derrida argues that one cannot talk about cultivating an ethics of hospitality, for,

> Hospitality is culture itself and not simply one ethic amongst oth-
> ers. Insofar as it has to do with the *ethos,* that is, the residence, one's
> home, the familiar place of dwelling, inasmuch as it is a manner
> of being there, the manner in which we relate to ourselves and to
> others, to others as our own or as foreigners, *ethics is hospitality*; eth-
> ics is so thoroughly coextensive with the experience of hospitality.
> (2001a, 16–17)[12]

Hospitality is seen as going to the heart of our relations to self and others.
Derrida's claim here that ethics and hospitality are coextensive can be traced
to his reading of Emmanuel Levinas's *Totality and Infinity* (2001), where he
reads Levinas's ethics as one where we respond to the other in welcome
(1999, 25, 50). So, the very basis of our ethical relation is that of responsive-
ness or receptiveness. This receptiveness is demonstrated in the welcome of
hospitality, but it is not completely passive, since we assume it. As a response,
it involves wonder as openness to the other and generosity as respect for
them as autonomous beings. It also involves the self-respect of generosity
because we cannot offer hospitality unless we are at home, unless we have
a strong sense of self that can be ethical to others.

Also in a Kantian spirit, Derrida affirms the ideas of progress and perfectibility, with the caveat that we sometimes need to have a break in this
progress when we rethink concepts such as the state, sovereignty, or citizenship of the world (2002, 26–27). That rethinking will involve wonder in the
sense of a respect for differences in languages and the production of new
idioms (2002, 44). Derrida's cosmopolitics involves a location that is beyond
the opposition between Eurocentrism and anti-Eurocentrism (2002, 9), and
a new cosmopolitanism must involve a new democracy, the *democratie à venir*
I discussed in the last chapter.

As Derrida acknowledges, the concept of hospitality involves the idea
of sovereignty, since the host determines the conditions of the visit. This
difficulty of an assertion of sovereignty in the very concept of hospitality
could be accepted or it could constitute a reason for believing that another
concept would be more appropriate. The notion of mastery and control that

is involved in conditional hospitality can lead to an arrogance in determining who can visit, under what conditions, and how long they are allowed to stay. This is a kind of distortion of the self-respect of generosity into the unjustified arrogance Descartes warns us of in *The Passions of the Soul*. Much of the distinction between legitimate refugees and so-called illegal immigrants or unlawful non-citizens rests on a particular sense of conditional hospitality—the idea of who has been invited and who has not. The good asylum seekers have applied through the proper channels, and the others have turned up "uninvited," "unauthorized," "irregularly," or have "jumped the queue" or are "bogus," so it is said.

In some cases, the concept of conditional hospitality can be used as a cover for racist views, when the most desperate asylum seekers, those who arrive by boat, are disparaged and harshly treated relative to visa overstayers, who are much more likely to be European and English-speaking. The distinction is made in terms of their mode of arrival but the ethnic differentiation is evident. This possibility does not demonstrate that hospitality is an inappropriate concept, but it shows that there are risks in the concept of conditional hospitality. The important thing about hospitality interpreted in this way is that the host has the right to decide who comes and under what conditions, so that the welcome is an extremely qualified one.

This is certainly how the former Australian government interpreted hospitality. The then prime minister, John Howard, claimed that "[n]ational security is . . . about this nation saying to the world we are a generous, open-hearted people taking more refugees on a per capita basis than any nation except Canada, we have a proud record of welcoming people from 140 different nations. But we will decide who comes to this country and the circumstances in which they come" (Marr and Wilkinson 2003, 245).[13] This statement is a clear expression of very conditional, limited hospitality, where the recipients and circumstances are determined by the state. In other countries, this attitude is expressed more in actions than in explicit statements. The High Court in the UK found that the Home Office "was operating a 'secret' policy of presumption of detention" (Phelps et al. 2009, 10).

Certainly, Derrida is aware that there are risks inherent in the concepts of hospitality and welcome, that the Latin *hospes* means host/ess, as well as guest, stranger, and foreigner, and there is a presumption in the offering of welcome. In *Adieu to Emmanuel Levinas,* he notes this difficulty, saying, "To dare to say welcome is perhaps to insinuate that one is at home here, that one knows what it means to be at home, and that at home one receives, invites, or offers hospitality, thus appropriating for oneself a place to *welcome*

[*accueillir*] the other, or worse, *welcoming* the other in order to appropriate for oneself a place and then speak the language of hospitality" (1999,
15–16). Here, Derrida is discussing the notion of welcome in the context
of his own lecture, but the point is clearly relevant to the wider issues he is
concerned with. To presume to offer hospitality (or to deny it) to refugees
is to presume that it is our place to do so. Therefore, the possible hostility,
arrogance, and lack of respect in the concept of conditional hospitality is
part of the contradictory logic that Derrida explores. It is also clear why
Derrida rejects a Kantian reading of his unconditional ethics in the case
of hospitality because, whereas Kant's categorical imperative is something
that we can aim to act on even if we cannot be confident of achieving it,
Derrida's unconditional hospitality is not only impossible but positively
destructive. That is, we need to have a home to provide hospitality. While
hospitality can be held out as an "impossible real" to improve our politics
and ethics, we do not want to come too close to it, unlike justice, and as we
will see in the following chapter, unlike forgiveness.

A number of thinkers, including Mustafa Dikeç (2002), Couze Venn
(2002), and Penelope Deutscher (2003), have enthusiastically embraced
Derrida's reworking of the concept of hospitality. Dikeç argues that we must
cultivate an ethics of hospitality, Venn supports Derrida's understanding of
cosmopolitanism, and Deutscher argues for the importance of unconditional
hospitality to issues surrounding colonialism and immigration. However, in
Strangers, Gods and Monsters, Richard Kearney criticizes Derrida's use of
the notion of unconditional hospitality, arguing that it does not enable us
to make ethical judgments about the other. He notes that Derrida accepts
that there must be immigration laws, but says his analysis "undervalues our
need to differentiate not just legally but *ethically* between good and evil
aliens" (2003, 73). For Kearney, we must reflect further on these questions
of ethical discrimination and judgment. And certainly Derrida's conclusion
that we must negotiate between unconditional hospitality and conditional
hospitality, just as we must negotiate between ethics and politics, seems to
be the beginning of thought on a set of important ethical and political
questions rather than the end of reflection. The Rwandan example, where
refugees from murder were left in refugee camps in Zaire along with their
potential murderers shows the necessity for both political and ethical distinctions (Gourevitch 1998, 187). Does Derrida's view of hospitality imply
that judgments of the kind Kearney believes essential cannot be made?

My argument here is that Derrida's view is more complex than Kearney allows. Derrida sees a gap in our negotiations between the ethics and

politics of hospitality. A quote I used earlier is again apposite: "Without silence, without the hiatus, which is not the absence of rules but the necessity of a leap at the moment of ethical, political, or juridical decision, we could simply unfold knowledge into a program or course of action. Nothing could make us more irresponsible; nothing could be more totalitarian" (1999, 117). What Derrida is proposing is that we not think we can resolve these questions through a schema or template that would determine in advance how we must answer questions concerning asylum seekers. We have to exercise our judgment in the context of particular ethical and political issues. He accepts that immigration must be regulated, but does not see his role as setting out those regulations.[14] Derrida asks, "How can the right to asylum be redefined and developed without repatriation and without naturalization?" (2001a, 7). Another alternative of course is temporary residence, which many countries use. Some refugees wish to stay permanently, but not all and the basis for refugee status can sometimes be eliminated by changes in the political situation of asylum seekers' country of origin. At this point, one needs to recall the need for analysis of particular cases and a range of solutions, as Derrida says, rather than either sending refugees to their country of origin or assuming they will become citizens of the other country. Nevertheless, there are certain practices, such as arbitrary and mandatory detention that should be ruled out, and there are also positive ways of ensuring that asylum seekers benefit from responses involving wonder and generosity.

Could the concept of cities of refuge, with new rights and greater sovereignty, help solve the problem? Derrida agrees with Hannah Arendt that international law is limited by the treaties made between sovereign states and not even a "world government" would solve the problem (Arendt 1976, 298). There is an implicit critique in his notion of "refuge cities" of Kant's idea of an international league based on sovereign states to make agreements of this kind. We have to take responsibility for the analysis of each particular situation, which is "unique and yet general" (1999, 115). Derrida's support of refuge cities is a particular response to the problems faced by dissident writers and artists. Some countries will find that hospitality to refugees will require more of a sacrifice than others, and some countries owe more to certain refugees than others due to their historical relationship of former colonization. Derrida's position does not preclude the specific ethical judgments Kearney seeks, although Derrida does not make them. The concept of hospitality needs to be made more nuanced to relate to specific circumstances.

The Limits of Hospitality?

While Derrida states that we must distinguish carefully between visitors, immigrants, and refugees, he appears to assume that the concept of hospitality alone is appropriate in all these circumstances. Hospitality is relevant for visitors and tourists of course, and all those attempting to communicate with the people of other nations. The terms *immigrant* and *refugee*, however, pose different challenges for the ethics of hospitality. Hospitality appears to be an inappropriate concept to apply to immigrants since they are not intending to visit but planning to stay. Immigrants need something more and other than hospitality because they want to become members and citizens of a new country. Their status then becomes one of unconditional acceptance, or perhaps conditional only in the sense that all citizenship is conditional. They have to be welcomed as something more than guests. The situation of the refugee is between visitor and immigrant as they may wish to stay for a short period, to reside or to become a citizen. This ambiguity makes refuge a difficult situation for the concept of hospitality to capture. Nonetheless, hospitality appears to be a useful concept for considering the issues that refugees have to face in initially being treated with respect for their human rights, and hospitality expresses wonder at differences. The fact of immigration and of refugee settlement shows that wonder and generosity are not static responses to fixed differences but fluid responses where those who initially offer hospitality may be changed themselves by the arrivals.

Another important aspect of asylum seekers' arrival is its complex relation to both ethics and politics. The definition of a refugee from the 1951 Convention and Protocol Relating to the Status of Refugees is a person who, "owing to well-founded fear of being persecuted for reasons of race, religion, nationality, membership of a particular social group or political opinion, is outside the country of his nationality and is unable, or owing to such fear, is unwilling to avail himself of the protection of that country" (Geneva Convention 1951, 16). If asylum is like visitation, what we require is more and better hospitality. Martha Nussbaum notes that our attitudes may fall short of the hospitality that is needed, so "we can always seek to enact constitutional protections for the alien on our soil, and for that alien's children" (1997, 49). In other words, the ethics of hospitality often does not reach the ideal, so must be supplemented with a politics of hospitality, as I argued should be the case generally. Derrida is very much in favor of improving the laws regarding asylum and immigration, saying in an interview, "I am for the Enlightenment, I'm for progress, I'm a 'progressist.' I

think the law is perfectible and we can improve the law. We have to improve
the conditions of conditional hospitality, we can change, we should change
the laws on immigration, as far as possible, given a certain number of constraints" (2001b, 100).[15] There is no doubt that more hospitality is needed
and that particular changes in laws and practices need to be made in many
countries.

There is a need for an immediate hospitality in being willing to consider the claims of asylum seekers to be refugees, to allow them to land and
not to incarcerate them while considering their refugee status. Hospitality
as a right to visit clearly condemns practices of arbitrary, mandatory, and
prolonged detention.[16] If hospitality were given greater political expression,
some of the worst excesses of government policies might be curbed.[17] Hospitality is also significant on a personal ethical level. Individuals in countries
such as Australia, Britain, France, and the United States have welcomed
asylum seekers under threat of deportation by the government into their
homes, risking prosecution. Even so, these demonstrations of hospitality
do not fundamentally change the situation of the asylum seeker when the
political policy is determined by the ungenerous and self-interested refrain
of "we decide whom we will be hospitable to and whom not." Asylum
seekers should not have to defer to the good will of their hosts. They are
claiming the right to have their claims considered, the minimalist claim
Kant characterizes in the *Metaphysics of Morals* as the right to try to interact
with the people of other countries (1996a, 6: 353). We need support for the
right of hospitality as well as a hospitable attitude.

There are a number of improvements to laws and conventions that
should be part of negotiations toward an ideal of hospitality. Derrida comments on the problem for refugees who are affected by financial hardship in
having their claims recognized. There needs to be an expansion of the categories of those considered to be genuine refugees, including persecution on
the grounds of sex, an issue that affects many women. While consideration
is given to the specificity of the persecution of women, this persecution is
not established as integral to the grounds for being considered a refugee
(UNHCR 2001). As Jane Freedman argues, the use of sexual violence and
rape in war is often not recognized as specific persecution of women, nor
is violence that occurs in the home, or threats of forced marriage or geni-
tal mutilation (2008, 416–18). The definition of a refugee in the Geneva
Convention also leaves out other just grounds for seeking asylum: persecution because of sexual orientation, expulsion from the country one is
a citizen of, stateless people who are expelled from a country, and those

fleeing famine. An improvement in the Geneva Convention and Protocol for Refugees and other international agreements is one way of ensuring protection for the rights of refugees and asylum seekers.

Nonetheless, refinement of the application of concepts of hospitality takes us only so far in fully understanding and responding to the precarious situation of those seeking refuge in foreign states. I suggest we need to refocus much of this discussion on the question of human rights—rights that go beyond the right to hospitality. One could see this as a way of ensuring that ethical principles are enshrined in politics, as Kant believes we should. We can reflect on the laws of hospitality by considering the question of human rights. Arendt wrote insightfully of the situation of refugees in relation to human rights in *On the Origins of Totalitarianism* (1976). Arendt argues that rights are only meaningful if they are accepted by the nations of the world. For her, the notion of natural human rights or the "Rights of Man" cannot have any purchase; rather, there has to be a guarantee: "We are not born equal; we become equal as members of a group on the strength of our decision to guarantee ourselves mutually equal rights" (1976, 301). Nature and history do not constitute essences or confer meaning on human rights; in Arendt's view, "Humanity, which for the eighteenth century, in Kantian terminology, was no more than a regulative idea, has today become an inescapable fact," so humanity itself has to guarantee the right to have rights (1976, 298). Arendt concludes that the right of asylum is an essential human right in the international context.

What is unclear is what Arendt sees as the solution—how we can ensure that the right to asylum will be taken seriously. She is skeptical about Kant's cosmopolitanism, for example, believing that perpetual peace would mean the end of politics as we know it (1968, 91). By this, she means that politics always concerns conflict and debate and perpetual peace implies the end of all such debate and so, for Arendt, the end of all political action. Action, for Arendt, is distinguished from labor, which is needed for our reproduction and sustenance and work, which is needed to create durable objects. Action and speech are what she sees as the activities that make us fully human, along with the life of the mind of thinking, willing, and judging. One interpretation of Arendt's claim concerning rights is simply that we must be more vigilant in enforcing the right to asylum.[18] Again, this suggestion could ameliorate the worst excesses of narrowly selfish governments and populations, but it does not constitute a new cosmopolitanism or the kind of rethinking of basic concepts that Derrida recommends. Alternatively, and more plausibly, one might think that "the right to have rights" (1976, 298) means everyone must have a right to citizenship on which a right of asylum can be based. There are ways of implementing Arendt's idea of the right to have rights or the right to be a citizen. For example, Michael Dummett argues that stateless people "are plainly entitled to be granted a national-ity" (2001, 30) and suggests that an international body should be set up by the UN to process the claims of stateless people and find an appropriate country to grant them citizenship. The body would consist of countries that agree to accept stateless people as citizens. Such a body may not be a world federation in Kant's sense, but it would be a coming together of countries on this particular issue. I believe Dummett's is a useful suggestion and would certainly improve the situation of refugees if implemented. These possibili-ties support asylum seekers' rights to be considered for refugee status or immigration and consider them as worthy of the respect given to others with security and peace.

Yet, there is still another, more important, way of interpreting and using Arendt's claim, which is to consider how rights that are more extensive than human rights could be guaranteed. Are all the rights of refugees like the right to visit? Her work on the relation between human rights and civil rights points to a significant gap in much of the discussion of rights of asy-lum. Refugees occupy a unique and unfortunate position in not being able to enjoy the conventional rights of citizens. Some asylum seekers would like to reside in the new country, and pathways to residency and citizen-ship are an important response there. However, not all refugees wish to become citizens of the country in which they are staying, and this should not mean they are forced to rely on human rights alone. It is often thought that all that is needed is somewhere to sleep and eat. Generosity to the asy-lum seeker should mean that one is recognized as worthy of expressing a view and being treated with dignity. A right to "political interaction" would guarantee that even if one is an asylum seeker or refugee one should have a voice in the political community. These rights should be a special way of contributing to political life—a voice for those who are not citizens but who nevertheless have a stake in government policies and practices. These would be public rights that are stronger and more extensive than human rights but are not the rights of citizens.

To see why there is a need for special rights for asylum seekers and refugees we need to take seriously their distinctive position in cosmopolitan affairs. In *On the Origins of Totalitarianism,* Arendt points out that the right to free speech could be freely exercised in concentration and extermina-tion camps, but such speech carries little import when it is not heard by the "outside world" (1976, 296). This free speech presumably goes on in refugee camps and detention centers today, but little of it is heard. Similarly, criminals often have better access to legal representation and appeal than those held in concentration camps or detention centers. This neglect is due to the policies of particular governments, but it is aided by philosophical neglect of the situation of the stateless.[19] Arendt is, of course, an exception, and Derrida's recommendation that we rethink the concepts of state, sovereignty, and cosmopolitanism is an injunction to redress that neglect.

The rights that asylum seekers and refugees are deprived of are public, political, and the rights of "action" in Arendt's sense—the rights to speak and to be heard in the public arena. As she says, action is only possible in the public sphere: "Action, as distinguished from fabrication, is never possible in isolation; to be isolated is to be deprived of the capacity to act" (1998, 188).[20] Action is essentially public and political, something that we engage in with and before others. This is a point governments understand very well, as shown by the prevalence of policies of arbitrary, mandatory, and indefinite detention of asylum seekers. The practice of holding asylum seekers in prisons, airports, and detention centers for long periods of time, carried out by many countries, prevents or at the very least hinders access of asylum seekers to the media, the parliament, and legal representation.[21] Rights to access these elements of political life would enable asylum seekers and refugees to play a greater role in the community without that role being one of a citizen. What is important is that refugees be able to make a contribution to the political life of the country in which they are staying.[22] While an unconditional right of hospitality may require that we not ask any questions of the stranger who arrives on our doorstep, that we regard them with wonder and accept their differences, concern with other rights and acknowledging them with generosity will make us want to ask and answer countless questions.

As Dikeç argues, hospitality is a *sensibility* as well as a set of actions that we can cultivate in "social relationships and interactions, as well as institutional practices" (2002, 235–36). Hospitality involves particular actions, but ideally it should include a wondering welcome of the other whether they are a neighbor or stranger, whether their culture is similar or very different. It should involve generous respect for their rights and an open and a benevolent response toward them. Wonder is an element in not judging or prejudging arrivals, and then it is important to cultivate generosity both in Descartes's sense and in the sense of being willing to give and share in terms of friendliness and in terms of resources. Furthermore, to be truly open to difference in others, communities have to change themselves rather than merely to expect refugees to adapt to the country that offers them hospitality in the form of asylum.

It is no accident that there has been a resurgence of interest in Kant's cosmopolitanism, as it contains suggestions that are immensely valuable for thinking through pressing contemporary questions. Starting from Kant's central insight that there is a universal right to hospitality, Derrida delineates both where cosmopolitanism is worthwhile and where it fails. The ethics and politics of hospitality Derrida develops promise to ameliorate the current situation of asylum seekers and refugees. The notion of hospitality, particularly unconditional hospitality, is a useful corrective to the mean-mindedness of many contemporary governments. However, there are difficulties in extending the concept of hospitality to account for all the complexities of immigration and refugee issues. Hospitality accounts for our initial response to asylum seekers and refugees, but does not articulate the terms of a continuing interaction, where people may stay for many years and eventually become citizens in the new community. Wonder and generosity have to be combined as part of that initial response and in our ongoing engagement with those who stay in our countries. A new politics of hospitality should enable stateless people to become citizens and extend the definition of refugee to acknowledge sexual persecution, expulsion, and the risk of starvation. It should also be supplemented by a means of public interaction with the community for those who are not citizens that is a fuller conception of generosity than providing accommodation. Hospitality is another kind of extension of wonder, generosity, and love, and an important one. In the next chapter I wish to address the question whether there are any cases where we should accept that neither wonder nor generosity are appropriate.

6

Wonder, Radical Evil, and Forgiveness

> I declared myself ready to forgive my enemies, and perhaps even to love them, but only when they showed certain signs of repentance, that is when they ceased being enemies. In the opposite case, that of the enemy who remains an enemy, who perseveres in his desire to inflict suffering, it is certain that one must not forgive him: one can try to salvage him, one can (one must!) discuss with him, but it is our duty to judge him, not to forgive him.
>
> —Primo Levi, *The Periodic Table*

In previous chapters, I have concentrated on the ways in which wonder and generosity could overcome sexist and racist oppression, bring about a more open, respectful, and loving ethics and politics and be part of a richer, more hospitable approach to asylum seekers. Yet some phenomena appear to challenge the resources of these two concepts. As I noted in the first chapter, evil presents a question for comprehending wonder, in the sense that it is a difference that we cannot simply wonder at, unlike sexual and cultural differences, for example. When we come to understand the world well enough we know what is "worthy" of wonder and what not. There may be differences we properly find threatening and frightening, when human beings are indifferent to the welfare of others or actively wish to destroy the lives of others. These are not like the differences that misogynists or racists perceive or magnify and distort in differently embodied others. In such cases, our feelings must very different from wonder and may stretch the limits of generosity or respect for others. While faced with some evil that we do not understand we may wonder at it due to the surprise, but once we grasp its nature, we must make a judgment. But how do we respond? Do we regard evil with horror or disgust or contempt or understanding and forgiveness?

It is useful to return to Descartes at this point because he, with Irigaray, is my starting point for thinking about wonder and generosity as responses to others and as he represents a philosophical and theological tradition that tries to explain evil in spite of the existence of an all-powerful benevolent God. First, Descartes believes that evil is only a privation, unlike good (1991, 269). He thinks we are likely to hate whatever we perceive as evil or harmful (1989, 53), and also to feel sad (1989, 54). Thus far, he is only speaking about "evil" in the sense of something that we do not value. That is one way of dealing with natural evil.

In relation to the problem of moral evil, Descartes, of course, believes that free will allows that possibility. In other words, he allows that people may do evil things. However, he believes that moral evil is based on mistaken judgments. In *The Passions of the Soul,* Descartes's conception of wrongdoing involves "weak souls" who, in spite of being aware of appropriate judgments concerning good and evil, allow themselves to be carried away by passions that represent situations in distorted ways (1989, 46). On the question of evil actions, Descartes says they cause indignation if done to others and anger if done to us (1989, 55). His only remedy is for us to remove ourselves from the presence of the cause of evil, and even that, he feels, may have disadvantages. In a very mild portrayal of an appropriate response to evil, Descartes suggests that hatred for "someone's evil habits likewise takes us away from his company; and we might otherwise find in the latter some good which we should be sorry to be deprived of" (1989, 94).[1] Furthermore, his view that generosity involves the recognition of the capacity for free will in others, which is the capacity to do both good and evil, suggests that generosity applies to someone who commits evil actions as much as it does to those who do good. This universal respect is one aspect of his thought that is a significant legacy and has implications for our understanding of evil, as I will discuss farther on in the chapter.

However, although Descartes's account of evil can deal with minor wrongdoing, he appears to have no sense of the great evils that can be perpetrated (although in fact he must have), and is inadequate to deal with the evils on a large scale of the twentieth century that have prompted thinkers such as Hannah Arendt to rethink evil. He also does not consider the evils of repeated violence and intimidation that can occur in the private sphere.

Hatred and sadness also seem inadequate as accounts of our response to evil and hardly suggest the kind of judgments that must be made. In the wake of the development of secular thought, a century of genocide and war, and growing liberation movements, philosophical discussion has shifted from Descartes's idea of evil as anything that is harmful to moral evil as deliberate wrongdoing of an evil. This kind of harm suggests that simply removing ourselves from the presence of the perpetrator may not be possible or be a sufficient response. In addition, feminists have addressed the question of domestic violence as a specific kind of harm, and I will consider the challenge it poses to forgiveness and its connection with shame.

If we feel indignation, resentment, and outrage, particularly in extreme cases of evil that seem unforgivable, should we try to overcome these feelings in order to forgive? It seems that these examples of extreme or radical evil are the ones that really test our capacity for generosity as respect for others, for wonder at difference, and for love and forgiveness, so I shall focus on them. Should one (indeed, can one) forgive the unforgivable, radical evil being an exemplary case of the unforgivable? And on what basis could we do so?

If we take Arendt's account of radical evil as incomprehensible or without ordinary human motivations seriously, radical evil seems to pose particular problems for the possibility of forgiveness, because there are no explanations, justifications, or excuses for radically evil actions. Furthermore, Jean Améry and Vladimir Jankélévitch both detail the reasons for not forgiving such evil in the case of torture and the Shoah. In other cases, evil can be partly accounted for by human weakness or passions, and our general susceptibility to these weaknesses suggests a reason for forgiveness. Arendt's argument that because radical evil transcends human concerns it is beyond human forgiveness is challenged by Derrida's view that forgiveness essentially involves forgiving the unforgivable, in other words, the forgiveness of radical evil. While Derrida does not explicitly state that we *should* forgive the unforgivable, my reading of his work on this point is that he implicitly sanctions such forgiveness. Derrida's view of forgiveness focuses on the logic of forgiveness, whereas Arendt focuses on the politics of forgiveness. Both see radical evil as beyond the human, whereas I argue that, regrettably, it is all too human and therefore our response has to take that into account. I contend that it is possible to forgive radical evil, but in general it is not a duty that directly follows from generosity and wonder.

Arendt on Forgiveness: The Impossibility
of Forgiving Radical Evil

The origin of the concept of forgiveness, like the concept of evil, can be located in religious ethical traditions, a connection that makes some philosophers skeptical about their usefulness for contemporary ethics or psychology. For example, Simone de Beauvoir claims in "An Eye for an Eye" that forgiveness or charity toward absolute evil is based on belief in original sin and in God as the ultimate judge (2004, 256–57).[2] However, while Arendt traces the understanding of forgiveness to a religious tradition, she sees no difficulty in understanding forgiveness in a secular way (1998, 238).[3] Similarly, I argue that while we should be aware of the origins of concepts such as forgiveness, we are able to rework them in a contemporary context and should not dismiss them out of hand. Forgiveness between human beings need not have a religious basis. Furthermore, the concept of forgiveness does work that other important concepts such as reconciliation do not do.[4]

A number of philosophers also believe that the concept of evil, even more so radical evil, belongs to the sphere of religion, so can have no place in secular discussions of ethics or psychology.[5] Alain Badiou, for example, claims that as radical evil invokes a measure that cannot be measured, it must be abandoned as being essentially religious (2001, 63).[6] By "measure," he means to make commensurable and he claims that theorists of radical evil, using the Shoah as their paradigm "example," are involved in incoherence. Badiou argues that the Shoah is used as the exemplar of radical evil, saying. "The Nazi extermination is radical Evil in that it provides for our time the unique, unrivalled—and in this sense, transcendent, or unsayable—measure of Evil, pure and simple" (2001, 62). He says that these thinkers maintain that the Shoah is incommensurable with other evils and yet constantly compare other evils to it, for example, when political leaders compare Nasser, Saddam Hussein, and Slobodan Milošović to Hitler. However, there are two problems with Badiou's analysis. One is that the claims of political leaders do not necessarily imply that there is a difficulty inherent in the concept of radical evil itself. Second, if we focus only on the issue of whether the Shoah can be compared to other evils, there is no incoherence in claiming that it is both incommensurable and a limit below which other evils can be compared to each other. One could argue that all other evils are measurable in a way that the Shoah is not.

The paradigmatic nature of the Shoah has led some philosophers to the view that radical evil is constituted by genocide. For example, Alessandro

Ferrara, after mentioning these paradigm examples of radical evil, concludes that "[c]onstitutive of radical evil seems to be the unleashing of violence on a victimized group unable to adequately react—targeting the individual only insofar as she is part of that group. Radical evil also seems to have to possess a characteristically systematic quality which episodic violence—for example, lynchings and pogroms—does not possess" (Lara 2002, 183).[7] Yet while genocide is the most obvious example of radical evil, I believe that the definition of radical evil is independent of it. Radical evil could be episodic, it could fall short of genocide or attempted genocide, and it could focus on a group that is not weak or victimized. It is different from racist and sexist oppression, which are evils, but which may not involve evil actions or intentions, although they sometimes do, when slavery, extreme humiliations, rape, torture, and even genocide are features of that oppression. Arguably, certain acts of terrorism are cases of radical evil.

Badiou's warning does have some force, in that the concept of evil should not be abused or too broadly applied, as in the "axis of evil" of the second Bush presidency. There is also a danger of attributing monstrosity to the perpetrators of radical evil and perversely, if unintentionally, glorifying criminal acts.[8] We need to be careful that we don't overlook the petty motives, stupidity, and shallowness of at least some perpetrators of terrible offenses. Nevertheless, as we shall see, radical evil delineates a specific category of evil and does not have to be tied to a religious tradition or its glorification.

Arendt, for instance, draws on religious texts, such as the Bible, in her analysis of forgiveness and evil, but does so within a thoroughly secular context. Throughout her work, Arendt is concerned with understanding the nature of evil, specifically as exemplified by the concentration and extermination camps in Nazi Germany, and in the Nazi and Stalinist regimes. For Arendt, the totalitarianism of those regimes represents a particular kind of evil—radical evil. She also touches on the question of whether we should forgive such evil in a number of texts. In that regard, Arendt has a short but very rich discussion of the concept of forgiveness in *The Human Condition* (1998). She says that the "faculty" of forgiving allows for the possibility of redemption from "irreversibility" or the problem of not being able to reverse what one has done (1998, 237). By redemption she means that if we are forgiven, we have the possibility of starting anew rather than being defined by the wrong we have committed. Furthermore, Arendt believes that forgiveness is essentially personal, although not necessarily private and individual, because we forgive a person for what they have done (1998,

241). My interpretation of this idea is that when we forgive, we always forgive a person their actions and we may do this in a public or collective way.

Arendt appears to tie forgiveness to wrong actions that have been committed "unknowingly" or without awareness of the depth of the wrong
(1998, 237, 240), a characterization that suggests forgiveness is only appropriate for a small subset of actions. However, she bases her view on the
thought that "crime and willed evil are rare" (1998, 240), so most wrongs
deserve forgiveness.[9] These wrongs are just part of the unpredictability of
human life. Radical evil can neither be forgiven nor punished in Arendt's
view, for it completely transcends the human realm (1998, 241). Her formulation presents the essence of the question: Is radical evil beyond the human
and therefore beyond the possibility of forgiveness?

Although Arendt references Kant's idea of radical evil, in my view they
are very different. For Arendt, radical evil is a kind of extreme evil. For
Kant, however, all evil is radical, although it appears in three different grades
or stages. Kant is credited with introducing the concept of radical evil in
Religion within the limits of Reason Alone (1996c). By "radical," he means that
evil is a deeply rooted human propensity, although always one that we can
choose against. The three different grades of the propensity to evil are, first,
that of frailty or weakness in following the good; second, impurity, when we
act according to duty but with mixed motives; and the third is corruption
or perversity, in which human beings put the principle of self-love and of
nonmoral motivations above that of duty (1996c, 6: 29–30).[10] Since Kant
also believes that we do not choose evil qua evil as an incentive, he argues
that in the third, corrupt stage, dishonesty or self-deception enables a person
to justify their actions and have peace of mind. This dishonesty, he writes,
"rests on the radical evil in human nature which (inasmuch as it puts out
of tune the moral ability to judge what to think of a human being, and
renders any imputability entirely uncertain, whether internal or external)
constitutes the foul stain of our species—and so long as we do not remove
it, it hinders the germ of the good from developing as it otherwise would"
(1996c, 6: 38). Dishonesty about our own propensity to evil will then result
in deceiving others, according to Kant.

Thus, Kant sees radical evil as fundamentally human, although still
blameworthy. There is potential, at least, for forgiveness, in that we all have
to deal with the difficulty of making moral choices. He does not specify
in this essay whether we should forgive radical evil, or rather the actions
done out of radical evil, but in *The Metaphysics of Morals* he says that human
beings have a duty to be forgiving, which is not to be confused with "*meek*

toleration of wrongs" or "renunciation of rigorous means (*rigorosa*) for preventing the recurrence of wrongs by others" (1996a, 6: 461). Forgiving is
part of the imperfect or conditional duty to be sympathetic to others, rather
than malicious.[11] Such a duty does not imply that one must forgive every
harm committed. Nevertheless, Kant's view that evil can always be understood in terms of self-interest is challenged by Arendt's accounts of radical
evil and the banality of evil, which also imply a different view of forgiveness.

In her writings, Arendt shifts from the language of radical evil to the
language of the banality of evil.[12] She discusses radical evil in an essay, "The
Concentration Camps," and in *The Origins of Totalitarianism* (1976, 459).
Arendt characterizes this radical or absolute evil as incomprehensible.[13] In
both works, she describes the processes involved in this particular form of
radical evil as they developed through concentration and extermination
camps. Totalitarian regimes, on her account, aim "to destroy the essence of
man [*sic*]" (1976, viii). Radical evil involves treating human beings as superfluous, meaning that the treatment even goes beyond violating what Kant
warns us against in the formulation of the categorical imperative in terms
of respect for humanity—treating others as mere means to one's own ends.
The obvious example of such evil is the Nazi treatment of Jewish people
and others whom they murdered when their work could have contributed
to the war effort.[14] To use Kant's terms, the victims of the camps have neither dignity nor price, as they are neither thought of as having a special
worth beyond price in themselves, nor are they thought of as useful. Arendt
says, "The concentration camp inmate has no price, because he can always
be replaced and he belongs to no one" (1976, 444).[15] The perpetrators also
treat themselves as superfluous, she argues, a phenomenon that has implications for an understanding of the nature of this kind of evil.

The process of making human beings superfluous involves, Arendt says,
eradicating first the juridical person, second the moral person, and finally all
spontaneity. The first is achieved by stripping people of their rights and placing the camps outside the usual judicial system in which there is a direct and
proportionate response to a particular crime. The second is done by "making
martyrdom impossible" since if one will be killed in any case, sacrificing one's
life has no meaning (1976, 451). Death becomes anonymous, and even suicide
is not an option. Furthermore, the SS implicated concentration camp inmates
in their crimes by forcing them to take part in the process of murder. The
third is the destruction of the individual's unique identity, the human person,
or spontaneity by torture and degradation. This spontaneity is also understood
by Arendt in terms of "natality," the possibility of doing something new that

is more than a reaction. Arendt argues that spontaneity or unpredictability is the greatest threat to total domination. She understands what went on in the camps as a destruction of the spontaneity and plurality of human beings. Plurality is destroyed since individual differences no longer matter.

On Arendt's account, this radical evil or absolute evil differs from other kinds of evil in that it cannot be explained by evil motives. "Ordinary" evil has some explanation, such as greed, status, anger, hatred, or revenge, that accounts for the motives of the perpetrator. Radical evil occurs where there is no practical benefit to the perpetrator. The way people are treated is characterized by "antiutility," Arendt argues, noting that the Nazis used precious resources on deportations and camps (1976, 445).[16] This lack of rationality and self-interested motives is the reason Arendt believes such evil is unforgivable. She argue that such actions cannot be forgiven because there are no humanly understandable motives such as selfishness, greed, fear, or even cruelty to explain what they have done. Likewise, there are no possible grounds for punishment.

I think it is clear that Arendt did not mean that the perpetrators of radical evil should not be punished, but rather that any form of punishment was incommensurate with the crime.[17] This view is made evident by her support for the death penalty for Eichmann: "Just as you supported and carried out a policy of not wanting to share the earth with the Jewish people and the people of a number of other nations—as though you and your superiors had any right to determine who should and who should not inhabit the world—we find that no one, that is, no member of the human race, can be expected to want to share the earth with you. This is the reason, and the only reason, you must hang" (1994b, 279). I do not agree with her on this point, for reasons that I will make clear later. Arendt says elsewhere that while our usual justifications for punishment are not applicable—protecting society, rehabilitation, deterrence, and retribution—since war criminals are not like ordinary criminals, "our sense of justice would find it intolerable to forego punishment and let those who murdered thousands and hundreds of thousands and millions go scot-free" (2003, 25–26). Clearly, it would be absurd to suggest that there be no punishment for crimes that are worse than any others.

In Arendt's examination of radical evil, the only motive she can attribute to totalitarian leaders is a desire for omnipotence (1992, 166). To return to Irigaray's characterization of wonder as recognition that the self is not alone, the perpetrators of radical evil refuse to accept that recognition and try to destroy it. They absolutely refuse both wonder and generosity. They have no respect for themselves in that they see themselves as part of a vast system, and they abandon any semblance of morality; they have no basic respect for others in that they are willing to degrade and kill them, and they have no wonder as they countenance no other way of looking at the world than their own.

Jean Améry makes a similar point in his book *At the Mind's Limits* (1980), where he analyzes the experience of torture and demonstrates how passions and values for both the victim and the torturer are perverted. Améry was a Jewish Austrian working for the resistance in Belgium when he was arrested and tortured by the Gestapo in 1943 and subsequently sent to Auschwitz (1980, 107). In his text, there are a few direct and indirect references to Arendt's work, suggesting he is critical of her approach to the horrors of the Shoah and to understanding totalitarianism. For instance, his argument that the Nazi regime is distinct and in no way analogous to Stalinism even at its worst is a clear and large difference between them. Améry's view is that torture belonged to the essence of Nazism in a way that it does not belong to any other political system (1980, 30–31). Yet their common existential basis to thinking through these questions means that Améry's discussion, based in his own experience, can augment and strengthen what we can learn from Arendt about evil and what it is like to suffer it. He denies the existence of banality of evil and suggests Arendt's experience of Nazi evil was limited (1980, 25). Nonetheless, his discussion of evil, especially torture, is relevant to understanding radical evil.

At the moment of what he calls "*the first blow,*" Améry realized that he had lost his "trust in the world." While this trust may involve basic beliefs about a functioning natural world, more significantly for him, it concerns our certainties about our relations with other human beings. He prefers this way of describing the wrong of torture to that of the loss of human dignity, a term he finds rather vague. While many authors focus on trust between individuals and entrusting something to someone (for example, Baier 1995), or on maintaining trust by not deceiving others, as Kant does, Améry centers on a trust in the world that is more general and I believe combines elements of both generosity and love. On the one hand, torture takes away our trust that our bodily integrity will be respected, which Irigaray argues should be enshrined in law: "More important as an element of trust in the world, and in our context what is solely relevant, is the certainty that by reason of written or unwritten social contracts the other person will spare me—more precisely stated, that he will respect my physical, and with it also my metaphysical, being. The boundaries of my body are also the boundaries of myself. My skin surface shields me against the external world. If I am to have trust, I must feel on it only what I *want* to feel" (1980, 28). Améry suggests that there are contexts in which retaliation may be a way of restoring trust in our own existence going on, but that is not possible under torture.

On the other hand, we lose the minimal care we trust others will give us. In a safe world we have a fundamental, taken for granted, supposition that if we are in trouble, if we have an accident, someone will come to help us: "The expectation of help, the certainty of help, is indeed one of the fundamental experiences of human beings" (1980, 28). At the first blow, Améry felt that trust, that secure feeling that others will come to help us, disintegrate. He knew that he was alone with his torturer and no one would render him aid. The power of the torturer is distinguished by Améry from the sovereignty of a king, who could be both cruel and kind, in that it is simply "the power to inflict suffering and to destroy" (1980, 39). He argues that the lost trust in the world cannot be regained, as the tortured remains forever tortured. He concludes that "[t]rust in the world, which already collapsed in part at the first blow, . . . in the end, under torture, fully, will not be regained" (1980, 40). The tortured person is left with fear and resentments that preclude forgiveness unless there is some sort of dramatic change in the relation to the past. Forgiveness is not possible, maintains Améry, until there is a full recognition of the wrongness of the Shoah and the Nazi regime as a whole. His account demonstrates how the breakdown of wonder and generosity appears at the extreme, and why forgiveness is so problematic in cases where a pure desire for sovereignty and power dominates. It also suggests that the experience of torture undermines the tortured person's capacity for wonder and generosity subsequently, as without trust we are suspicious of others and their motives.

On Arendt's account, we cannot connect the desire for omnipotence we see in torturers and the perpetrators of genocide with the usual human weaknesses and passions that we all share, although psychoanalysts may attempt to.[18] This is why forgiveness is not in question in this context for her. She sees forgiveness as a human concept, and radical evil goes beyond the human. What Arendt does not make entirely clear is whether such a desire for omnipotence can still be seen in Kantian terms, as a motivation of self-love or self-interest, (albeit) a very extreme one to which the moral law is subordinated, or whether the perpetrators in totalitarian regimes were entirely rejecting the moral law and choosing evil qua evil. The idea that ordinary human motives play no important role suggests the latter. Another point Arendt makes is that the usual moral order was reversed so that good took on the quality of temptation rather than evil (1994b, 150). Richard Bernstein argues it is evident that Arendt denies the Kantian view that spontaneity cannot be eliminated without destroying agency, as she maintains that spontaneity is destroyed in the camps (2002, 208). However, it is the spontaneity of the *victims* that is destroyed, which may well imply that they are no longer morally accountable, at least while they are in that state, the state Giorgio Agamben refers to as the nonhuman but also human (1999, 82–83).

Moreover, Arendt hints that the spontaneity of the perpetrators is also destroyed. For instance, she comments with regard to totalitarianism that "[t]he manipulators of this system believe in their own superfluousness as much as in that of all others, and the totalitarian murderers are all the more dangerous because they do not care if they themselves are alive or dead, if they ever lived or never were born" (1976, 459). The system requires the perpetrators to be indifferent to their own lives as well as that of the victims. Arendt also implies that freedom as spontaneity and as autonomy disappears, so that the only "freedom" is the preservation of the human species (1976, 438). Thus, the suggestion is that the perpetrators were not truly free, and yet Arendt believes that they are morally accountable for their actions. It is reasonable to conclude that she is denying the Kantian framework where even the worst evil is committed in the light of the categorical imperative and evil is not chosen for its own sake.

As I noted earlier, in *The Human Condition* Arendt refers to Kant's concept of radical evil as if she is using the same concept (1958, 241). Later, after the Eichmann trial in Jerusalem, Arendt distinguished between radical evil and extreme evil. After reflecting on Eichmann's appearance in the court, she contends that evil cannot have the depth required to call it radical (1978, 250–51).[19] Rather, it is like a fungus that spreads over the surface of things. Bernstein points out that "[i]nsofar as 'radical' suggests digging to roots that are hidden, she no longer believes that evil is radical in *this sense*" (2002, 218). He also argues that Arendt shifts in her thinking from the concept of superfluousness to that of thoughtlessness to explain evil (1996, 142–43).[20] She emphasizes Eichmann's lack of thought and reflection on what he was doing in carrying out the work of extermination.

However, I argue that these two concepts are compatible in that one focuses on the way perpetrators treat the victims—rendering them superfluous—and the other emphasizes the condition of the perpetrators—their state of thoughtlessness. Both conditions are relevant to understanding radical evil. The perpetrators do not reflect on their actions, and their actions have the result of rendering others superfluous. Bernstein concludes that "radical evil is compatible with the banality of evil" (2002, 231). He sees Arendt as shifting her focus to the intentions of the perpetrators, but still presupposing that the evil is radical. What Bernstein insightfully observes as being original to Arendt's theory is the splitting apart of the evilness or wickedness of the intentions or motives from the evilness or monstrosity of the deeds. Monstrous actions can be committed from the most banal and trivial of motives, such as the petty ambition that appears to have motivated Eichmann.[21]

Nevertheless, there is a complication in that not all radical evil is also banal. Some perpetrators, such as Hitler, commit incomprehensible crimes out of monstrous motives.[22] Radical evil can be committed from a variety of motives or no motive at all. One could also argue that "banality" gives an explanation of the evil but a very inadequate one. There is a large gap between the triviality of the motives and the horror of what they have done, but it is not completely incomprehensible. What the explanation does not explain is how, from a psychological point of view, such banal motives could have been thought to justify such monstrous deeds. Whether it is called radical or banal, such evil involves utter lack of consideration of the individuality or the perspective of the victims, in other words, no generosity. This lack of respect for others implies the converse, that the perpetrators also lacked proper self-respect. Arendt's idea that the Nazi perpetrators were seen as superfluous and also regarded themselves as superfluous supports this point, as so many perpetrators saw themselves as carrying out the will of some outside force—Hitler or history—and so many committed suicide as soon as the war was over. Radical evil also implies an absence of wonder as no consideration is given to cultural, sexual, or racial differences. While it might be argued that genocidal killers are hyper-focused on the difference of their victims, without a basis of respect, their attention to difference becomes destruction of difference. In the world of the concentration and extermination camps, inmates had to learn the language and rules of those camps that applied to all, albeit with their own hierarchies.

For Arendt, our initial response to such radical evil, particularly the destruction of individuality and spontaneity, is horror (1976, 454). She also says that we may be "apathetic and baffled" by accounts of the concentration and extermination camps because what happened there is so much more extreme than typical injustices and oppression (1948, 743). From such an initial reaction, Arendt argues, we have to pursue the difficult task of trying to understand what appears to be incomprehensible. However, this search for understanding does not mean we do not hold the perpetrators responsible or that we fail to judge them. At this point we can address the initial question of how we should respond to such evil. There is a risk that radical evil, due to its enormity and our difficulty in understanding it, may be responded to with wonder or awe. I take it that Arendt, among many others, dedicated her life's work to countering any such response.

We may initially respond with wonder and disbelief on hearing of some terrible atrocity, as when we hear a surprising piece of news, but once we find out more about it, understanding and judgment become our primary reactions. Our judgment here is different from the prejudiced reaction of the sexist or racist person discussed in chapter 3, because it is founded on an attempt to understand, not on a baseless rejection. Of course, there may be times when we are confused, when we think we are making a reasoned judgment and ethical response and we are wrong about that. Due to that risk, we have to be vigilant and reflective about all our dismissals and hatreds of others, to determine if have failed in our thinking and in generosity and wonder. Finding an understanding of the specificity of evil is what Arendt tries to do, to investigate the history and context of Nazism and Stalinism and to explain it insofar as that is possible. Furthermore, her argument is that we must judge it and judge as wrong, as something that "*ought not to have happened*" (1994a, 14).

Again, we have to be wary of thinking what can be achieved by explanation and understanding. What we would hope not to arrive at is an imaginative identification with the perpetrators that makes us complicit in their crimes.[23] We also may have different responses depending on the perpetrator. The banal perpetrator may provoke our contempt and scorn, whereas the extreme perpetrators may, properly, horrify us. We may also respond with a lingering puzzlement, given that we do not *fully* understand what they have done. But that puzzlement is different from the openness of wonder Descartes and Irigaray describe. In relation to generosity, both Descartes and Kant insist that we cannot refuse all respect even to a vicious person, and that is where the idea of generosity gives us a way of thinking about the limits of punishment, even where one believes that is necessary. Such punishment should not be cruel or humiliating, in order to be consistent with generosity. This discussion focuses on the negative responses, so to speak, toward perpetrators of radical evil. The other question is whether these perpetrators can be forgiven.

The apparent incomprehensibility of radical evil, and the relative inexplicability of banal evil, implies for Arendt that the acts of the perpetrators are beyond forgiveness. On Arendt's view, forgiveness is a human thing and we cannot forgive the inhuman. The casting of evil as banal does not alter this claim, since the "banal" perpetrator has not unknowingly acted, even if they may have tried to avoid reflecting on what they were doing. I agree with Arendt that forgiveness is a human thing but I do not agree that radical evil is inhuman. Perhaps what Arendt leaves out is a leap to forgive that goes beyond understanding of motives. This leap appears to be exactly what Jacques Derrida is suggesting.

Derrida on Forgiveness: Forgiving the Unforgivable

Derrida takes up the question of forgiveness in "On Forgiveness" (2001) and "To Forgive: The Unforgivable and the Imprescriptible" (Caputo et al. 2001). Just as he argues that true hospitality is unconditional and limitless, Derrida maintains that we can only *truly* forgive the unforgivable crime or harm[24] (2001, 32). He also compares forgiveness (*le pardon, un pardon*) to the unconditionality of the gift, but notes that forgiveness is related to the past, so cannot be reduced to the gift (Caputo et al. 2001, 22) True forgiveness is unconditional and not premised on an understanding of the evil committed, so it includes forgiveness of radical evil. Pure forgiveness is aneconomic; it is beyond repentance, atonement, or any account of the weight of the crime, Derrida says. Once we begin to think of repentance and negotiation, healing and reconciliation, Derrida claims that we have entered the realm of impure or conditional forgiveness that is too simple. True forgiveness is a kind of madness, beyond such considerations. True forgiveness is forgiveness of the "*guilty as guilty*" (2001, 34). In his view, forgiveness cannot be of those who have atoned, because then they are no longer guilty.

Furthermore, conditional forgiveness does not exemplify the open generosity of true forgiveness. Such forgiveness is "corrupted" by the calculation of the value of the crime and of repentance (Caputo et al. 2001, 46) Derrida traces the idea of unconditional forgiveness to what he calls the Abrahamic religious tradition in order to include Judaism, Christianity, and Islam, yet argues that such forgiveness goes beyond that tradition, insofar as the tradition contains the contradictory or auto-deconstructive call for forgiveness only in proportion to repentance (2001, 35). This self-deconstruction is supposed to follow from the call for repentance, as he thinks that this undermines the generosity of forgiveness and makes the penitent no longer in need of forgiveness. He concludes that the unconditional and conditional forms of forgiveness are heterogenous, irreducible, yet none-theless indissociable, as are unconditional and conditional hospitality (2001, 44–45). Unconditional forgiveness includes forgiving the unforgivable, a position in direct contradiction of Arendt's view.

While Derrida briefly refers to Arendt's view of forgiveness (to note she does not claim that forgiveness has a juridical dimension, although she believes it is correlative to punishment in being a way of responding to the problem of irreversibility), he considers Vladimir Jankélévitch's argument that the perpetrators of the Shoah cannot be forgiven because "forgiveness died in the death camps" (Jankélévitch 1996, 567) in some detail in both "To Forgive" and "On Forgiveness" (1996; 2001).[25] Jankélévitch first published his essay "Should We Pardon Them?" in 1966, when there was debate concerning the decision in France in 1964 to have no statutory limitations on crimes against humanity such as the deeds of the Nazis. The essay was republished in English in 1996. Here, he relates this legal issue to the more personal one of forgiveness. Jankélévitch argues that there should not be any legal statute of limitations on those crimes: they are imprescriptible. One reason he gives is that any particular cutoff point in time is arbitrary. Another is that the full horrors of the crimes are not realized immediately but over time. More importantly, they are crimes against humanity, on a different scale from ordinary crimes; therefore they should be regarded differently. Jankélévitch says that it contradicts morality to consider pardoning such crimes (1996, 556).

Furthermore, these crimes are so great they cannot be redressed: they are "inexpiable," and for the inexpiable forgiveness can have no meaning. Jankélévitch's argument here is similar to Arendt's, in that he believes that once punishment cannot be proportionate and is almost irrelevant, the crime is inexpiable (1996, 558). He is clearly thinking of the crimes of the Shoah as radical evil. Jankélévitch says that the Shoah is a "crime out of all proportion to everyday wrongdoing" and "an unnamable, unmentionable, and terrifying thing" (1996, 553, 554). He also refers to "ontological wickedness," or "the most diabolical and gratuitous wickedness that history has ever known" (1996, 556). Since their crimes were unmotivated, he says, the perpetrators were monsters. The crimes of the extermination camps are different from other war crimes, such as terror bombing, due to their "directed, methodical, and *selective* character" (1996, 563).

Jankélévitch refers to the "refined sadism" of the perpetrators of the Shoah (1996, 563). Améry also explores sadism in the Nazi torturers, taking from Georges Bataille an existential psychology that sees sadism "as the radical negation of the other" (1980, 35).[26] He shows how the sadist is extreme in their denial of human existence. Amplifying Jankélévitch's account, Améry writes, "[T]orture becomes the total inversion of the social world, in which we can live only if we grant our fellow man life, ease his suffering, bridle the desire of our ego to expand. But in the world of torture man exists only by ruining the other person who stands before him" (1980, 35). Hence, there is no generosity, no wonder, no love, only a lack of the restraint so important to ethical life, a desire to enlarge the reach of sovereignty.

As a response to the crimes of the Nazis, which Améry contends are unique, he advocates holding on to resentment, rather than forgiving as a result of social pressure (1980, 72). Nevertheless, he believes that forgiveness would be possible or that resentment could be given up if history were made moral through a total repudiation of the entire Nazi period and all its works, a prospect he sees as unlikely at the very least (1980, 78–79).[27] According to Jankélévitch, the unforgivability of these crimes proceeds from the knowingness, from their deliberate character. Moreover, he argues, no one ever asked to be pardoned, so they should not be.[28] Jankélévitch argues that a pardon could only be justified by the "distress and dereliction of the guilty," but he finds them complacent and unconcerned (1996, 567).

Derrida counters Jankélévitch's claim that there is a need for forgiveness to be asked for in "To Forgive" by saying that there is

in the very meaning of forgiveness a force, a desire, an impetus, a movement, an appeal (call it what you will) that demands that forgiveness be granted, if it can be, even to someone who does not ask for it, who does not repent or confess or improve or redeem himself, beyond consequently, an entire identificatory, spiritual, whether sublime or not, economy, beyond all expiation even. (Caputo et al. 2001, 28)

The notion of forgiveness here is one of reaching out to the other, extending our forgiveness, without being asked to do so or expecting anything in return.[29] Derrida says it is hard to follow Jankélévitch's logic and is surprised that he has changed his mind from an earlier work, *Le Pardon* (1967), where he was more sympathetic to the idea of unconditional forgiveness.[30]

The gaps Derrida sees in Jankélévitch's logic are between the inexpiable and the unforgivable and between finding a crime unforgivable and concluding that we cannot forgive it. For Derrida, this conclusion cannot follow because the unforgivable calls for our forgiveness and "because this logic continues to imply that forgiveness remains the correlate of a judgment and the counterpart to a *possible* punishment, to a possible expiation, to the 'expiable'" (2001, 36). Derrida questions such a correlation since he sees punishment and forgiveness as quite separate and distinct, and sees forgiveness as not tied to judgment.[31] He finds the idea of the imprescriptible points beyond the law to the concept of the unforgivable, and therefore, true forgiveness (2001, 53). Furthermore, Jankélévitch is only alleging that pardon has not been asked for (2001, 35).

What Derrida finds most problematic in Jankélévitch's account is the idea that "*forgiveness must have a meaning*" (2001, 36). He finds no reason to assume that forgiveness depends on a human possibility. Derrida challenges both Arendt's and Jankélévitch's view that forgiveness is "a human thing" or on a human scale (Caputo et al. 2001, 30–31), suggesting that pure forgiveness somehow goes beyond the human. What he perhaps has in mind is that a God seems able to forgive because such a being would be beyond the particular entanglements of guilt and harm (Caputo et al. 2001, 46). Thus, while he is not supporting a theistic approach to forgiveness, he is accepting that true forgiveness is somehow transcendent.

Derrida questions the idea that forgiveness cannot be a response to radical evil or the "inexpiable" in the name of a hyperbolical ethics, an ethics that is exaggerated, which goes beyond an exchange of demands and expectations. The unforgivable is radical evil for Derrida or perhaps even something worse (if that was possible). He says that such evil involves "an absolute hatred" and "destructive hostility" (2001, 49). This ethics "therefore . . . carries itself beyond laws, norms, or any obligation. Ethics beyond ethics, there perhaps is the undiscoverable place of forgiveness" (2001, 36).[32] According to Derrida, Jankélévitch's view concerning the unforgivability of the Shoah falls into an "economic" logic of exchange as he believes that an apology is necessary for forgiveness. In contrast, hyperbolical ethics concerns itself with the impossible, therefore the unforgivable.

Surprisingly, Derrida "privatizes" forgiveness even more than Arendt, because Arendt connects forgiveness with judgment and punishment in the political realm (1998, 241), whereas Derrida argues that pure forgiveness has nothing to do with judgment. For him, forgiveness is between two people only, the victim and the perpetrator (2001, 42). He accepts that some people cannot bring themselves to forgive and that such a decision is a private matter, citing the example of a woman who said at the Truth and Reconciliation Commission in South Africa that only she, the victim, could forgive and she was not ready to forgive. Derrida's idea is that the "democracy to come" he champions would allow for the secret and the inaccessible, and experiences such as those of the Truth and Reconciliation Commission demonstrate the importance of allowing for such secrets (2001, 55). Louise Du Toit criticizes Derrida for accepting that victims of rape "could not testify about this before the commission" (Derrida 2001, 60; Du Toit 2009, ch.1). He seems to imply that rape victims should keep silent to avoid "exposing themselves one more time, by their very testimony, to another violence." More emphatically, he says in "To Forgive," "that women in South Africa were often raped and could not come forth and bear witness before the commission because they would have to tell the stories of their being raped or they would have to show the scars and expose their nakedness" (Caputo et al. 2001, 59). He has accepted rather too readily one response and way of dealing with the problem of testifying about rape that links with his idea of the need for the "secret." The more general point he is making about the importance of there being a space for private decisions concerning whether or not and when to forgive is one that I am arguing for here. However, there is a strain in Derrida's thought on forgiveness that goes against his acceptance of nonforgiveness.

While Derrida's account of true forgiveness may be of a forgiveness that does not, cannot, exist, he claims it is essential to provide us with a means to think about the nature of forgiveness, to understand acts that fall short of forgiveness. The impossibility of pure forgiveness should guide our thinking about forgiveness based on repentance, mourning, and exchange. Ultimately, as we negotiate between ethics and politics, we will negotiate between pure forgiveness and its impure forms. Derrida's characterization of forgiveness addresses the logic of forgiveness, rather than the ethics or psychology of forgiveness. He does not make a claim as to when we should forgive and when not.[33] However, I argue that we must read his view of forgiveness as implicitly arguing for the "madness" or leap beyond any conditions of pure forgiveness, for two reasons.

First, Derrida's criticisms of Jankélévitch and Arendt suggest not only that their account of forgiveness is conditional but also that their particular views about whom and when we should forgive are objects of his criticism. For example, Derrida seems scandalized by Jankélévitch's angry tone in writing about the Shoah and his remarks concerning Martin Heidegger.[34] Derrida quotes a passage from Jankélévitch's essay, and then warns, "What follows are remarks of such polemical violence and such anger against the Germans that I do not even want to read them or cite them" (Caputo et al. 2001, 28). Of Jankélévitch's view of Heidegger, Derrida writes, "And a little further on, as often elsewhere, Jankélévitch violently attacks Heidegger" (Caputo et al. 2001, 36).[35] Jankélévitch does make a number of remarks about Heidegger, for example, "The pedantic tone of German racism reminds me of . . . the gibberish of Heidegger" (1996, 564). These remarks are certainly unsympathetic to Heidegger, but there are several rather than many and the reference to "violent attacks" builds up a picture of Jankélévitch as an irresponsible writer, at least in this piece.

Furthermore, Derrida links Jankélévitch's waiting for a word of sympathy from the perpetrators and his criticisms of Heidegger with Paul Celan's poem, *Todtnauberg*, often interpreted as an expression of disappointment that Heidegger did not ask for forgiveness. He quotes the first verse from the poem: "Arnica, eyebright, the / draft from the well with the starred die above it, / in the / hut, / the line / —whose name did the book / register before mine?—, / the line inscribed / in that book about / a hope, today / of a thinking man's coming / word / in the heart. . . ." (Celan 1988, 292–93). Derrida sets aside the question of the poem's interpretation and makes the point that Celan's poem itself is a gift, an expression of forgiveness: "*Todtnauberg* remains thus to be read, to be received—as gift or forgiveness themselves, a gift and a forgiveness which are the poem before being, possibly, its themes or the theme of the poet's disappointed expectation" (Caputo et al. 2001, 38). (Apparently, Celan sent it to Heidegger, who loved it [Joris, 1988, 5].) This interesting interpretation contrasts Celan's generous forgiveness (he was not asked for forgiveness by Heidegger) with Jankélévitch's view that without a request for forgiveness he cannot and should not forgive. Implicitly, Jankélévitch is unfavorably compared to Celan because he is less forgiving.

Second, Derrida's positive account of true forgiveness implies that it is an ideal that we should try to live up to insofar as it is possible. We should aspire to true forgiveness, that is, to forgiving the unforgivable. He uses normative language in defining pure forgiveness, for example, "Forgiveness is not, it *should not be,* normal, normative, normalizing. It *should* remain exceptional and extraordinary, in the face of the impossible: as if it interrupted the ordinary course of historical temporality" (2001, 32).[36] Derrida also says that a hyperbolical ethics "would command precisely . . . that forgiveness be granted where it is neither asked for nor deserved, and even for the worst radical evil" (Caputo et al. 2001, 29). Conversely, Derrida's association of impure forgiveness with calculation and corruption implies that we should avoid this impurity by not considering the conditions for forgiveness, such as repentance and atonement (2001, 27; Caputo et al. 2001, 46), although he notes that once we have to make a decision in a particular case, forgiveness must "engage in a series of conditions of all kinds (psycho-sociological, political, etc.)" (2001, 45). These conditions are like a falling away from extraordinary forgiveness.

In the sense of holding out impossible ideals, or as he calls them, "reals," Derrida is a stern moralist. When exactly Derrida believes we should give way to the madness of pure forgiveness is another question. His remarks concerning the South African Truth and Reconciliation commission accord with Jankélévitch's point that others cannot forgive on behalf of the dead: "The survivor is not ready to substitute herself, abusively, for the dead" (2001, 44; Jankélévitch 1996, 569). Here, the impossibility of forgiveness is a practical one, in that the victim is not in a position to forgive. Derrida also says that "I always risk perjuring myself by forgiving, of betraying someone else by forgiving, for one is always doomed to forgive (thus abusively) in the name of another" (Caputo et al. 2001, 49) However, it appears that he is willing to accept that risk in the name of forgiveness.

As we have seen in the previous chapters, Derrida believes we have to negotiate between the unconditional and the conditional: "It is between these two poles, *irreconcilable but indissociable,* that decisions and responsibilities are to be taken" (2001, 45). However, there is an important difference between Derrida's accounts of unconditional hospitality and forgiveness. Both are impossible, but in the case of hospitality, as we saw, Derrida warns of a number of specific, catastrophic dangers of unconditional hospitality. The visitor can become an invader or colonist. Conquest is an abuse of hospitality. In any case, hospitality can only be offered if we have a home, so pure hospitality without conditions is ruled out. But there is no correlative list of the dangers of pure forgiveness, of the harms that might arise from its untrammeled progress. Derrida makes one point concerning the possible arrogance and assertion of sovereignty in presuming to forgive (2001, 58).[37] Not everyone wishes to be forgiven. Nevertheless, he adds that forgiveness that is unconditional but without sovereignty is possible. Sovereignty does not appear to be undermined by forgiveness in that way that it is by hospitality. Another difference is that Derrida speaks of the right to hospitality, but he does not speak of a right to forgiveness or a duty to forgive.[38] I believe that is appropriate. However, by taking forgiveness to its logical limits, Derrida creates an implicit expectation that pure, mad, true, forgiveness is a good, and it is one that we should expect of ourselves and that others may expect of us.

A possible implication of Derrida's account is that we should be less forgiving of the unforgiving, for they do not aspire to true forgiveness, a paradoxical outcome. He references Hegel's view that "all is forgivable except the crime against spirit, that is, against the reconciling power of forgiveness" (2001, 34).[39] Derrida's position seems to imply that the perpetrators must be forgiven no matter what they did. Furthermore, his account of forgiveness puts the onus on the victims to forgive rather than the oppressors to atone. This point could be a little unjust, as Derrida says that his concern is what he calls the comedy of forgiveness and what he has in mind are those who presume to forgive on behalf of others, such as heads of state (2001, 50).[40] Ultimately, he claims, he remains torn between the purity of forgiveness and the pragmatism of reconciliation. However, the weight of Derrida's argument lies on the potential forgivers. This presumption adds a further burden to the victims of radical evil, and cannot constitute an ethical injunction in every case.[41] Nevertheless, Derrida's idea that there is a call for forgiveness is an appealing one. What would an ethic of forgiveness that takes into account both these insights and these difficulties look like?

Why Might We Forgive?

A gap in both Derrida's and Arendt's account of forgiveness is a precise characterization of the psychological nature of forgiveness. Their views certainly provide hints of what such an account might look like, providing constraints on the account, for example, by saying whether forgiveness is "a human thing" or not, and whether it involves forgiving the unforgivable. Forgiveness is generally opposed to resentment, so we might say that forgiveness involves the giving up of resentment, or as Uma Narayan says, giving up "our sense of grievance" (1997, 171).[42] Giving up that grievance does not mean that one has to trust again or deny the original wrong. Narayan notes that we may feel a range of emotions toward the offender, including moral anger and hurt. "Hurt" may seem an inappropriately trivial term to use in the context of radical evil, but I believe that it can be a component in our response to extreme racism and anti-Semitism, for example, as such treatment can be experienced as a betrayal. The evil of genocide can be carried out by friends, neighbors, and family, as it was in the Rwandan genocide. Letting go of these particular feelings does not entail forgetting of the original offense or excusing it, but a willingness to think of that person as other than an enemy or wrongdoer.[43] The nature of the relationship between victim and offender will of course affect the nature of forgiveness. Unilaterally forgiving a person whom one does not interact with will be a very different affair from forgiving a former friend or neighbor. The consequences and the feelings of both the victim and the perpetrator will be very different when they have to live or work together.

In Derrida's account, the idea of repentance or apology is left out of the process of forgiveness, and this is one area where I disagree with him. I argue that there is an important, if complex, relationship between repentance and forgiveness. It appears that just as one can forgive without being asked to, one can and should offer an apology and repent without expecting forgiveness. As we have seen, Jankélévitch argues that we cannot forgive the perpetrators of the Shoah because they have never asked for forgiveness, and Derrida counters with his view that true forgiveness does not depend on apology. To be fair to Derrida's view, it should be noted that an injunction to forgive without apology does not correspond to an excuse for not apologizing.[44] However, I would take this point farther, and say that victims should not be blamed for wanting or expecting an apology even when they cannot forgive. Another central question concerning forgiveness is whether it is essentially personal.

I will discuss these issues in more detail in the following chapter, where I examine the relation between forgiveness and apology. At this stage, I wish to note that the final decision concerning when and whether to forgive is a personal one in the sense that it concerns only victims who have directly suffered harm and those very close to them. Arendt accepts the idea of collective harm, arguing that the Shoah was "a crime against humanity, perpetrated upon the body of the Jewish people" (1994b, 269). If that interpretation is correct, it appears that others may be able to forgive the perpetrators of the Shoah and other crimes against humanity (provided they are considered forgivable at all). Eve Garrard (2002) argues that this aspect of the Shoah makes it possible for everyone to be hurt by the crime and therefore in a position to consider forgiving that crime. Derrida implies we can forgive such crimes when he argues that there is no conceptual limit to forgiveness, in that we all inherit crimes against humanity (2001, 32), although he says that we cannot forgive on the behalf of victims. It seems to me that the second point is more important and has a stronger basis. The notion of crimes against humanity does not really make all of humanity victims of genocidal killers, for example, but makes us all feel shame that we are part of a group capable of such crimes. This idea of a shame that we feel because of a wrong that we have done or feel connected to is one that I will return to.

Derrida is right to separate forgiveness from juridical and political considerations, I argue. For instance, forgiveness is quite separate from the question of punishment. Punishment is a legal issue that must be determined according to the rule of law. However, our response to the humanity of the perpetrators entails that we treat even the worst offenders with respect, which means following due process and, in my view, that both "cruel and unusual" punishments are out of the question, as is the death penalty. Universal generous respect for others is not defeated by evil actions. The basic respect advocated by Descartes and Kant is quite compatible with negative feelings toward others and even with punishment, but not, I believe with the death penalty. As I mentioned in chapter 4, this is one area where Kant's view is inconsistent. In *The Metaphysics of Morals,* Kant says that if a person "has committed murder he must *die*" (1996a, 6: 333). Where I see the inconsistency is that Kant expressly rules out mistreatment and upholds respect for the humanity of the criminal: "The retribution . . . must be freed from any mistreatment that could make the humanity in the person suffering it into something abominable" (1996a, 6: 333); yet he fails to acknowledge that capital punishment destroys the humanity of the person. It is inadequate to assert that someone's humanity is being respected in executing them. Arendt's argument in support of the death penalty in *Eichmann in Jerusalem,* which I quoted earlier, is also weak and based on a concept of revenge that does not sit well with many of her other views. Although she does not elaborate how far she sees this argument extending, her idea that those who do not wish to share the earth with others should be executed would include many beyond Eichmann. Furthermore, her remarks demonstrate that she had not moved so very far away from her earlier conception of radical evil as inhuman.

Forgiveness must be understood quite differently. My argument is that we cannot expect or demand forgiveness as a right. We can only hope for it or try to bring about the conditions for it, by showing repentance, making atonement and reparations. Toward the end of his essay, Jankélévitch says there can be no reparations for the Shoah (1996, 571), and while it is an understandable view, the offering of reparations is still an essential expectation of the perpetrator, even if they are refused. I also contend that forgiveness of radical evil is possible, although unlikely for practical reasons.

Arendt believes that forgiveness of radical evil is impossible. Some philosophers suggest there are other difficulties with forgiving radical evil. Carlos Pereda warns of the dangers of what he calls "forgiveness and oblivion" in a political context (Lara 2001, 210–22). While he believes we need to forsake revenge, he argues we need warnings for the future, so we must remember the atrocities of the past. His view emerges from the commonly made connection between forgiveness and forgetting.[45] However, these two acts can be separated. Forgiveness is perfectly compatible with continuing to remember the wrongdoing.

There is an interesting connection between the idea that we should forgive the perpetrators of horrible crimes because of their common humanity with us, and the contrasting view that they are so utterly different from ordinary people, so evil, that they should not be forgiven. The basis for forgiveness in the political sphere, Arendt argues, is respect, rather than love, which is its basis in the private realm: "Respect, at any rate, because it concerns only the person, is quite sufficient to prompt forgiving of what a person did, for the sake of the person" (1998, 243).[46] On her account, however, the perpetrators put themselves outside the realm of respect and therefore forgiveness. Garrard argues that forgiveness, even of the unforgivable, must be based on respect or our common human nature and so provides a basis for forgiveness (2002, 164). The idea of generosity, of the respect owed to all members of the human community may seem to be undermined by acts of radical evil because the acts put the perpetrators outside the human community. However, if we take the basis of respect to be common human freedom, particular acts, no matter how abhorrent, do not have this effect of placing evil people outside the community. For example, Gitta Sereny found that Franz Stangl, the commandant of Treblinka, after many hours of discussion, could come to feel the enormity of what he had done and could experience remorse (1974). Not all perpetrators will come to feel remorse for their crimes, but we should treat them in ways that make it possible for them to develop moral feelings, even when they are being punished.

Nevertheless, I argue that generosity provides only the preliminary basis for forgiveness, and does not mean that we must forgive. Garrard concedes that our common human nature provides a weak reason to forgive (2002, 163).[47] However, common human nature is not just a weak reason, it is simply not enough. If respect were a sufficient reason to forgive, our decision to forgive should be universal: either we should forgive all wrongdoers or we should forgive none. The actual decision to forgive is more like an act of love, because it is and must be voluntary and dependent on the particular case. I do not mean that we can forgive as an act of will, but that we can cultivate forgiveness in ourselves, just as we can cultivate love and wonder. We may forgive without realizing we have done so, and may believe we have forgiven when we have not. To forgive is partly to decide to act as if we have forgiven, and to hope that our passions and attitudes will change with time. Generosity or respect for others, then, is important but not enough for forgiveness. Perpetrators differ in their actions, their choices, and motivations, but share other features with everyone. Nevertheless, the crime of treating some others as of no value whatever, without generosity or wonder, which I take to be characteristic of radical evil, cannot be met with the same response as lesser acts. In trivial cases a failure to forgive can appear churlish and be a sign of an unforgiving character, but not in the case of radical evil.

Like Jankélévitch, I believe that forgiveness is partly dependent on an expression of remorse and repentance on the part of the perpetrator. This signals that they acknowledge their wrong, the harm to the victim, and are attempting to change. However, the victim is not under a strict obligation to forgive, since forgiveness is discretionary. The perpetrator's remorse prepares the way for forgiveness but does not determine it. Love, understood as sympathy for the other, cannot be an unconditional or perfect duty. It is a responsibility or duty to be a forgiving person over the course of a whole life, for that is to be a better person, but it cannot be a duty to forgive in any particular case. Kant's account of perfect and imperfect duties, which I discussed in chapter 4, makes sense of this distinction. He defines a perfect duty as "one that admits no exception in favor of inclination" (1996, 4: 422), whereas an imperfect duty is one that is virtuous and worthy to fulfill but it is not culpable not to do so unless that is made into a principle (1996, 6: 390).[48] Therefore, my argument is that *forgivingness* is an imperfect duty, so that to a great extent, in specific instances, it is a matter of personal discretion whether to forgive. However, we should try to be forgiving people and should not make a determination never to forgive. There may be cases where the considerations in favor of forgiving are so strong that the imperfect duty of forgiveness becomes almost like a perfect duty in that the person has apologized, has fully atoned, is remorseful, no one else could forgive them and forgiveness is extremely important to them. These cases are rare, but could occur in relation to relatively small wrongs.

Moreover, the extreme harm of radical evil makes the latitude of imperfect duties even wider. In any case, since forgiveness is related to the acknowledgment of responsibility for one's acts and genuine regret and remorse, forgiveness of radical evil may only be possible in very unusual cases. This is for the simple reason that known examples of perpetrators of radical evil who are remorseful or who make atonement for their actions are very rare. Lawrence Thomas has to invent a fictional repentant Nazi in his paper on forgiving the unforgivable (2003). One actual example I am aware of is described in Simon Wiesenthal's *The Sunflower* (1998).

Wiesenthal explains how a dying SS man, Karl, asked him for forgiveness for his participation in atrocities against Jewish people. Wiesenthal silently listens to the man's confession and then leaves the room. Later, after the war, he visits Karl's mother, and does not tell her about Karl's murderous actions. Wiesenthal invited a range of theologians, philosophers, and psychologists to read his memoir and to ask themselves what they would have done in the same situation.

The responses divide between recommending forgiveness and rejecting the idea, primarily depending on how they interpret the SS man's attitude. If commentators see his remorse as genuine, they are likely to suggest forgiveness is at least possible, but if they interpret his behavior as arrogant, denying Simon Wiesenthal's humanity and not fully recognizing the wrongs of his own actions, they dismiss the idea of forgiveness.[49] On the one hand, Karl is repentant, but on the other hand, he had called for "a Jew," any Jew, to be brought to his bedside to hear his confession and he says that the people he killed "died quickly, they did not suffer as I do" (1998, 52). Even in this very rare circumstance of a direct request for forgiveness from a perpetrator, it seems unjust to expect forgiveness or to criticize Simon Wiesenthal for withholding forgiveness since it is his decision to make.

Forgiveness could be worthwhile for the victim because it may be a way of coming to terms with the past. However, no one can dictate the terms under which someone should reach the point of forgiveness.[50] Being forgiving may be a good, but it is not one that can be forced on people. Nor should we judge others for not being forgiving enough. We might say that they are being impractical or making things worse for themselves by not forgiving, but we should not condemn them by holding them to impossible standards. Lack of forgiving as a consistent trait is problematic, but generally it is not in particular instances. In the end, forgiveness is a leap even when it is related to repentance and apology. This would also be true even in the cases of mutual forgiveness that Trudy Govier alerts us to (2002, viii), as both parties would need to reflect on the possibilities and reasons for forgiveness. That said, forgiveness is a valuable ethical action that can be an expression of generosity and love, as long as it does not entail condoning evil. There may be cases where forgiveness does amount to a kind of acceptance of wrongdoing.

One example is that of ongoing domestic violence. Judith Boss links the question of forgiveness to the oppression of women, since violent, sexual abuse of women is prevalent in many societies. She argues that it is morally wrong for women to forgive the perpetrators of domestic violence in the context of ongoing abuse in these situations. By forgiveness here she means the giving up of feelings of anger and resentment (1997, 236). Drawing on Kant's account of self-respect, Boss sees forgiveness as constrained by the need to maintain self-respect. As I suggest, she sees a need for genuine repentance of the part of the abuser for forgiveness. Thus, "Forgiveness, in order to be consistent with self-respect and moral equality, is appropriate only when the offender ceases to hold a degraded view of his victim and repents of his wrongful actions" (1997, 237). This is an important example for generosity, in that it is possible for forms of forgiveness to undermine generosity in the sense of both self-respect and respect for others. Murphy and Hampton also contend that forgiveness can be a vice if it implies lack of self-respect (1988, 17). They make the additional point that failure to resent can imply a lack of respect for others. If we think of a wrong done to us by others as unworthy of our resentment, we may be disregarding their moral agency and value. Inappropriate forgiveness or failure to resent a wrong could actually undermine our capacity for generosity. If we cannot respect ourselves, we will find it more difficult to respect others. In other words, it may be more ethical to resent the perpetrator than to forgive them.[51]

Furthermore, in such cases of continuing abuse, women can lose their respect and love for self and feel themselves deserving of abuse. Boss sees this as a misdirection of the anger and resentment that should be felt toward the abuser. In circumstances where genuine repentance and a change of behavior is shown, forgiveness is still the victim's choice, she maintains. Her way of expressing the voluntary nature of forgiveness in this case is to say that it is "supererogatory" and so worthy of admiration rather than expected (1997, 244). Boss also mentions that victims of abuse may blame themselves and others may blame them for the abuse. Being and feeling oneself a victim may be a cause of shame, a shame that one has been so badly treated, shame before the world as a victim and shame before oneself as someone who cannot escape the torment.

There are two senses of shame that are relevant here. One is a pervasive sense of shame feminists have argued that women and others in an oppressive culture are more likely to be disposed to. The other is the particular shame that someone may feel in relation to some wrong they have done. Both are undermining of generosity in that they make it difficult to respect the self, to feel esteem and to forgive oneself and others. Perhaps the most famous discussion of shame occurs in Jean-Paul Sartre's *Being and Nothingness,* where he discusses shame as a phenomenon that reveals the mode of Being-for-Others (2003). He describes the situation of a person who is caught, or who experiences themselves as being caught, peering through a keyhole. Through this look of the other seeing one as a voyeur, shame is experienced. Sartre's argument is that we feel shame in the face of others. While shame is "an intimate relation of myself to myself . . . it is in its primary structure shame *before somebody*" (2003, 246). His elucidation of shame as in its essence relational is generally accepted.[52]

Sandra Bartky, for example, while criticizing Sartre for thinking of shame as before the other too literally, concedes that shame "requires if not an actual audience before whom my deficiencies are paraded, then an internalized audience with the capacity to judge me, hence internalized standards of judgment" (1990, 86). Like Sartre, she also takes it that in a significant way we are as we appear. What she means by this is that we become or experience ourselves as we are seen by others, even if that judgment is unjust. Shame may be a recognition that we have failed in some way but it may also be a result of how we are viewed and treated by others, and can be detrimental to the cultivation of generosity. Shame is also generally distinguished from guilt as being more closely focused on the entire self, rather than a particular act (Bartky 1990, 87; Ahmed 2004, 105). Bartky understands pervasive shame as a mode of attunement for women and even more so for women of color.[53] Then, in the case of the oppressed person who is subject to domestic violence, for example, their feelings of self-worth would always be experienced in this context. Her point is that shame in this sense is not an opportunity for assessing oneself and becoming a better person, but more likely to lead to self-obsession, self-destructive rage, and, in general, disempowerment. Shame in this sense is injurious to the development of generosity in its obvious threat to self-respect. I argue that this shame would also be corrosive of wonder, as it is bound to regarding others as menacing and intimidating.

The second type of shame is one that those who transgress properly feel as a result of their own actions. In that case, for perpetrators, there is also the problem of forgiving oneself. While it might be thought that perpetrators tend to be far too ready to forgive themselves, the possibility that it might be harder than forgiving others must be conceded. They may also feel shame and find that they can no longer respect themselves. This is the kind of shame Dan Zahavi calls "repenting, self-reflective shame," felt, for example, by a man for committing atrocities in the Rwandan genocide (Zahavi 2010, 219). Forgiving yourself involves generosity or proper self-respect, and while it could be argued that we should respect ourselves simply as human beings, some acts may make a person feel unworthy of that basic respect, let alone a fuller esteem. Similarly, shame can make one feel unworthy of the respect of others. Forgiveness of oneself may be as difficult and even as inappropriate as the forgiveness of others in cases of radical evil. Robin S. Dillon argues that a perpetrator needs to take full responsibility for what they have done, repent and atone, but they may still need to reproach themself for what they have done (2001, 78). She stresses that an ethical response may not only be forgiveness or its lack, but may also include a deeply ambivalent view of the self that still includes guilt and shame.

Unlike philosophers who examine the conditions of self-forgiveness, such as Dillon and Uma Narayan (1997), Arendt does not believe that one can forgive oneself, as she sees forgiveness as based on the plurality of the human condition and on the experience that only others can have of us. However, I contend this claim puts too stringent conditions on the basis of forgiveness. For, while we cannot see ourselves as others see us, we can experience our past actions as surprising, wrongful, and harmful to ourselves when we reflect on them.

Asked whether we can forgive ourselves, Derrida gives a very interesting answer: "There is in me someone who is always ready to forgive and another who is absolutely merciless, and we are constantly fighting. Sometimes I can sleep, sometimes I cannot" (Caputo et al. 2001, 61). The suggestion here is that there is a barrier to self-forgiveness, not the barrier of lack of otherness that concerns Arendt, but the barrier of pluralism within the self that blocks complete self-forgiveness. Perpetrators of radical evil might be able to forgive themselves if they were able to both understand what they had done and to see a change in themselves. Or they might maintain an ambivalent and conflictual attitude to themselves. In many cases, forgiveness of radical evil may be too much to expect. All the perpetrator can do is make atonement by acknowledging their guilt and attempt at reparation without expectation of forgiveness or reconciliation.

Radical evil poses challenges for understanding both wonder and generosity, as evil is not a difference we should regard with wonder, since it must be judged and it stretches the limits of our respect for the other. I have focused on radical evil as extreme evil not properly accounted for by everyday motives. It is possible to forgive radical evil, but such forgiveness cannot be demanded or expected. Radical evil's lack of comprehensibility does not place it in a different category of evil or wrongdoing with respect to forgiveness, although forgiveness in such a case is more complex and difficult. The treatment of the victim is one lacking in wonder and generosity itself and is likely to damage the victim's own capacity to respond ethically, as they lose the trust in the world Améry so starkly shows us is lost in experiences such as torture. Both victims and perpetrators can be filled with a shame that undercuts their self-respect. More important than the lack of or inadequacy of motivation as an explanation for radical evil is the subsequent attitude of the perpetrator and their apology and repentance. Only their humanity, their repentance, and, finally, the victims' responses can provide a basis for forgiveness. Forgiveness needs generous respect and love in the form of sympathy. As I showed, Jankélévitch and Améry both argued that there had to be a major moral change in the attitude of the perpetrators for forgiveness to be possible. Derrida's view of forgiveness focuses on the logic of forgiveness, which nonetheless has ethical and political implications, whereas Arendt focuses on the politics of forgiveness. In this shift of focus from logic to ethics and politics there has to be a shift in our expectation of forgiveness. Derrida states that forgiveness *is* forgiveness of the unforgivable or radical evil, and as I argued, implies that we must forgive the unforgivable. He believes that forgiveness is beyond the human. Arendt put the unforgivable or radical evil beyond the human and finds it truly unforgivable.

However, both forgiveness *and* radical evil, unfortunately, are human. In my judgment, while it is not ethical to demand or expect forgiveness from victims, it is a human response that may be worthwhile for both victim and perpetrator even in extreme cases. Forgiveness is asymmetrical in that while the perpetrator cannot expect forgiveness, the victim can have reasons for trying to forgive, both as part of their own process of healing and in attempting to see a connection between everyone and those who commit evil actions. Yet in the end, the decision whether to try to forgive is one that only the victim can make. In some cases, the decision to forgive would not be the ethical one as it would undermine the self-respect of generosity. Conversely, the perpetrator can only attempt to atone or bring about the conditions for reconciliation or forgiveness.

In the following chapter I explore the relation between reconciliation, forgiveness, and apology. Derrida's and others' shifting of the focus from the perpetrators to the victims raises very important questions about the connections between these acts, wonder and generosity, and their place in both ethics and politics.

7

Apology, Forgiveness, and Reconciliation

This vicarious responsibility for things we have not done, this taking upon ourselves the consequences for things we are entirely innocent of, is the price we pay for the fact that we live our lives not by ourselves but among our fellow men.

—Hannah Arendt, *Responsibility and Judgment*

My discussion of evil and forgiveness in the previous chapter leads us to the very important question of the nature and value of official apologies for wrongdoing. Are they part of a political life where wonder, generosity, and love are taken seriously and expressed? In recent years, many governments around the world have made official apologies for injustices perpetrated by previous governments.[1] However, some governments have been reluctant to make apologies, and the reasons for this reluctance need to be both understood and challenged. Russian Prime Minister Vladimir V. Putin did not apologize for the massacre of more than twenty thousand Polish officers by the Soviet secret police even though he joined with Polish officials in the commemoration of the murders (Schwirtz, 2010). Other examples of refusals to apologize are Britain's, the United States', Spain's, Portugal's, and Holland's refusals to apologize for the transatlantic slave trade and colonialism at the 2001 UN Conference against Racism, Racial Discrimination, Xenophobia and Related Intolerance until any possibility of reparations or an admission that slavery was a crime against humanity was excluded (Castle 2001). The U.S. House of Representatives and the Senate have at last apologized for slavery and segregation. British Prime Minister

David Cameron apologized for "Bloody Sunday" (1972) in Ireland, when British troops shot Northern Irish Protesters (Bono 2010). For a long time, the Australian government refused to apologize to aboriginal Australians for the policy of removal of aboriginal children from their parents, until in 2008 the recently elected prime minister did so. Yet these apologies are almost always issued reluctantly a long time after the event, with many fears and doubts about their meaning and the possible repercussions.

It is surprising that the thought of a number of philosophers and political theorists, particularly Hannah Arendt and Jacques Derrida, whom I discussed in previous chapters, appears to support these reluctant stances. In Arendt's case, it appears that her critique of collective guilt undermines the case for an official apology because apologies are thought to depend on an assumption of collective guilt. In Derrida's case, it is his account of forgiveness as independent of apology I examined in the last chapter that appears to obviate the need for or even justify the lack of an apology. The concept of reconciliation has also been criticized on the grounds that reconciliation implies a former unity that never existed and fault on both sides and looks toward an impossible harmony.

In this chapter, I wish to explore the question of an apology in order to show that these apparent objections to an official apology are not as they appear, and to show more clearly what such an apology means and why it is an obligation. I argue that the apology to aboriginal Australians and apologies for the slave trade do not have to involve a corresponding expectation of forgiveness. That is one feature of the asymmetry between them. They also differ in their relation to generosity, wonder, and love. Contemporary political theorists, such as Peter Digeser (1998), Bert van Roermund (2001), and Andrew Schaap (2003), have argued for the value of political forgiveness. To sustain this view, apology and forgiveness must be understood, either explicitly or implicitly, as symmetrical in one or more of three ways: as both based on respect (van Roermund 2001, 182; Schaap 2003, 82), as both perfect duties (van Roermund 2001, 182–83), or as both potentially public acts (Digeser 1998, 704).

Against these positions, I contend that there are a number of important implications following from the nature of apologies, since they are based on the respect for others of generosity, and of forgiveness, which is based on love, as I argued in the previous chapter. In many cases, the apology that is needed for previous injustice or oppression is one that involves wonder, in the sense that it involves a recognition of the completely different culture that existed or, in some cases, the different cultural position that exists partly as result of that oppression. One asymmetry is that apologies are a perfect duty or obligatory whereas forgiveness is an imperfect duty or discretionary. A further asymmetry is that apologies are (or can be) public acts whereas forgiveness is essentially personal. Accounts of both forgiveness and reconciliation have conceived them as a kind of deal or pact so that it seems that if forgiveness is not part of such a pact, then there is no need for an apology. Although forgiveness cannot be expected, it is possible to progress toward reconciliation, if reconciliation is properly understood as a willingness to work together without a presumption of having overcome the past, rather than as necessarily involving forgiveness, as Desmond Tutu assumes (1999, 209). An apology is an important feature of reconciliation, along with practical measures to overcome past oppression and injustice. The lack of generosity in refusals to apologize tends to obstruct the reconciliation process and make the possibility of loving forgiveness very remote. This lack of recognition of past injustice is like a tear in ethical and political life.

I will begin by discussing a number of refusals to apologize, and then examine Arendt's and Derrida's apparent support for this refusal. In relation to Arendt, I show that in fact her work allows us to comprehend the nature of collective responsibility. In Derrida's case, I argue that his analysis puts the burden of forgiveness on the colonized rather than the colonizers and neglects the asymmetry between apology and forgiveness, an asymmetry that I show runs along the three main lines sketched above. Finally, I will explore the implications of this asymmetry for our understanding of reconciliation.

Refusals to Apologize

In this chapter, I will focus on examples where governments have refused to apologize. My discussion of these examples has implications for official apologies in general and sheds light on the nature of apology itself. In the U.S. case, an apology to Native Americans, made as part of the Indian Health Care Bill, was passed in the Senate but not voted on in the House in 2008 (Brownback 2008). It was finally signed into law by President Barack Obama in December 2009 as part of a defense appropriations bill (McKinnon 2009). The U.S. House of Representatives and the Senate apologized for slavery and for the mistreatment of African Americans under Jim Crow laws (Fears 2008). In the past, U.S. presidents seem to have avoided the issue of apology rather than directly refusing to apologize. For example, President

Clinton set up a President's Initiative on Race but did not make an apology one of the issues the initiative should examine (Nobles 2008, 105–106). However, during this period the Assistant Secretary for Indian Affairs apologized for the harms caused by the Bureau of Indian Affairs (Rebecca Tsosie, in Barkan and Karn 2006, 185–212). In Canada, Prime Minister Stephen Harper apologized for the residential schools in which Canadian native children were abused and neglected (Campion-Smith 2008).

The former Liberal government in Australia refused to acknowledge responsibility or officially apologize to the aboriginal people for past practices of removing children from their parents, although John Howard, the prime minister, offered a personal apology and passed a motion in parliament expressing regret. This case is particularly interesting in understanding the nature of public apologies, as he put the arguments against them openly and on record. It is also distinct in that there was significant active public support from indigenous and nonindigenous peoples alike for such an apology. The reason Howard gave for not supporting a government apology is that present generations should not have to accept guilt and blame for the actions of previous generations (Healey 2001a, 8). Likewise, implicitly, the present government cannot be held responsible for the actions of previous governments. Furthermore, he said that "to apply retrospectively the standards of today in relation to the behavior of some who were very sincere in their actions does them immense injustice" (Healey 2001b, 10). Howard articulated an understanding of guilt, responsibility, and history that is behind refusals to apologize.

On the one hand, it was argued that an apology necessitated an admission of responsibility and in the government's case, a legal responsibility to provide compensation (Healey 2001b, 21). (Different conclusions were drawn about whether that meant an apology should be made.) On the other hand, it was argued that an apology constituted a sincere expression of regret for the suffering of aboriginal people, an interpretation which, if appropriate, would make the government's refusal to apologize more shocking.[2] Some were willing to say sorry without being sure to what extent they were accepting responsibility in order to express their regret for past and present harms to indigenous Australians. However, regret alone is not enough. As Martin Golding notes, "Merely being regretful, even appropriately regretful, is not adequate to constitute moral amends: the regret must be expressed in an apology to the injured party" (1984–85, 132). Saying "sorry" is an important step in reconciliation because a proper apology must use a term that accepts responsibility in the sense of acknowledging that one has an obligation to make amends. Regret can be expressed by a person or group who is not connected with the past wrongs in any way at all. My argument is that an apology in this situation and other similar situations is an essential act of generosity that shows respect for those who have suffered and in many ways is a sign of a robust self-respect, as a willingness to take responsibility. An apology is also linked to wonder in that it recognizes the distinct position of indigenous peoples and other oppressed groups both in the past and currently.

The call for an apology to the people known as "the stolen generations" came as a result of the inquiry into the policy of child removal, the *Report of the National Inquiry into the Separation of Aboriginal and Torres Strait Islander Children from Their Families,* generally known as the *Bringing Them Home Report,* which I briefly discussed in chapter 3 (Human Rights and Equal Opportunity Commission 1997).[3] Between 1910 and 1970, approximately one in ten aboriginal children was forcibly removed from or otherwise coerced or deceived into leaving their parents by government officials (Manne 2001, 25). These children were placed in institutions or with foster families. They were often lost to their families or were prevented from having contact with them and in many different ways excluded from their languages and culture. Many were neglected, abused, and maltreated in their new environments. "Half-caste" children—children with one nonaboriginal parent—were targeted in an attempt to assimilate them into the white population. The policy was supported by aims at cultural assimilation (through reeducation) and biological assimilation (through marrying nonaboriginals). As I have shown in previous chapters, this treatment involves failures of wonder in the policy of assimilation and failures of generosity in not respecting the family relations or often the basic needs of aboriginal children.

Although it is difficult to separate the effects of removal from the general disadvantageous context within which many aboriginal Australians live, many of those who were removed from their families suffered and continue to suffer ongoing psychological problems of depression, anxiety, self-harming behavior, and drug and alcohol abuse, and there is evidence that aboriginal people removed in childhood are more likely to have been arrested and are likely to have worse health than those not removed (Human Rights and Equal Opportunity Commission 1997, part 3).[4] Children deprived of their language, land, culture, and contact with their immediate and extended family lose a sense of their identity and their place in the world and this sense is not replaced by nonaboriginal culture.[5] Aboriginal children suffered extreme forms of racism and were often treated with neither generosity nor wonder, as I explained in chapter 3. For instance, aboriginal children were often not accepted into white culture, yet at the same time aboriginality was disparaged, and later they experienced difficulties in returning to their original communities. There was no wonder at the traditions of the oldest living culture in the world. The removal of children also affects whole communities through the generations by disrupting the links that provide continuity, security, and confidence in self and culture due to the trauma and because they cannot pass on their traditions to the next generation. Their basic self-respect, or capacity to be fully generous, is undermined. Furthermore, for those not brought up in loving homes, their facility for self-love is made into the difficult struggle Irigaray describes it as for women.

An official apology is supposed to acknowledge the injustice of past treatment of aboriginal people as well as their suffering and to act as a statement of intent to henceforth behave justly. Philosophical analyses of apology incorporate expressions of regret, acceptance of responsibility, acknowledgement of the suffering of and offense toward the victims, and "making a gesture of respect" or generosity that acknowledges that the victim should not have been treated unjustly (Kort 1975, 78–87). Similarly, Joyce describes apologies as involving "the expression of regret, the admission of responsibility, and an acknowledgement of a wrong committed to the addressee" (1999, 167). An apology is interpreted by both governments and more widely as acknowledging the responsibility of current governments, so the question of responsibility needs to be explored.

Guilt and Responsibility

Arguments against government apologies rely on the idea that we only meaningfully apologize for wrongs that we have committed personally, not as a designated representative of a collective. John Howard's statement that "Australians of this generation should not be required to accept guilt and blame for past actions and policies over which they had no control" resonated with some (Healey 2001b, 7). As I noted in my introduction to this chapter, at first glance Arendt appears to support Howard's position. Arendt is critical of the notion of collective guilt, saying, "When all are guilty, nobody is" (2003, 147), and, "Where all are guilty, nobody in the last analysis can be judged" (1978, 230).[6] Her argument is that professed guilt for crimes one has not committed is a way of evading the genuine guilt that can only accrue from an action that a particular person has performed. For example, Albert Speer's formal assumption of responsibility for *all* Nazi crimes can be contrasted with a genuine acceptance and acknowledgment of his guilt for his own specific actions, an acknowledgment he avoided for most of his life (Sereny 1995, 703–704, 707–708). Arendt's criticisms of the notion of collective guilt might seem to support the case against apology.

However, Arendt's point is that while guilt is personal, responsibility can be more general and indirect. On her view, collective responsibility is political, rather than moral or legal. She says that "[t]wo conditions have to be present for collective responsibility: I must be held responsible for something I have not done, and the reason for my responsibility must be my membership in a group (a collective) which no voluntary act of mine can dissolve" (2003, 149). A typical example of collective responsibility is when a government accepts responsibility for the actions of preceding governments. Arendt believes that "[e]very government assumes responsibility for the deeds and misdeeds of its predecessors and every nation for the deeds and misdeeds of the past" (2003, 149). Her argument is that we are necessarily implicated in the actions of others when we are part of a community, saying that "[t]his vicarious responsibility for things we have not done, this taking upon ourselves the consequences for things we are entirely innocent of, is the price we pay for the fact that we live our lives not by ourselves but among our fellow men" (2003, 158). In other words, by living in a community our obligations become connected with the actions of others.

As Arendt notes, guilt and responsibility are often confused, but responsibility has a second sense that guilt does not have. We use the terms *guilt* and *responsibility* to apply to individual cases of direct personal involvement in an action by saying they are guilty or they are responsible. The term *responsibility* is *also* used in cases of indirect and collective involvement when the collective is not directly responsible for the action but nevertheless is held to be responsible or assumes responsibility—we take it upon ourselves, in Arendt's words. The term *guilt* implies that we are guilty *of* something for which we may be condemned or punished. The connotations of responsibility are very different; when we become responsible *for* something, we have a set of obligations to care for those who have suffered the wrong and to try to make reparations. The fear of having to make reparations has often prevented or delayed apologies being made, and many apologies are accompanied by a very explicit claim that reparations will not be involved in any way.[7]

Parents are often held responsible for the actions of children, CEOs for harm to employees, and governments for the actions of previous governments. It makes sense to hold a collective responsible for past actions in a way it does not to hold a collective guilty of past actions. When we are held responsible or assume responsibility for past wrongs, we may not feel personal guilt, but we are connected in a way different from a bystander or group in no sense responsible. In such a case, we are likely to feel shame, rather than guilt or remorse. We feel shame as belonging to that group and how we might be seen by others. Sara Ahmed argues, in a consideration of comments in "sorry books," that collective expressions of shame can be two-sided in that expressions of shame over past actions can be bound to a desire to feel pride in the present (2004, 110–13).[8] How deeply felt the shame might be, is another question. The shift to a concentration on responsibility rather than felt guilt or shame, means that an official apology is not dependent on individual members of the government, for instance, feeling guilt or shame. But it is dependent on them being willing to demonstrate respect for others. For these reasons, an apology is not premised on collective guilt but on collective and representative responsibility and so cannot be ruled out on the grounds of improper ascription of guilt. Individuals may experience guilt for *present* injustices, but that is another matter. Confusion between guilt and responsibility in public debate is one of the factors that can lessen support for an apology.

The issue of responsibility was also debated in Australia because the government's claim was widely interpreted to include responsibility as well as guilt.[9] Many writers on political issues and activists argue that current generations can have a responsibility for past injustices in general and that contemporary Australians, particularly government and institutional representatives, have responsibility for past injustices committed in Australia. The case for the moral responsibility of the present government and indeed contemporary nonindigenous Australians has been made in a number of ways. For example, Janna Thompson argues that nonaboriginal Australians have a responsibility for historical injustices against aboriginal people since they participate in the moral practice of making commitments and expecting others to keep them across generations (2000). In this case, Thompson argues that "by assuming responsibility for sovereignty over Australia predecessors of non-Aboriginal Australians were in effect making a commitment to protect Aborigines and their communities—a responsibility they failed to fulfil" (2000, 339). Her argument supplements Arendt's by explaining one of the pertinent factors of belonging to a community, that is, that we participate in common moral practices.

Robert Sparrow also argues that nonaboriginal Australians have such a responsibility, but do so in virtue of the continuity between present injustices and the invasion of Australia and dispossession of aboriginal people (2000). This argument applies in those cases where we can see these connections, and means that such responsibility may diminish over time or when the connections are difficult to trace. T. L. Zutlevics argues that the current Australian government shares moral responsibility for what past governments have done as it is essentially the same entity, and that a genuine apology is important because it shows a recognition of the wrong done and also "reflects a degree of empathy towards the one harmed" (2002, 71). This argument applies to all situations where continuity between present and past governments can be located. Zutlevics's statement also suggests the need for a recognition of the equal moral worth of the other central to wonder and generosity. Although their reasons differ, these authors accept the responsibility of present generations for the injustices committed by past generations and the importance of an apology. Arendt's distinction between guilt and responsibility and her account of collective responsibility clarifies how responsibility can be general and indirect, unlike guilt.

In my view, these arguments demonstrate that the case for responsibility is overdetermined in the Australian context and other cases of recent colonialism, in the sense that each of these arguments is sufficient to establish responsibility, without demonstrating that collective responsibility continues in perpetuity. In what follows, I will focus on the question of what this responsibility implies about the necessity and the nature of an apology. It is often thought that if there is an obligation to apologize there must be a reciprocal obligation to forgive, and I contest this assumption in what follows.

Derrida's View of Forgiveness and Apology

In this section, I return to Derrida's work to show that his analysis of forgiveness, because it implies that an apology is unnecessary, puts the burden of forgiveness on those who have suffered the most. This is not what he explicitly argues; yet I will show that his discussion has this subtle implication. Derrida's discussion of forgiveness and apology is particularly relevant to concerns about collective responsibility and the possibility of forgiveness, as he believes that recent apologies and requests for forgiveness are tied to the delineation of crimes against humanity after World War II (2001b, 25). This connection between the need for apology and such extreme crimes is one that is at work in the Australian context, in South Africa, and elsewhere.[10] In considering what I see as a problematic account of forgiveness and apology, I should note that Derrida, personally, was in favor of an official apology by the Australian government to the aboriginal people.[11] However, Derrida's philosophical account of apology suggests an apology is unnecessary in a case such as this and not a responsibility falling on governments.

This interpretation of Derrida on apology follows from his argument that there is no conceptual limit to forgiveness. Derrida's account of forgiveness is that *true* or *pure* forgiveness is, paradoxically, forgiveness of the unforgivable: "There is only forgiveness, if there is any, where there is the unforgivable" (2001a, 32).[12] As I discussed in the previous chapter, true forgiveness, on his view, is not coincident with a legal or political response to wrongs but is an ethical response to the call for forgiveness. His argument is that any other, conditional, forgiveness is not forgiveness of the guilty as guilty. Such forgiveness becomes an exchange or pact in which the guilty person repents or atones and thus is no longer guilty and no longer in genuine need of forgiveness. There is something appealing in this view if we see the relationship between forgiveness and repentance or atonement as a kind of exchange or calculation, where so long as a perpetrator atones to a certain extent then the victim must forgive. However, I would argue that one can take an apology, and other attempts to make amends, to be important to forgiveness without assuming that would make forgiveness a deal or bargain. I will elaborate on this point further on.

In Derrida's view, *practical* or conditional forgiveness puts limits on the possibilities of forgiveness and expects apologies, reparation, and atonement. As quoted in the previous chapter, he concludes that "[i]t is between these two poles (of forgiveness), *irreconcilable yet indissociable,* that decisions and responsibilities are to be taken" (2001a, 45).[13] Again, although Derrida does not claim that there should be collective forgiveness of, for example, the proponents of the apartheid regime, his view intimates such a response is appropriate.[14] His characterization of true or pure forgiveness as forgiveness of the unforgivable and its functioning as a necessary, underlying limit implies that victims should forgive, and moreover, that they should do so without demanding and receiving an apology.

Derrida's interest in forgiveness partly stems from the relatively recent wave of official apologies, which he views with some skepticism. While he sees something positive in these apologies he also contends that "simulacra, the automatic ritual, hypocrisy, calculation, or mimicry are often a part, and invite parasites to this ceremony of culpability" (2001a, 29). From his skeptical position, these simulacra have little to do with true forgiveness. As Derrida writes, "So if there is a reconciliation in the colonial context, this doesn't require forgiveness, that is something else, some other process, and if there is forgiveness, it doesn't necessarily lead to reconciliation" (2001c, 89). He strongly separates forgiveness and reconciliation, saying, "Forgiveness does not, it should never amount to a therapy of reconciliation" (2001a, 41). Whereas Derrida says that "no one would decently dare to object to the imperative of reconciliation," he also says that "it is only a political strategy or a psycho-therapeutic economy" (Derrida, 2001a, 50).

There are a number of important and compelling claims in Derrida's account of forgiveness and reconciliation. First, there is no doubt that an insincere apology can be harmful. As an example, Trudy Govier and Wilhelm Verwoerd describe the circumstances of F. W. De Klerk's unsuccessful apology to black South Africans. While his initial apology sounded sincere, he gave no promises to make amends and tried to deny responsibility for violations of human rights (Govier and Verwoerd 2002, 77–78). I should note here that in the case of an official apology, it is not the state of mind or passions of the representative making the apology that is important to its being sincere. The insincerity of De Klerk's apology came from its limited value as an act of apology that demonstrated generosity. This is more important than his state of mind, although his actions were revealing of his attitudes. While it might be preferable if the representative has the appropriate passions and attitudes, what is essential to the sincerity of such an apology is a full acceptance of responsibility and a commitment to address past injustices that shows respect, a commitment that should be upheld.

Second, I agree with Derrida that forgiveness and reconciliation are two very different things. What I do not accept is that forgiveness must apply in circumstances such as that of the stolen generations. Perhaps the "only" in Derrida's statement that reconciliation "is only a political strategy or a psycho-therapeutic economy" should be questioned and the importance of certain kinds of political strategies and attempts at healing upheld. While Derrida clearly does not intend to provide an excuse for not apologizing in his injunction to forgive without receipt of an apology, his account encourages such an interpretation. As he says, an apology is part of a practical process of improving a situation. Furthermore, it is a responsibility more central than that of forgiveness. By emphasizing forgiveness in his account and by placing apologies on the seemingly lesser, practical plane, Derrida has reversed priorities in this case and placed the onus on victims to forgive rather than on those responsible for injustice to apologize.

In his discussion of forgiveness in *Memory, History, Forgetting* (2004), Paul Ricoeur focuses on the broad notion of "fault" in relation to forgiveness. The concepts of guilt and responsibility are both narrower and more specific than the notion of fault. In Ricoeur's view, guilt is a symbol of fault, along with stain and sin (2004, 465). A fault is a mistake or wrong that may or may not be acknowledged by the person at fault. If you are at fault, then you will generally be held responsible. Ricoeur's concern is primarily with the *experience* of fault, an experience that can be independent of whether one is guilty or responsible. He agrees with Derrida that forgiving includes forgiveness of the unforgivable and that we cannot separate the guilty person from their act (2004, 468, 490). However, Ricoeur believes that forgiveness is like love, and that forgiveness is paired with the "inaugural gesture" of repentance (2004, 467, 490).[15] He concludes that "it does not seem that the vocabulary of the unconditional and the conditional, inherited from the antinomies of the dialectic of pure reason, is appropriate for the problematic of forgiveness and repentance. . . . Possessing an irreducibly practical nature, it can be uttered only in the grammar of the optative mood" (2004, 493). Unlike Derrida, Ricoeur does not hold up forgiveness as an aspiration, but as something we wish or hope for. Between what he calls the "depth of fault" and the "height of forgiveness," there is a possibility, though difficult, of responding to past events. These basic features of Ricoeur's view, in my judgment, are more appealing than that of Derrida's. Nevertheless, he does not articulate an ethics of forgiveness, nor does he consider the nature of apology. In the next section, I will demonstrate why I believe there is a fundamental asymmetry between forgiveness and apology.

Forgiveness and Love; Apology and Generosity

First, as I noted, an essential asymmetry between forgiveness and apology is that forgiveness is based on love and apologies are based on generosity in both the sense of self-respect and respect for the other. What I believe is wrong with Derrida's understanding of forgiveness is his implicit assumption that forgiveness is based *solely* on respect for the other or is a response to the humanity of the other. From his account, it might appear that unconditional forgiveness is based on love, as an extraordinary gesture, and conditional forgiveness is based on respect, because that is an attitude the guilty can expect from others. However, I take Derrida to be assuming that both unconditional and conditional forgiveness are based on respect, since in both cases he does not see forgiveness as a personal decision. Unconditional forgiveness is given for no reason at all, or only for the reason that the perpetrator is human, whereas conditional forgiveness is given for that reason and in addition some action such as apology or repentance. It is not dependent on a personal relation to the other. If the obligation to forgive is based on respect alone, then victims have a responsibility to forgive those who have wronged them, whether or not they apologize or atone. Although unconditional forgiveness itself is beyond the human, according to Derrida, and can forgive crimes that are also beyond the human (2001b, 30, 47), such unconditional forgiveness can only be based on some fundamental feature that all human beings share regardless of whether they apologize or atone for what they have done. It is only human beings that we forgive. As I argued in the previous chapter, forgiveness is not based on respect for others, or rather respect alone is not enough to make forgiveness a duty. If the duty to forgive was based on respect then it would be a universal responsibility and not dependent on repentance or apology. Generosity is significant here as respect for others in acknowledging their worth and as respect for the self since it takes self-respect to admit wrong rather than evading that knowledge. Nevertheless, a full comprehension of forgiveness involves the response to the "who" of the other or love in the form of sympathy.

Second, a further distinction follows from the fact that forgiveness is based on love. As I argued in previous chapters, love cannot be an unconditional or perfect duty, although we should try to create the conditions for love and to cultivate love in ourselves, as Irigaray suggests. We should try to develop a forgiving character, for that is a way to be more ethical, but we cannot say it is a duty to forgive except perhaps in relatively trivial instances and where the offender has repented. Such conditions do not necessarily mean that forgiving becomes a perfect duty in general but that the case for forgiving is sometimes overwhelming and we might believe it is a sign of poor character not to forgive. Nevertheless, the point that *forgivingness* is an imperfect duty, so that to a great extent, in particular cases, forgiveness is discretionary, remains.

One reason given that victims should forgive is that we all might be perpetrators if we were unlucky enough to be in the wrong historical circumstance (Van Roermund 2001, 182–83). However, not all people become perpetrators even in terrible circumstances, and not all perpetrators demand forgiveness. Recognition of human frailty is a reason to be forgiving, but not for victims to forgive in a particular case.[16] A victim could accept that they might have been a perpetrator but still feel that if they had been they should not be forgiven.

Apologies, conversely, are based on generous respect for others and are necessary to justice. They acknowledge the fundamental human dignity of the other person and their right not to be ill-treated. It is natural to say that one *owes* another an apology, but not that someone owes us forgiveness. That makes it the duty of governments to apologize for past injustices. This asymmetry between forgiveness and apology also explains why an official apology makes sense, whereas official forgiveness, unlike official pardon, does not.[17] Since forgiveness is a personal response based on love rather than respect, forgiveness is something only individuals can properly enact. Only individuals can forgive, and only individuals can decide when and whether it is appropriate to forgive.

There are a number of reasons why forgiveness may not be an appropriate response. In Australia's case, it is not clear that there is any reason for aboriginal people to forgive nonaboriginal people for past and present injustices.[18] While apology and forgiveness are commonly associated,[19] I argue that they can be separated—one can apologize without asking for forgiveness and ask for forgiveness without apologizing.[20] Again, this is grounded in the different moral psychological character of forgiveness and apology. People should not expect that a loving response—forgiveness—be exchanged for the performance of a duty based on respect—apology. Of course, victims of injustice may choose to forgive their oppressors for their own benefit, because they find it the only or the best way to get on with their lives. I also accept that forgiveness of past wrongs is allowable if some steps to atone have been taken. My argument is that victims in these kinds of circumstances are not ethically *obligated* to do so.

A third difference between apology and forgiveness is that an apology is an act that one can be (reasonably) sure has been performed, whereas forgiveness is much more mysterious—individuals can believe they have forgiven and come to realize they have not, and vice versa. Here, I disagree with Ricoeur's and others' view that forgiveness is a speech act, like that of apology (2004, 485). For example, Digeser maintains that "at the very least, forgiveness requires that one says (or does not say) and/or does (or does not do) certain things when one has forgiven another" (1998, 704).[21] He proposes that any psychological conditions for forgiveness be set aside and replaced by public external conditions, such as agreeing never to mention the original wrong again. Forgiveness will often make some change in our actions as well as our passions, although it may not. However, forgiveness is primarily opposed to holding resentment against perpetrators, so that forgiveness involves giving up that resentment, or trying to. Forgiving involves a change of heart, although it may not mean giving up all our hard feelings against the perpetrator. It means giving up our grievance against them for particular acts, but not necessarily all the hurt and anger they have caused. Forgiveness also may not imply that one trusts the person again.

The difference between forgiveness and apology on this point is apparent in the irrelevance of the state of mind of a representative making an apology to their ability to do so. It would be preferable if the individual making an apology on behalf of others had the appropriate attitudes as well, but it is not essential, as it is in the case of forgiveness. Official apologies are not identical to personal apologies that express the heartfelt remorse that comes from an acknowledgment of personal guilt. Collective responsibility and the necessity of a representative making the apology mean that some of the personal aspects of individual apologies are not relevant.[22] Nevertheless, official apologies can and should involve expressions of a change of attitude or an undertaking, on behalf of the group, not to repeat or continue the injustices of the past or to perpetrate news ones. Such undertakings are part of what justifies an attribution of sincerity to an apology in that they reveal respect for the other.

Furthermore, in cases of official apologies, an expectation of forgiveness and the expression of apology should be strictly separated. Most of the apologies or acknowledgments of wrongs committed made in Australia have not included a request for forgiveness. One exception is the Churches of Christ Federal Aborigines Board who wrote, "To the degree to which were a part of the destruction processes we seek forgiveness and offer our repentance" (Human Rights and Equal Opportunity Commission 1997, Part 4, Submission 411). It is not clear in this case how the board understood the relationship between their offer of repentance and their request for forgiveness. A request for forgiveness, of course, is not a demand for forgiveness, nor need it express an expectation of forgiveness. It may be a forlorn request.

The decision whether to forgive, whom to forgive, and what for is a completely independent decision that should not be preempted by the form and character of an apology. The Australian Declaration towards Reconciliation at one point refers to the idea that "one part of the nation apologizes and expresses its sorrow and sincere regret for the injustices of the past, so the other part accepts the apologies and forgives" (2000), but this has not been a popular conception, and for good reasons. As I have argued, the decision to forgive is a personal one, dependent on context, which cannot be demanded or expected as an obligation or duty. Furthermore, an expectation of forgiveness in this case would be a further imposition on aboriginal people that itself would be ungenerous in the sense of disrespectful.

Derrida's view that unconditional forgiveness does not require an apology appears to place the onus on the victim to forgive without apology. Instead, the disconnection between forgiveness and apology should be taken to work the other way: that an apology does not create an ethical obligation to forgive.[23] An apology may certainly be an important condition for forgiveness. Nevertheless, an apology may not constitute ample grounds for feeling that there has been a real change and moreover, the decision to forgive is that of the sufferers themselves. The seriousness of what occurred to the Australian aboriginal people and other sufferers of historic injustices does not mean an apology is irrelevant, but it does mean that forgiveness is not necessarily in question.

What I have said about forgiveness raises the question of what role, if any, it could have in politics. Ricoeur, for example, discusses Arendt's view of forgiveness in politics. For Arendt, forgiveness can be political, as it is an action to remedy the irreversibility of deeds affecting others. As I discussed in the previous chapter, she believes that such political forgiveness is based on respect: "Respect, at any rate, because it concerns only the person, is quite sufficient to prompt forgiving of what a person did, for the sake of the person" (1998, 243). She also says that love "is not only apolitical but antipolitical" (1998, 242). Ricoeur, putting together his view that forgiveness is based on love and Arendt's view that love is antipolitical, concludes that "[t]here is no politics of forgiveness" (2004, 488). Now, while I agree that forgiveness is based on love, I think the situation is more complex than the way either Arendt or Ricoeur portrays it.

Love, because it is personal and in a sense elective, cannot or rather should not be subjected to the whims of politics to make a politics of forgiveness. However, forgiveness, like love, can have a place in politics. While my argument that forgiveness is a personal decision means that forgiveness cannot be demanded or expected, the conditions that would make forgiveness more likely could be created, just like those which provide a context for love in general to flourish, as I argued in chapter 2.[24] I take it that is the best way to interpret the role of forgiveness in the South African Truth and Reconciliation commission. While some might have spoken strongly about expectations of forgiveness, the disclosures of the perpetrators are a step or condition in making forgiveness possible, not in determining forgiveness. Even more specifically, it makes it more likely that victims can try to forgive, though it may be difficult or impossible. The perpetrators were promised amnesty or immunity from prosecution rather than forgiveness. Claire Moon points out that "[b]ecause the TRC offered the incentive of amnesty in return for 'full confessions,' it *disturbed* the interpersonal and spontaneous economy of 'ideal' forgiveness" (2004, 191). Apologies and confessions do not make those responsible no longer guilty, as Derrida suggests, and forgiveness is still a leap beyond the conditions that make it more likely. I accept that there may be political reasons for forgiveness, as Schaap (2003) argues, as long as those reasons are not taken to imply ethical obligations to forgive in particular cases.

As I noted earlier, the failure to apologize can alter the position of the government from one of being responsible for past injustices to perpetuating injustice. Considering the South African context, Govier and Verwoerd describe how that failure to acknowledge past wrongs constitutes a second injury to the victims: "It further damages these vulnerable people because *moral contempt can be as devastating as the original wrong itself*" (2002, 71). A refusal to apologize is an instance of moral contempt because it fails to demonstrate generosity or respect for the victim; it fails to acknowledge that they deserve not to be treated badly. It is a sign of lack of self-respect as we should all be able to acknowledge our flaws in the context of moral worth. Such a refusal is also likely to be undermining of the victims' self-respect. Without an apology involving a resolution to overcome injustice, injustice almost certainly continues into the future.

An official apology could also create a better environment for individual apologies by providing an affirming and legitimating context for them. Individuals and institutions in Australia apologized in spite of the former government's stance, yet a more just situation has existed since the government apologized. Governments place themselves at fault by not apologizing. I would not say, as Michael Ignatieff does of the Chilean president Patricio Alwyn's apology for the victims of Pinochet's oppression, that a government apology is *necessary* to create "the public climate in which a thousand acts of private repentance and apology [became] possible" (1996, 121–22).[25] Individuals are capable of making apologies independently of governments. However, a government apology creates a context in which individual and institutional apologies are affirmed rather than delegitimated. That context would be one in which genuine reconciliation would take place. The nature of such reconciliation is the final issue I consider in this chapter.

Reconciliation and Forgiveness

My understanding of the asymmetry between apology and forgiveness helps us to properly conceptualize reconciliation, the meaning of which is persistently debated. Since forgiveness is based on love and so an imperfect duty and a personal decision, it is not necessary for reconciliation, although an apology is. The former Australian government implied that practical reconciliation makes an apology unnecessary,[26] as if engagement in one form of reconciliation can only occur at the expense of the other. However, there is no need to choose between an apology, conceived as symbolic reconciliation, and practical reconciliation. All the other processes of reconciliation and overcoming the effects of past and present injustice must continue simultaneously. Again, Derrida's analysis suggests why concerned persons could be skeptical of reconciliation's contribution to justice. Derrida's idea of reconciliation is something that the state offers to past offenders, such as Nazi collaborators in the French occupation, as a kind of pardon. In such an offer, he writes, "there is always a strategical or political calculation in the generous gesture of one who offers reconciliation or amnesty, and it is necessary always to integrate this calculation in our analyses" (2001a, 40). However, the Australian notion of reconciliation, where the government is the perpetrator and a part of the population the aggrieved, is very different. To describe an act as strategic and calculating sounds derogatory, but at times such strategy is preferable to an unbending unwillingness to compromise.

On my account, forgiveness is not a necessary feature of reconciliation. One reason that forgiveness may be expected is due to a conception that reconciliation and forgiveness must go hand in hand. For example, Desmond Tutu believes that countries with a history of injustice are faced with a choice of "forgiveness and reconciliation rather than their opposites" (1999, 209). Tutu's conception of reconciliation is explicitly theological; in his account, he states, "It is and has always been God's intention that we should live in friendship and harmony" (1999, 212). He asked victims to forgive those who told the truth to the TRC about their past actions, and even those who refused to (Tutu 1999, 220; Elshtain 2003, 63).[27] In North Carolina, the Greensboro Truth and Reconciliation Commission was established by residents to investigate the Greensboro massacre. Unlike forgiveness, compensation is an important part of reconciliation. So, The U.S. government's payment of $3.4 billion to settle claims concerning Native American trust funds is a significant aspect of a "sincere reconciliation," as

Barack Obama states (Savage 2009). The tasks of reconciliation can go on without forgiveness. It is the refusal to apologize, to properly express regret and to deny responsibility that halts or slows the process of reconciliation and makes even the idea of forgiveness impossible.

Importantly, reconciliation is not offered as a "gesture" but as a process that whole countries must work through. Tutu rightly says that "reconciliation is liable to be a long drawn-out process with ups and downs, not something accomplished overnight and certainly not by a Commission, no matter how effective" (1999, 221). However, this characterization of reconciliation also suggests it is different from forgiveness in being an ongoing and collective process rather than an individual decision.[28] An official apology is one step in that process.

One criticism of reconciliation in cases where representatives of perpetrators are reconciling with victims is that it presumes fault and blameworthiness on the part of the victims. Raimond Gaita ruefully noted, "How extraordinary then that our current government treats reconciliation as though it were substantially a two-way affair, as though we had something serious for which to forgive the Aborigines" (2000, 129). A suspicion of calculation may remain concerning the motives of particular individuals taking part in reconciliation, and reconciliation itself, like apology, should not be conceived as a kind of deal or bargain in the sense that what both parties to reconciliation should do must be somehow equivalent. If reconciliation is interpreted in this way, it does appear to be a problematic notion. While, like Derrida, we may be skeptical of the motives of politicians who rush to reconcile, we should be even more skeptical of politicians who refuse to take the basic steps of reconciliation. However, reconciliation does not need to presume fault on both sides. Fault can be primarily or even exclusively on one side. It is only in the sense that both sides are partners in reconciliation that it is a two-way affair.

Another criticism of reconciliation is expressed in the form of a question: How can there be reconciliation when there was never a friendship that can be reconciled? For example, Rosalyn Diprose argues, "It is highly unlikely that reconciliation as defined would ever be fully realized given that this would require restoration of an original harmony that to my knowledge has never existed between indigenous and nonindigenous Australians" (2002, 148).[29] My argument is that reconciliation is possible because it is really about pragmatically working together rather than achieving a lost wholeness, although in certain cases a prior good relationship may have existed.

Moon maintains that theological conceptions of reconciliation impose a "prelapsarian" ideal onto this pragmatic view (2004, 195), and Schaap says that the "restorative conception of reconciliation therefore makes a presumption of what in fact it must achieve" (2001, 762). However, these prelapsarian and restorative conceptions can be resisted. It is possible to be reconciled without forgiving. From a political point of view, reconciliation can even be more valuable than forgiveness. Forgiveness entails a change in attitude but not necessarily a willingness to have a further relationship with the person. In contrast, since reconciliation entails being willing to interact and form some kind of relationship with others, it can contribute more in a practical sense to people living and working together than forgiveness. Reconciliation could help to further the conditions for the development of wonder, generosity, and love. By working together, different groups could come to respond openly to each others differences, to respect each other's differences, and to come to feel sympathy and benevolence for each other.

In a useful discussion of reconciliation, Govier distinguishes between what she calls the minimal and maximal concepts of reconciliation. The minimal is simply nonviolent coexistence, whereas the maximal is acknowledgment, then "repentance, restitution, forgiveness by victims, and eventual attitudes of warm acceptance" such as Tutu's concept of reconciliation (2002, 144). Maximal concepts of reconciliation place great importance on changing people's feelings and attitudes by modeling reconciliation between groups on reconciliation in intimate personal relationships. Her preference is for an intermediate concept of reconciliation that involves "building or restoring trust in the wake of wrong-doing" (2002, 144) with more modest expectations of changes in attitudes, and this is close to what I am advocating.[30] The Australian Declaration towards Reconciliation refers to "a commitment to go on together in a spirit of reconciliation" and to the hope of achieving justice and equity (2000). Such reconciliation must involve an acknowledgment of past injustices through a respectful apology and working together to address the legacies of those injustices. This ideal is different from an attempt to reach friendship and harmony and does not dictate the particular passions that should be experienced by any of the parties to reconciliation. What is needed is willingness to participate and to treat each other with generosity and wonder rather than expectations of friendship and warm acceptance, although such feelings may develop. Reconciliation shares with an apology the features of being based on respect or generosity and being able to be primarily expressed through public and political actions. Yet it can also lead to wonder and love.

Governments frequently argue that they should not have to accept guilt or responsibility for the practices of previous governments and thus apologies for past injustices are not warranted. I have argued that these apparent objections to an official apology are based on a misunderstanding of the nature of responsibility, and of apology and its distinction from forgiveness. Despite appearances, Arendt's analysis enables us to distinguish between guilt and responsibility and accept that the government is not guilty. However, I argued that it is reasonable to hold governments responsible for the actions of previous governments. Likewise, Derrida's account of forgiveness as independent of apology appears to preclude the need for or possibly justify governments' failure to apologize. Accounts of both forgiveness and reconciliation have conceptualized them as similar to a contract, so it appears that if forgiveness can exist without apology an apology is not necessary. In this vein, Derrida's analysis concentrates only on the idea that forgiveness without apology is possible, and in spite of his personal support for political apologies, implies the victim is obligated to forgive.

That is only one aspect of the asymmetry between apology and forgiveness. My view is that apology without forgiveness is also possible and in cases where there is a history of injustice, may be the most appropriate response. Official apologies for past injustices can be made, indeed should be made, without a corresponding expectation of forgiveness. An official apology such as in the case of slavery or the treatment of indigenous people are based on an acknowledgment of respect for the people concerned, a generous respect that is owed as a perfect duty and is expressed in a public way. This apology both demonstrates self-respect and helps to restore the self-respect of those harmed. Such an apology can involve wonder in recognizing the distinct forms of culture that were ignored or dismissed by preceding generations. An apology at the very least expresses regret and sorrow, demonstrates respect for the victims, and acknowledges suffering and wrongs. Such an apology is a gesture toward reconciliation that improves the conditions for further action. An official apology is a central feature of reconciliation that supports practical measures to overcome situations of injustice. In contrast, forgiveness cannot be expected from oppressed groups, because forgiveness is based on love, understood as sympathy, and must be a discretionary or imperfect duty as well as a personal decision. Reconciliation in such circumstances is best understood as a willingness to work together without assuming that the past has been overcome, rather than as a restoration of unity after mistakes made on both sides.

I would like to end this chapter with the text of the apology that was made, after years of arguing about the value of such an apology, in Australia. On February 13, 2008, Prime Minister Kevin Rudd's apology motion was made in Parliament:

> Today we honour the Indigenous peoples of this land, the oldest continuing cultures in human history. We reflect on their past mistreatment. We reflect in particular on the mistreatment of those who were Stolen Generations—this blemished chapter in our nation's history. The time has now come for the nation to turn a new page in Australia's history by righting the wrongs of the past and so moving forward with confidence to the future. We apologise for the laws and policies of successive Parliaments and governments that have inflicted profound grief, suffering and loss on these our fellow Australians. We apologise especially for the removal of Aboriginal and Torres Strait Islander children from their families, their communities and their country. For the pain, suffering and hurt of these Stolen Generations, their descendants and for their families left behind, we say sorry. To the mothers and the fathers, the brothers and the sisters, for the breaking up of families and communities, we say sorry. And for the indignity and degradation thus inflicted on a proud people and a proud culture, we say sorry. We the Parliament of Australia respectfully request that this apology be received in the spirit in which it is offered as part of the healing of the nation. For the future we take heart; resolving that this new page in the history of our great continent can now be written. We today take this first step by acknowledging the past and laying claim to a future that embraces all Australians. A future where this Parliament resolves that the injustices of the past must never, never happen again. A future where we harness the determination of all Australians, Indigenous and non-Indigenous, to close the gap that lies between us in life expectancy, educational achievement and economic opportunity. A future where we embrace the possibility of new solutions to enduring problems where old approaches have failed. A future based on mutual respect, mutual resolve and mutual responsibility. A future where all Australians, whatever their origins,

are truly equal partners, with equal opportunities and with an equal stake in shaping the next chapter in the history of this great country, Australia. (http://australia.gov.au/about-australia/our-country/our-people/apology-to-australias-indigenous-peoples)

The event of such an apology also provides another reason for thinking that apologies are worthwhile and supporting them. What is really interesting about the Australian apology is that making such an apology also puts pressure on government leaders in other countries to make similar apologies and, in some cases, to make reparations and compensation for the harms that were done. They can help the development of wonder and generosity at both the political and ethical level. In the following year, Rudd also apologized for the child migrant program, where children from the UK were taken to Australia after World War II, often to cruel and harsh treatment in orphanages. The British prime minister made an apology to those child migrants in 2010. Harper's apology for residential schools in Canada came in June after Rudd's apology in February, and the United States made its apologies for slavery in 2008 and 2009 and its apology to Native Americans in 2009. Of course, there are many other factors involved, including the nature of the government, the individual leader at the time, whether it be Kevin Rudd or Barack Obama, the opinion polls on the matter, the level of demand or expectation of an apology, but it is clear that governments pay attention to what happens in other nations, particularly when there are similar events in their history. Making an official apology can lead to a genuine change in the extent to which generosity and wonder are *lived* and on an international scale.

Conclusion

Throughout this book I have argued that our strategies in overcoming oppression, injustice, evil, and abuse must be twofold. We need both generosity, in Descartes's sense of proper self-respect that leads us to regard others with respect, and wonder, as articulated by both Descartes and Irigaray. We should relate to others as similar to ourselves in the sense of our having the ability to make choices, and as distinct in the choices we make. I also argued that the passion of wonder can and should be encouraged and cultivated as a virtue and is relevant to all kinds of differences between human beings, not only sexual difference. I have focused primarily on sexual difference, and racial and cultural difference and specific forms of oppression, injustice, and evil. While I began with the view that wonder and generosity are essential to ethics and should be combined, they do not provide a complete ethics. They need to be linked with other passions, such as love, and developed into virtues, and actions, such as hospitality, apology, and forgiveness. Furthermore, the relationship between ethics and politics needs to be carefully set out.

I developed this ethics of the passions further by elucidating the relationship between love and respect as it appears in Kant's and Irigaray's work. Kant's distinction between love and respect is very useful for developing the ethics of wonder and generosity because he discusses them in more depth and with more precision than Descartes. However, his ethics is incomplete, since he believes that love's relevance to ethics is only as a form of practice, and he sees love and respect as opposing forces. Irigaray has much more to say about love as a feeling, an aspect of love that is essential to its value.

Kant should have taken the passionate aspects of love more seriously in major works such as *The Metaphysics of Morals* (1996a), which he does in certain other texts, such as "The End of All Things" (1996c). Nevertheless, philosophers interested in liberation should take up his idea that love and friendship should not involve self-abandonment. This idea is one that incorporates generosity as self-respect. While Irigaray does not use Kant directly in her texts, she extends this idea of distance in love by showing how love incorporates wonder and requires a certain distance between ourselves and others, even when we are close to them in some senses. She also demonstrates how love and respect are interconnected, so that love and friendship are possible rather than impossible ideals, as Kant thought. Both love and respect are essential to ethics but there is an asymmetry between them, as love should be based on respect yet respect does not need to be based on love. This difference between them does not mean that love is completely ephemeral. Although love is felt for particular others, we can encourage love as part of ethical life. Certain political conditions are needed for love between human beings, and Irigaray suggests what some of those conditions might be. Moreover, ethical love can also enable a transformation of political conditions themselves. I am not suggesting that love is perfect or never painful, but that, like wonder and generosity, love has a potential as a force for good that should be furthered, and we should take that into account when thinking about political organization.

In chapter 3, I considered in detail the structure of prejudices that can prevent wonder, generosity, and love from being developed as virtues. Our response to all forms of oppression must be one that respects the humanity of others, in other words is generous, while at the same time responding with wonder to difference and perhaps also with love. Irigaray's work on issues connected with race and class difference need to be taken farther, and there is a need to focus on the specificity of particular oppressions. While she has a point in saying that sexual difference is irreducible, this does not mean that other differences are reducible to sexual difference, nor that they are only elaborations of sexual difference. I discussed a range of feminist and antiracist approaches to sexism and racism and found that they tend to emphasize either wonder in terms of difference, as Irigaray tends to do, or they stress generosity alone.

This is where I believe that Simone de Beauvoir's approach is helpful, as she focuses on the complex interaction between our identity as human beings and as women or men or as raced and sees them as having varying salience. Using this as a framework, we can see how racism and sexism take different forms, depending on whether it is difference or sameness that is emphasized. So likewise, strategies for overcoming oppression have to be sensitive to these nuances. I contend that the most extreme forms of prejudice tend to focus on difference interpreted in an exaggerated and demeaning way and when that is the case it must be countered by generosity. In the ideal situation, however, generosity, wonder and love will all be in play, so to speak, in a way that emerges not as a reaction to oppression but from ethical relations between everyone.

In the following chapters, I further explored how an ethics and politics of wonder and generosity can help us both to understand and to respond to difficult issues affecting oppressed groups, and enriched the discussion by introducing the ethical acts of hospitality, forgiveness, and apology. I pursued a general understanding of how ethics and politics should relate to each other by considering Kant's and Derrida's work on this issue. Discussion of their work, as well as that of Hannah Arendt, suggested a conception of ethical politics that can deal with the difficulties they raise. The account of the relation between ethics and politics that can best enhance the expression of wonder and generosity is one that is both proper and generous—that conforms to standards of right, as Kant outlines—and is generous or virtuous, in Derrida's sense. Derrida's setting up of unconditional ethics brings the imperfect duties of Kant to the forefront of politics and suggests how we might take them seriously. In addition to the focus on generosity, wonder, and love, Derrida introduces the concepts of hospitality and forgiveness. While these are not passions, they are actions that involve passion, exemplifying the openness of wonder and love as well as generosity in Descartes's sense as self-respect and respect for others. They are also virtues in the sense that being hospitable and being forgiving can be stable traits of character.

The thinker who provides the strongest contrast to Kant's and Derrida's views of the relation between ethics and politics is Arendt. She maintains that there is no place for ethics in politics at all, except in the most extreme situations. Arendt considers ethics to be too superficial, because she sees ethics as like mores or customs that can be easily changed. However, I argued that a better explanation of what happened in Germany and other countries during the Nazi period, for example, is that ethics were not encouraged in any deep way. Therefore, politics has to be thought about in terms of incorporating ethics into the very structure of political arrangements. Arendt also believes that ethics is primarily concerned with the self, not with the world, but I think she is mistaken here, as our ethical decisions always place us in relation to others and the world and have broad implications. I do not accept Arendt's view of politics as a public realm quite separate from the realm of morality or ethics. Rather, taking Derrida's introduction of virtue concepts such as hospitality and forgiveness into the political sphere seriously, I believe that every aspect of our lives is colored by politics and what is needed is a conception of political life that enables that life to be ethical. Politics affects everyone's lives, so politics can and should play a central part in enabling us to act with wonder, generosity, and love toward others and ourselves.

Derrida's insistence on the importance of unconditional ethical demands to politics forces us to think more carefully about that role and about the responsibility of both ethics and politics to each other. So I adopt these features in developing an ethical politics and responding to specific ethical and political issues. The features of ethics that are relevant to politics are both the "right" or rights Kant argued for and Derrida's unconditional duties. However, I argued that we should retain Kant's distinction between perfect and imperfect duties and consider the duties of love to be imperfect ones. My view is that combining these features of Kant's and Derrida's ethical politics makes it possible to genuinely and fruitfully negotiate our way between ethics and politics. This negotiation involves generosity or respect for others, wonder, and love as well, so an ethical politics is one that aims to promote these responses.

In chapters 5, 6, and 7, I showed how this conception of the relation between ethics and politics and a framework of wonder and generosity as responses to difference and similarity, and their relation to love, help us to think about contemporary ethical and political issues. I investigated the importance of hospitality, in both an ethical and political sense, for asylum seekers and refugees. Hospitality exemplifies some of the characteristics of wonder in its openness to the other, and is a kind of loving way to relate to others. Derrida sketches some of the features of cosmopolitanism and hospitality, using Kant as his primary source. Derrida's conception of hospitality suggests ways that we can improve the situation of asylum seekers and refugees, particularly on an individual level. The notion of unconditional hospitality is a valuable counterweight to the narrowly conceived self-interest we see expressed by many contemporary governments in their policies and practices toward asylum seekers and as characterizing the initial response to asylum seekers. However, unconditional hospitality is an insufficient basis on which to respond to the ethical and political challenges of asylum.

Wonder and generosity have to be combined in our first response to asylum seekers and in our ongoing engagement with those who stay in our countries The concept of hospitality as such is too narrow to incorporate a full response to immigration and refugee issues, as once asylum seekers spend a reasonable length of time in a country they are no longer "visitors" who need hospitality or charity of any kind. This is where generosity or respect is even more important, because it is essential that basic proper treatment for asylum seekers is thought of as a right and must be extended to all. Stateless people and refugees should be able to become citizens. This need for citizenship is how I interpreted Arendt's idea of "the right to have rights." Furthermore, this politics of hospitality should extend to enabling those who are not citizens to have a voice in public life. Genuinely just and generous policies toward asylum seekers are a significant example of where harmony between ethics and politics is needed. Right provides the basis for just treatment and hospitality, and an ethical sense provides the kind of spirit and mode in which individuals should respond to the difficulties of asylum seekers and refugees.

To this point in the book, I considered the way wonder and generosity and love could help us to overcome instances of injustice and oppression. Yet there are others kinds of cases that challenge this way of thinking about ethics and politics. Evil could be considered a category that goes beyond any such response, and particular evils, such as genocide, terrorism, or repeated abuse, do not seem to be accounted for by theories of oppression and injustice. Thus, evil, especially radical evil, understood in Arendt's original sense as evil that cannot be accounted for by common human motives, raises a special difficulty for my idea that we should respond to difference with wonder, or indeed with forgiveness. I argued that wonder is not an appropriate response to evil actions, but that we should still be generous and respect the person who has done those actions. The other side of the coin is that evil actions reveal a lack of wonder and generosity.

The question of forgiveness is central here, since it appears to be a respectful or loving way in which we can respond to evil. I considered Arendt's position that radical evil cannot be forgiven, and Derrida's view that the only true forgiveness is forgiveness of such evil, as well as Améry's and Jankélévitch's arguments for keeping our resentment in the face of a lack of proper recognition of the evil. Furthermore, I examined the link between the suffering of the evils of torture or abuse, and the loss of trust and the experience of a shame that undermines generosity.

Arendt and Derrida agree that radical evil and forgiveness are beyond the human. My contention is that forgiveness, and, unhappily, radical evil as well, are human. Radical evil's lack of comprehensibility does not mean it is in a different category of evil in relation to forgiveness, although forgiveness is harder, and often the conditions for it are not met. It is rare for a perpetrator of radical evil to seek forgiveness. I argued that it is essential for the perpetrator to apologize and to repent before forgiveness is an ethical possibility. Such forgiveness should not be demanded or expected. Nevertheless, forgiveness may be ethically valuable for both victims and perpetrators even in cases of radical evil. While forgiveness is not a duty, the victim can have reasons for trying to forgive, both as an aspect of recovering from the harm committed and seeing how the perpetrator is possibly deserving of a generous respect, even though they should be punished.

In the final chapter, I explored the relation between reconciliation, forgiveness, and apology further in the context of recent official apologies and refusals to apologize, especially the former Australian government's refusal to apologize for a previous practice of removing aboriginal children from their parents. Derrida's shifting of the focus from the perpetrators to the victims in his work on forgiveness raises very important questions about the relations between these acts and their place in both ethics and politics. Derrida's skepticism about official apologies makes it worthwhile to reflect on cases of refusals to apologize. In the Australian case, the government argued that it should not have to accept guilt or responsibility for the practices of previous governments and so an apology to aboriginal people is not necessary. I argued that these apparent general objections to an official apology are based on a misunderstanding of the nature of responsibility, of apology, and the distinction between apology and forgiveness. In my view, it is reasonable to hold the government responsible and in general to hold current governments responsible for the actions of previous governments.

Accounts of both forgiveness and reconciliation have conceptualized them as like a contract, so if forgiveness without apology is possible an apology is not needed. Derrida's analysis of the logic of forgiveness focuses on this idea that forgiveness without apology is possible and suggests that the victim has a duty to forgive. I argued that apology without forgiveness is also possible and is the most ethical response in cases where there is a history of injustice. An official apology, such as that given in the Australian case and in the case of apologies for slavery in the United States, is based on generosity as respect for the people harmed, as well as showing the mature self-respect of those that apologize. This respect is a perfect duty and an apology is a public way of expressing that respect, as well as regret for past suffering and acknowledgment of continuing responsibility. However, forgiveness cannot be expected from aboriginal people or other victims of past extreme injustice, as forgiveness is premised on love, and is an imperfect or elective duty. An official apology is an important feature of reconciliation and I argued that such apologies support practical ways of improving people's living conditions rather than being a substitute for them or being in opposition to them. I also argued that reconciliation in a political context should be regarded as a commitment on the part of different groups to work together, not in forgetfulness of the past or under the illusion of some kind of mythical harmony. Coming together in a practical way engenders a response to difference of wonder and generosity, rather than indifference or contempt.

Apologies of this kind are an ethical political gesture. They are one respectful step that can be taken on the way to relations that involve wonder and love, a step that is central to any attempts to right past wrongs and to begin to properly develop ethical and political life. Wonder and generosity lead us toward responses to some of the most difficult ethical and political questions and to a more positive conception of our relations with others.

Notes

Chapter 1. Wonder and Generosity

1. Irigaray is also interested in the way Descartes's view in *The Passions* moves beyond the rigid dualism of his earlier work. As Naomi Schor says, "In Irigaray, Descartes functions both as the philosopher who irrevocably sunders body from soul and the one who most brilliantly reunites them" (1995, 58). Schor is referring to Irigaray's earlier reading of Descartes in *Speculum of the Other Woman* (1985a, 180–90) and the essay on wonder.

2. Elizabeth of Bohemia asked Descartes to clarify the role of the passions in our everyday life and to answer the question of how can they help us to lead a good life. See Shapiro (2007, 110–11) and Nye (1999, 59). *The Passions of the Soul* (1989) provides Descartes's answers to these questions.

3. It should be noted that desire has no opposite either, in Descartes's view (1989, 66).

4. This strength depends on two things—the novelty of the object and the fact that the movement that it causes has its whole strength from the start of the experience. Descartes thinks that wonder affects unusual parts of the brain, which are tender (because they are not used often), and this increases the effects of the movements of the animal spirits in the body (1989, 58).

5. Both Plato and Aristotle said that philosophy begins in wonder. Plato, in "Theatetus," says, "Wonder is the feeling of a philosopher, and philosophy begins in wonder" (1999, 155d). Aristotle, in the *Metaphysics,*

states that "it is owing to wonder that men both now begin and at first began to philosophize" (1984, 982b12–27), and in the *Rhetoric* he says, "Wondering implies the desire of learning, so that the object of wonder is an object of desire" (1371a31–b10).

6. Descartes discusses sexual difference in *The Passions* in relation to the desire that arises from delight when we feel "as though one were only half of a whole whose other half has to be a person of the other sex" (1989, 69). Elsewhere, he says that a father's love of his children is the most pure and perfect love because it does not expect any return or involve any desire for possession (1989, 63–64).

7. Irigaray discusses Aristotle's conception of the female in *Speculum* (1985a, 160–67), and his notion of place in relation to women in *An Ethics of Sexual Difference* (1993a, 34–55).

8. For an exploration of Irigaray's critique of Levinas, see Dana McDonald (1998). For an elucidation of Levinas on these points, see Claire Katz (2001).

9. Anne Caldwell notes that Irigaray posits a reciprocity that does not "collapse the difference" between self and other (1997, 49).

10. One can take as an example how wonder relates to the problem of other minds, which Descartes discusses in the *Meditations* (1984, 21). This problem makes little sense if we consider that in wonder the other strikes us first.

11. In his work on ethics, Cordner also sees wonder as "a mode of registering Otherness," as accepting that the Other is beyond our grasp (2002, 143).

12. This is an important claim in Irigaray's work, and I will discuss it in detail in chapter 3, where I focus on sexual difference in relation to other differences between human beings.

13. Although Irigaray is critical of Levinas's view of the feminine, her understanding of ethics has been influenced by his conception of ethics as an attempt to respond to the alterity of the other, who is prior to the subject. See her essays "The Fecundity of the Caress" (1993a) and "Questions to Emmanuel Levinas" (1991a).

14. Wittgenstein says that the experience of wonder—"seeing the world as a miracle"—suggests the supernatural character of ethics (1993, 43).

15. In a later article, Cheah and Grosz defend Irigaray from the charge that her work is "heterosexist" by arguing that the interval of sexual difference concerns only the basis for social change, that respect for sexual difference will also positively affect homosexual relations, and

that implications for reconceptionalizing lesbianism outside current social structures can be drawn out from her work (1998, 28–29).

16. Young gives three telling examples of nonsymmetrical differences: between disabled and nondisabled people, between Native and non-Native Americans, and between African Americans and non-African Americans (1997, 41–44).

17. See my paper "Sublimation, Love, and Creativity" (2000) for a discussion of this creative potential.

18. See my book *The Analytic Imaginary* (2002) for a sustained discussion of this view of the power of the imagination in a number of philosophical areas.

19. In chapter 6 I examine the way shame can be damaging to self-respect.

20. Other philosophers have noted the fruitfulness of Descartes's work. For example, Michèle Le Dœuff remarks, "I do know, it is true, of a philosophy of the subject which does not include the idea of a social possession of women in its text, and this is the Cartesian theory" (1993, 405). Her view that "universality demands that I respect humanity in others and in myself, while justice relates to the idea that people's relations between themselves and with things can be impersonally defined and that that definition includes me" (1991, 279) seems close in spirit to the notion of generosity. Anthony David states that Descartes is "in short, an unwitting feminist" (1997, 370). Descartes certainly was egalitarian in many ways, and there are resources in his work for the purposes of feminist and other liberation projects.

21. At one point, Descartes notes that he prefers the term *generosity* to the term *magnanimity* because "the Schools" do not understand this virtue (1989, 109).

22. Rosalyn Diprose, in her book *Corporeal Generosity,* also uses an extended concept of generosity, through the work of Nietzsche, Merleau-Ponty, and Levinas. She notes that Descartes is a precedent for "understanding generosity as a giving that enhances the self through the other" (2002, 200, n. 2).

23. As we will see in the following chapter, Kant distinguishes between esteem and respect, as he sees esteem as more comparative than Descartes does.

24. Aristotle thought that only those who have physical and moral excellence can be considered great.

25. See Vance Morgan for an interesting discussion of this issue (1994, 207–10).

26. See also (1996, 104).
27. The point of not wondering at everything is also relevant in a different way—that we should come to understand the world enough to know what is "worthy" of wonder and what not. For example, there may be human beings that we should not wonder at, whose difference we may properly find threatening and frightening, such as the psychopath or serial killer. In such cases, our feelings would be very different from wonder. I will discuss this problem in detail in chapter 6.
28. Arendt interprets Plato's notion of wonder as admiration, and affirmation of the world (1978a, 141–52).
29. See Sara Heinämaa for a very interesting reading of Irigaray's work on wonder as the development of the notion of self-criticism (1999). Debra Bergoffen develops the understanding of a wonder that lasts through Beauvoir's work (2003).
30. In my joint book, *Integrity and the Fragile Self* (2003, 41–72), we discuss the role of integrity in living a moral life.

Chapter 2. Love and Respect

1. See Michèle Le Dœuff (1989, 57–99) for a discussion of the provisional nature of Descartes's ethics in the *Discourse*. She argues that Descartes did not mean his ethics to be provisional at all since the term he uses is *par provision,* a juridical meaning an installment awarded by a judgment to a party in advance. On this reading his ethics provides adequately for his purposes. If we take *The Passions of the Soul* (1989) as the development of a proper ethics this makes the interpretation that his previous remarks on ethics were only provisional more plausible. Anthony David argues that such an installment can be overridden if the final judgment goes against the party (1997, 368).
2. This view is in great contrast to the search for certainty of Descartes's metaphysics.
3. This occupation provides satisfaction for Descartes, though it is not clear how others could gain a similar or analogous satisfaction. Not everyone is a philosopher, and not everyone can live the retiring life Descartes did.
4. Patrick Frierson argues that Kant gives a stronger argument for connecting free will and a person's value by connecting free will to moral responsibility, rather than to praise and blame, as Descartes does (2002,

322). See Descartes (1989, 103). However, Frierson believes that Descartes's other argument that free will is worthy of wonder because in that we resemble God is a more promising one.

5. This question of the importance of love to ethics is prior to any ethics of care that delineates the precise way we should care for others. See Gilligan (1993).

6. Irigaray's only extensive discussion of Kant appears in *Speculum,* and focuses primarily on his metaphysics (1985, 203–13). See Rachel Jones (20111, 114–29) for a detailed discussion of this section of *Speculum.* Joanna Hodge (2003) discusses Irigaray's relation to Kant's view of time and space, taking her cue from two asides in *An Ethics of Sexual Difference* (1993a).

7. See Frierson (2002) for a detailed discussion of Descartes's view of love.

8. Our duties to ourselves are to preserve ourselves and to develop and perfect ourselves (1996a, 6: 422–47). Kant writes: "*Love* and *respect* are the feelings that accompany the carrying out of these duties" (1996a, 6: 448). It is surprising that he says "feelings" here because in the rest of his discussion he makes it clear he is not referring to feelings, but rather duties. Marcia Baron notes this peculiarity (1997, 32).

9. Allen Wood rightly says that because Kant is not concerned with love as an inclination his is not an ethics of love (1999, 271). However, Kant's position on this issue is not quite as clear-cut as Wood suggests, as we shall see.

10. See Wood for a discussion of Kant's distinction between ambition and "proper self-respect" (1999, 263). Paul Guyer argues that self-respect in Kant is linked both to carrying out duties to the self and that these duties can sometimes be the means to fulfilling duties to others (2010, 150).

11. There must be limits to the extent we make others' ends our own, as it would involve a violation of respect to appropriate their ends.

12. Wood says that love and respect are in conflict as empirical inclinations because love is based on taking pleasure in others whereas in respect we experience pain through the limiting of our vanity (1999, 271). However, Kant's point is that love and respect conflict as duties as well.

13. Marcia Baron notes that it is hard to see why and love and respect (as maxims) would pull us in different directions. She points out that rather than being in conflict, there is an overlap between respect and love, because love includes respect. Kant speaks as if love and respect are symmetrically dependent on one another. However, they seem to be

asymmetric—love (as a maxim) requires respect but the reverse is not true (1997, 33). Wood (1999, 272) quotes Kant as saying that we more likely to love those we do not respect, and in *Lectures on Ethics*, Kant says that "we can also love a bad man, while not respecting him in the least" (1996b, 27: 358). As an ideal, Kant seems to think that love will be related to respect: "The *tender* lover shows respect" (1996b, 27: 26). See Backström (2007) for a criticism of the view that love requires respect.

14. The original German derives from *abstoßen,* which means to push off or away, or to repel or repulse.

15. Baron argues that there are duties of respect that should be understood as positive (1997, 35). For example, Kant's claims that we should not be contemptuous of others and should suppose that people's judgment has some truth can both be seen as positive duties (1996a, 6: 463). He also distinguishes three vices that violate the duty of respect: arrogance, defamation, and ridicule.

16. Nietzsche, most probably with Kant's views in mind, claims that the idea of "love" and "love of one's neighbor" leads to the destruction of the individual (1982, #132).

17. See Derrida, *Of Grammatology,* for a discussion of the double meaning of supplement, as both that which is needed to make up a deficiency and that which is in excess of what is needed to make the original lack complete (1982, 144–64).

18. I take up the relationship between sexist oppression and other forms of oppression in the subsequent chapter.

19. In an interesting article, Randy Cagle argues that Kant believes emotions and feelings can be cultivated (1996).

20. Irigaray describes this ideal love, negatively, as involving: (1) a time that is neither pure nostalgia for the past nor an appeal to the future with regard to the unique; (2) neither a fragmentation that puts its reassemblage off to some past or future day nor a putting off until tomorrow its need to discharge and recharge; (3) nor a simple part of the self in the other of the same or of the other, but a voyage through the other that returns to the self and constitutes the self through the space-time of nostalgia and hope (both past and future) (1993a, 61).

21. Irigaray compares love of self to an icon, as opposed to an idol or a fetish. She says that an icon irradiates the invisible, whereas the idol attracts the gaze but blinds it, and the fetish destroys in seduction the power of the invisible (1993a, 70).

22. Irigaray argues that self-affection for women has to be protected or it

may be absorbed by men's need for women for their own self-affection (2008a, 104).

23. Hegel also holds the view that lovers become a unity: "What in the first instance is most the individual's own is united into the whole in the lover's touch and contact; consciousness of a separate self disappears, and all distinction between the lovers is annulled" (1970, 307).

24. Krzysztof Ziarek argues that Irigaray's ethics of sexual difference can be understood through the notion of proximity, but he notes that "the amorous proximity allows something to be reserved and withheld, making the economy of giving exceed the parameters of proximity" (2000, 150). Irigaray conveys this reserve through the contrasting notion of distance. See also Irigaray (2002b, especially 20, 65–66, 150), where she describes ways of meeting with the other that do not involve integrating them. Baron also notes that love is dependent on respect, but she means as maxims (1997, 34).

25. Kelly Oliver describes Irigaray's view of love as "We can love another only through vigilant self-limitation" (2007, 133).

26. In order to have a sense of other that is not projective or selfish we need an intuition of the infinite, Irigaray claims. This intuition can be of a god or a divine principle *or* "the intuition of a subject that, at each point in the present, remains unfinished and open to a becoming of the other that is neither simply passive nor simply active" (1993a, 11–122). In *Conversations,* Irigaray says that we need to cultivate respect for the other (2008b, 132).

27. In many discussions of friendship, friendship is connected with the notion of political community understood as a kind of brotherhood, a feature Derrida emphasizes throughout his analyses. See his discussion of Kant's account of friendship (1997, 252–63). An obvious example is the slogan of the French republic: "Liberty, Equality, Fraternity." Le Dœuff argues that "fraternity should be replaced with 'solidarity' to overcome the exclusiveness of the term" (1991, 95). Thus, it is understandable that Irigaray connects the exclusions made in the name of love and friendship with social and political conditions.

28. Derrida notes that Montaigne also attributes a similar saying to Aristotle, although it is not to be found in his texts (1997). In Kant's *Lectures on Ethics,* Socrates is supposed to have said it. Kant explains: "This was as much as to say that no friendship ever matches the Idea of friendship; and he was right about this, for it is not in fact possible" (1996b, 27: 424). Another example of Kant's excessive pessimism is his claim

that once respect is violated, it cannot be regained (1996a, 6: 470). In contrast, Descartes believes "that there is no man so imperfect that we cannot have a quite perfect friendship for him when we think ourselves loved by him, and have a truly noble and generous soul" (1989, 64).

29. Wollstonecraft makes a point about this kind of lack of respect in relations between women and between women and men, in *A Vindication of the Rights of Woman*, in the chapter on "Modesty—Comprehensively Considered, and Not as a Sexual Virtue" (1988, 121–31).

30. In *Lectures on Ethics*, Kant says, "We must so conduct ourselves to a friend, that it does us no harm if he were to become an enemy" (1996b, 27: 429). Annette Baier notes that Kant is limiting the role of love in our lives, trying to ensure that we do not humiliate others by getting too close to them, and recommending we avoid the risk of exposure and vulnerability (1995, 34–36). She argues that in his account of friendship and love, respect "trumps" the ideal of loving fellowship (1995, 36). However, she may be interpreting the point a little strongly, as we can read him as saying not that respect trumps love, but that it must always be an element in friendship.

31. Irigaray criticizes this view of love (as a means) in Plato's *Symposium* in "Sorcerer Love: A Reading of Plato, *Symposium*, 'Diotima's Speech'" (1993a, 20–33). Velleman (1999) discusses how Kant's view that love does not have an aim differs from that of Freud and many analytic philosophers.

32. Kant also says, "Sexual inclination . . . is a unique kind of pleasure (*sui generis*), and this ardor has nothing in common with moral love properly speaking, though it can enter into close union with it under the limiting conditions of practical reason" (1996a, 6: 426).

33. Interestingly, Descartes says that there is not an important distinction between benevolent love and concupiscent love because they concern only the effects of love and not its essence (1989, 63).

34. Descartes conceptualizes all love this way, although he believes that a father's love is the most perfect of this kind, and friendship less perfect (1989, 63–64).

35. Derrida says that Montaigne "discreetly introduces . . . heterology, transcendence, dissymmetry, and infinity" into his account of friendship (1997, 291).

36. Morny Joy also questions Irigaray's reliance on an "idealization of the couple" and on the view that sexual difference is of more importance than other differences (2000, 123).

37. Christopher Cohoon argues that we have to alter Irigaray to think of the sexed other, who could be the same sex, rather than the other of a different sex (2011, 485). This change addresses the issue of including homosexual relationships, but not the broader question of including other differences between people.

38. Here, Kant again uses the analogy with metaphysics and physics, and says that there should be a schematism that shows how we can make the shift from the metaphysics of morals to nature or application (1996a, 6: 468). See Sarah Kofman (1982), Natalie Alexander (1999), Mason Cash (2001), and Wood (1999) for discussions of the relationship between Kant's ethical theory and his anthropological views, particularly his views of women.

39. Hannah Arendt argues that "love, by its very nature, is unworldly, and it is for this reason rather than its rarity that it is not only apolitical but antipolitical, perhaps the most powerful of all antipolitical forces" (1998, 242). Arendt would think that love does not have a place in politics and that politics should not concern itself with love. I take her point that love is not directly political but I do not accept that love is antipolitical or undermining of politics. How we conceptualize love and its role in our lives is relevant to politics.

40. In relation to the question of which kind of changes are more urgent, she says that juridical changes "seem most pressing as changes in custom require more time to take effect" (1996, 131).

41. See Alison Stone (2006, 161–92) for a very interesting discussion of Irigaray's interpretation of Hegel.

42. Irigaray argues that there are at least four rights specific to women: "the right to physical and moral inviolability," voluntary motherhood, culture, and "a preferential and reciprocal right for mother and child (ren)" (1996, 132).

43. Stone has an illuminating discussion of Irigaray's conception of sexuate rights. Her interpretation is that Irigaray means that "all rights should be 'sexuate' in that they should serve, directly or indirectly, to secure for women and men the all-important ability to express their sexed natures culturally" (2006, 184).

44. In Ziarek's view, Irigaray's focus on the particular encourages respect for all kinds of differences (2001, 163).

45. Kelly Oliver points out the importance of love as motivation to transcend self-interested political action and therefore forms of domination (2001, 218).

46. Although Irigaray does not express her view in such terms, her idea of love as appreciating the other in their specificity and autonomy is compatible with Velleman's Kantian reading of love as an appreciation of the incomparable value or dignity of each person (1999, 367).

Chapter 3. Responding to Difference and Similarity

1. Some feminists have taken the implications of Spelman's (and others') work to be that one cannot make any generalizations at all about women's experiences. For example, Pettman argues that aboriginal women find family a place of comfort and validation (1992, 67), so attacks on the family by white feminists are a problem when aboriginal families are already being attacked by a racist state. However, Bordo points out the need for generalizations in feminist theory (1990). A more realistic conclusion is that greater care is needed when making generalizations—in describing stereotypes, roles, experiences, and characterizing oppression. Spelman suggests that while theorists should respect the variety of women's experiences, what unifies women is "the overwhelming evidence of the worldwide and historical subordination of women to men" (1988, 131). The claim that all women are oppressed is compatible with the existence of many varieties of oppression.

2. It should be noted that these arguments concerning the biology of sex are different from arguments pertaining to the biology of race, because the arguments about race do not depend on breaking down a two-part distinction. Cases of indeterminate sex are thought to be more problematic for the sex distinction than they are for race. As in the case of race, it is also argued that because the idea of sex has been used in an oppressive way, it should be abandoned or deconstructed. Butler (1990) and Fraser (1997) hold this view, although for slightly different reasons.

3. In a more recent paper, she introduces the terms *whitely* and *whiteliness* "as terms whose grammar is analogous to that of 'masculine' and 'masculinity'" (2001, 87).

4. See Fuss (1989, 1–21) for a discussion of different understandings of essentialism and constructionism.

5. See, for example, Huntington (1997), Deutscher (1998), and Joy (2000).

6. See Young (1997), Bloodsworth (1999), and Ziarek (2001), for example.

7. Deutscher evaluates this work as not being critical of Eastern traditions: "Arguing that the west is culturally impoverished, her work [Irigaray's]

contributes to an idealized depiction of the east serving the denuncia-
tion of western culture" (2002, 168). Her view is that Irigaray is insuf-
ficiently self-reflexive about her own relation to Eastern culture and
ultimately adopts an appropriative stance toward it.

8. On this point, Jones agrees with Deutscher that what is needed is "the
same kind of detailed critical analysis of the depiction of race and cultural difference as Irigaray has undertaken with regard to sexual difference" (2011, 223).

9. On this point, Irigaray appears to agree with Engels's analysis in "The
Origin of the Family, Private Property and the State" (1968).

10. Wingenbach argues that Irigaray's idea of justice is more attainable than
Derrida's because it has a more specific focus (1996). I say more about
Derrida's views of ethics and politics in the next chapter.

11. Alison Martin (2004) explains how a report on citizenship for the
European Union worked on by Renzo Imbeni and Irigaray, and based
around these ideas, was undermined by right-wing amendments and
voted down.

12. Deutscher's interpretation is that Irigaray's problem is how "to agitate
for equality in the name of possible difference" (2002, 17).

13. Le Dœuff also criticizes the French parity movement, the movement
aimed at gaining equal representation of women in parliament, for not
developing a specific political platform (2002, 26). This way of thinking
implies that one has to combine equal representation with a concern
for issues that affect women.

14. Young-Bruehl criticizes Beauvoir for trying to argue both that there is
an analogy between racism and sexism *and* that sexism is unique (1996,
119–20). This is a coherent position provided that that one does not
take unique to mean: "shares no features with other forms of oppression." Racism and sexism can have some similar features, overlap and
occur simultaneously, and both can still be unique.

15. Simons describes the influence on Beauvoir of Richard Wright's
descriptions of the way that oppression affects psychological development, his emphasis on the lived experience of racism, and his belief
in the necessity of race consciousness (Simons 1999). He was in turn
influenced by W. E. B. Du Bois's idea of double-consciousness, or seeing
oneself through the eyes of others (Du Bois 1986).

16. Beauvoir is often claimed to hold the view that women must reject
femininity and to be an equality feminist. Irigaray says that her own
"thought on women's liberation has gone beyond simply a quest for

equality between the sexes," unlike Beauvoir (1993b, 11). Schor also argues that Beauvoir risks "saming": the view that women must be the same as men (1995, 52). However, some recent commentators have taken issue with this interpretation, as I do. See Heinämaa for a discussion of the similarities between Beauvoir's and Irigaray's views of embodiment and femininity (2003, xvii–xix), and Bergoffen discusses both their uses of the concept of wonder (2003).

17. Deutscher argues that sometimes Beauvoir treats race and sex, for example, as if they are separate, and makes the interesting suggestion that Beauvoir could have made use of her concept of ambiguity to articulate the relationship of sex and race (2008, 131–35).

18. Le Dœuff (1991, 28–29) argues that a feminist view is one that acknowledges that sometimes sex is irrelevant and sometimes it is very important.

19. In a different use of the term *generosity*, Scarth argues Beauvoir's work implies that we should act to ensure other's freedom and be guided by "receptive generosity—an openness to the foreignness of the other" (2004, 171).

20. Zack is one of the few feminist philosophers who argues against "intersectionality"—the view that distinct kinds of oppression interact to form a new kind. She writes, "Politically, it easily leads to a fragmentation of women that precludes common goals as well as basic empathy" (2005, 7). She says that women can be defined in relation to a category that includes being designated female at birth, being biological mothers, or the heterosexual object choice of men (2005, 8).

21. Alcoff takes up the idea of lived experience to argue that race is an aspect of lived reality and so we cannot give up on it as a concept (Bernasconi, 2001).

22. One criticism of this approach is that it suggests that oppressed people can determine the relevance of their group membership in an arbitrary and inconsistent way. This does not appear to be a problem because so much thought has already been put into working out a consistent way of thinking about these issues. The criticism itself is the expression of racist and sexist views that oppressed people are incapable of thinking through these matters seriously.

23. We continue to need the concept "race" because there has been so much cultural loss for some groups that "ethnicity" does not suggest their exceptional historical situation. For example, in the Australian context, ethnicity connotes cultural variation, a notion that does not

do justice to the unique situation of indigenous people. Ethnicity relies on particular aspects of culture, such as the idea of a shared language or religion, whereas the idea of race used in a positive sense can suggest other connections. Indigenous people may not have that shared language but have a particular set of relations to history and the land. We may not always need the idea of race; it is possible that it will be abandoned in a utopian future. That future is simply farther off than is sometimes imagined, and ways of thinking about these questions have to take into account the contemporary situation of oppressed groups.

24. It should be noted that Beauvoir does not use the term *Negroes* in her original text. Rather she uses the expression "*les noirs d'Amérique*" (1949, II: 47).

25. For a discussion of black "double consciousness," see Ernest Allen (1997).

26. Thus, I disagree with Genevieve Lloyd's view that what connected the policies was "a failure to recognize difference" (2000, 36). That is an important feature of what happened, but the analysis needs to be complicated through understanding that a failure to respect similarity was also involved.

27. This characterization of racism itself may seem to need explaining— for example, by arguing that racists hold the views they do in order to gain a sense of self-worth. Although this is a significant consideration, I will leave it aside here to focus on the structure of racist thinking. See Young-Bruehl (1996) and part II of Levine and Pataki (2004) for a discussion of the psychological background of racism.

28. The One Nation party in Australia, a minor conservative party, trades on the idea that its assimilationist policies are not racist because they simply demand equal (the same) treatment for everyone.

29. In chapter 7 I will show what is deeply problematic about this failure to apologize.

30. For example, a white artist, Elizabeth Durack, adopted indigenous painting techniques and exhibited her work as an aboriginal man under the name "Eddie Burrup."

31. I will discuss issues affecting asylum seekers and refugees in more detail in chapter 5.

32. Fuss's (1989, 3) characterization of Beauvoir simply as an antiessentialist misunderstands her view. See also my (1994) paper that discusses Beauvoir's understanding of female bodies and sexuality in the light of issues concerning essentialism and constructionism.

33. A number of antiracists and feminists have argued against the ideals of color-blindness and sex-blindness (Spelman 1988; Young 1990).

Chapter 4. The Relation between Ethics and Politics

1. In the *Groundwork,* Kant argues that because we are autonomous we are bound by the moral law: "If, therefore, freedom of the will is presupposed, morality together with its principle follows from it by mere analysis of its concept" (1996a, 4: 447).
2. Kant further distinguishes between natural or private right, which includes rights to property, contracts, and domestic right, and public or civil right, which concerns the rights of a state, of nations, and cosmopolitan right. The doctrine of virtue includes duties to ourselves and the duties to others of love and respect that I examined in chapter 2.
3. The doctrine of right concerns the a priori basis of ethical laws. One might disagree with Kant's view that politics is the doctrine of right put into practice, and argue, for example, that ethics and politics are two separate spheres, as Arendt does. I will discuss Arendt's conception of politics farther on in this chapter.
4. See Kant's discussion of radical evil in *Religion within the limits of Reason Alone,* which I will examine in chapter 6 (1996b).
5. In Bobbio's four-part categorization of theorists of ethics and politics into rigid monism, flexible monism, and apparent and real dualism, Kant appears as a rigid monist, or one who believes that politics can be reduced to ethics. He also sees Kant as arguing that being a moral politician will lead to success, an argument Bobbio finds unsupported by history or experience (2000, 49). Kant does warn of the uncertainties and dangers of trying to calculate how to achieve an end once one abandons the categorical imperative.
6. This argument is based on a presumption of reasonableness of "everyone." If people's judgment were perverted, perhaps their resistance would not indicate injustice, but their lack of understanding of the maxims.
7. There has been a great deal of interest in Kant's condemnation of rebellion here, particularly since he is a well-known supporter of the French Revolution. See, for example Hutchings (1996, 46) and Arendt (1982, 44–51). See also Kant (1996a, 6: 320–23). Derrida believes that a system of law can only be justified by what comes after its institution, in that

such systems rest on a mystical, nonjustified, violent foundation (1992, 35). Kant's view is the reverse—that systems of law are justified by their foundation. Once they are founded, however, they should not be overthrown. I will say more about this issue farther on.

8. Cosmopolitan right is very interesting as it concerns the relations between individuals and states where the power imbalance is wildly differential. Presumably, individuals could not make known, say, their intentions to overthrow states, whereas states could make known their intentions not to respect the rights of individuals such as the right to hospitality. However, Kant again could be relying on the presumption that all reasonable people would object to and resist such a principle. I will discuss Kant's cosmopolitanism and the right of hospitality in the next chapter.

9. In "On the common saying: That may be correct in theory, but it is of no use in practice," Kant defines the principles of a civil state as: "1. The *freedom* of every member of the society as a human being. 2. His *equality* with every other as a *subject*. 3. The *independence* of every member of a commonwealth as a *citizen*" (1996a, 8: 290). In *Perpetual Peace*, Kant says that the principles of a *Republican* state are freedom, equality, and the *dependence* "of all upon a single common legislation (as subjects)" (1996a, 8: 350).

10. The first and two last should be implemented immediately, whereas Kant allows that there may be some delay, depending on circumstances, in acting on the other three (1996a, 8: 347).

11. Kurt Huber, a philosophy professor who took part in "The White Rose," an anti-Nazi resistance group, wrote, "I asked myself, following Kant's categorical imperative, what would happen if these subjective maxims governing my actions were to become universal law. To this there can be but one answer: public order, security, trust in the government and in our political life will be restored. . . . This is not illegal; rather, it is the restitution of legality" (Scholl 1983, 64–65).

12. See the *Groundwork of the Metaphysics of Morals*, for Kant's distinction between perfect and imperfect duties (1996a, 4: 422).

13. I am not suggesting that individuals should be compelled to follow imperfect duties but that politics should encourage their fulfillment both at an institutional and individual level.

14. Levinas's influence on Derrida's ethics has been more thoroughly explored than Kant's. See for example, Simon Critchley (1999a) and (1999b), Diane Perpich (1998), and Miriam Bankovsky, who also

considers the relation of both to Kant. Beardsworth discusses the relation between Kant and Derrida on law and violence (1996, 46–70). Derrida discusses Levinas in "Violence and Metaphysics: An Essay on the Thought of Emmanuel Levinas" (2001b) and *Adieu to Emmanuel Levinas* (1999). On Kant and Derrida on hospitality, see the next chapter. For discussions of Derrida's relation to feminism, see Feder, Rawlinson, and Zakin (1997).

15. Critchley has a very good, albeit brief, discussion of what Derrida means by democracy to come (2000, 463–64).

16. On Perpich's reading of Levinas, ethics and politics are commensurable. Although they in a sense anticipate each other, there is always a gap between them, in that the third alters the ethical relation, and the ethical relation interrupts the political. She explains that ethics is "the condition of justice and political institutions, not in the sense of being a cause, ground, or logical fundament, but in the sense that it is ethics that endows justice with meaning" (1998, 5). I understand her to mean that ethics in this sense concerns particular relations but then always becomes bound up with relations with others in a more general sense, while politics is always "interrupted" or conscious of the need to be just to the singular in its universal laws.

17. Another way that Derrida expresses this problem is by writing, "The hiatus, the silence of this non-response concerning the schemas between the ethical and the political, remains. It is a fact that it remains, and this fact is not some empirical contingency, it is a *Faktum*" (1999, 116).

18. In a later paper, Critchley presents Derrida's account of the decision more sympathetically, by describing it as nonfoundational but nonarbitrary and necessarily contextual (2000, 461–62).

19. Levinas also believes that we have to negotiate between ethics and politics. Bernasconi says that Levinas is not concerned to resolve conflicts between ethics and politics, yet "the task of negotiating in practice the conflicting demands under which I find myself, involves the use of reason, that is, the third person perspective" (1999, 81). In his view, while Levinas "favors" ethics over politics, they are not in opposition for him.

20. Mary-Jane Rubenstein argues that Derrida's deconstruction of these concepts is itself a work of wonder because he makes us see their impossibility, and then shows that impossibility is their possibility (2011, 182).

21. Derrida also says he hesitates to conflate his idea of justice with a Kantian regulative idea (1992, 25). He repeats his reservations in *Rogues* (2005, 83–85) concerning democracy.

22. A further difference is that Kant accepts that hospitality is conditional and that forgiveness is an imperfect duty, as I note in the following chapters.

23. Hutchings's reading of Foucault connects his understanding of Kant to Kant's aesthetics, where the genius follows an earlier example of genius but goes beyond the constraints of the example and thereby creates a new rule (1996, 121–22) (Kant 2000, 5: 318). Custer also explores the parallels between Kant and Foucault on the question of freedom, arguing that they both understand freedom as a practice of invention like artistic creation (1998).

24. Kant considered how an ethical community could be cultivated, for example, in his discussion of ethical communities in *Religion within the limits of Reason Alone* (1996c, 6: 97–102). He thought of them as a church organized like a household or family.

25. It is interesting to note that one Descartes's commentator, Marshall, believes we can understand his ethics in terms of perfect and imperfect duties. Marshall includes a prohibition against suicide (perfect), the duty to cultivate our intellect (imperfect), the duty to look after our health (imperfect), and the duties of justice (perfect) and benevolence (imperfect) (1998, 158–66).

26. Kateb also discusses this question in another essay, "Political Action: Its Nature and Advantages" (Villa 2000, 130–48). Here, he sees a certain moral code in Arendt's account of authentic political action involving her concepts of forgiving and promising in *The Human Condition* (1998), which he finds inadequate due to her "rather eccentric notion of how morality has traditionally been conceived" (Villa 2000, 144). I consider her conception of forgiveness in the next chapter.

27. Arendt says that "the inhumanity of Kant's moral philosophy is undeniable . . . because the categorical imperative is postulated as absolute and in its absoluteness introduces into the interhuman realm—which by its nature consists of relationships—something that runs counter to its fundamental relativity" (1995, 27).

28. Arendt quotes without referencing Machiavelli as saying that those who will not resist evil allow the wicked "to do as much evil as they please" and Aristotle as warning against philosophers acting in politics. The point she ascribes to Aristotle is that because philosophers are so unconcerned with their own good they cannot be trusted with the good of others or the good of the community (Aristotle 1984, *Nichomachean Ethics*, Bk.6, 1140b9 and 1141b4). Here, a different sense of

good is introduced in contrast to her earlier point concerning the moral
good of the self. "Good" is understood as our worldly interests, or "the
down-to-earth-interests of the community" (1968, 245).

29. There's a very important distinction between Arendt's view and mine
   in her conception of what is required for right action. She believes that
   it is central that we put ourselves in the place of others, and that is the
   failure of the banality of evil (1982, 73; 1968, 241–42). I agree with her
   that a failure to put oneself in the place of others is often the basis for
   cruel and indifferent treatment of others, but a recognition that our
   own way of seeing the world is not the only one and that we cannot
   enlarge one's view as a sheer act of will is also important. We have to
   recognize others' difference from ourselves.

30. Nevertheless, respect plans a significant role in Arendt's account of forgiveness, as we will see in chapter 6.

31. Foucault's concern is that the subject is free to practice ethical relations
   with themselves and others (1997, 281–301).

32. Bernasconi argues that Kant's cosmopolitanism is "severely compro-
   mised" by his thinking about race (2003, 19). I agree that tensions arise
   in Kant's work because of his views on race, including tensions with his
   own critique of colonialism in "Perpetual Peace" (1996a).

33. The two kinds of killing Kant argues should be exempt from capital
   punishment are that of a mother who kills her illegitimate child and a
   soldier who kills another soldier in a duel (1996a, 6: 336–37). Derrida
   does not address this question of how important Kant takes the death
   penalty to be, although he emphasizes Kant's connection of the *jus
   talionis* (law of retribution) to the basis of criminal justice (2004, 148). I
   would argue that one could retain this conception of punishment and
   still maintain an abolitionist stance. I am against both retributive justice
   and capital punishment, but a discussion of these issues in sufficient
   detail would take me beyond the concerns of this book.

Chapter 5. Cosmopolitanism, Hospitality, and Refugees

1. See, for example, Chandler (2003), Cheah and Robbins (1998), Lu
   (2000), Mertens (1996), Robbins (2002), Papastephanou (2002), and
   Venn (2002).

2. Kant's notion of cosmopolitanism in *Anthropology from a Pragmatic Point*

of View, where he says we must "pursue diligently" the principle of cosmopolitanism, is closer to what contemporary theorists see as useful in cosmopolitanism (1974, 191).

3. See Beck (Kant 1957, vii–xiv) for an account of the relationship between the elements Kant sees as necessary for perpetual peace. The preliminary articles are: a genuine peace treaty, no acquisition of an independent nation by another, the abolition of standing armies, abolition of foreign debt, no interference with the constitution and government of another nation, and no flagrant breaches of trust during war.

4. The other two are a requirement that all states be republican and that the right of nations should be based on a federation of free states, as I noted (1996a, 8: 349–57).

5. Covell distinguishes between Kant allowing here for "a right of resort," or "presenting" oneself to other societies, whereas the "right of a guest" implies a right of settlement, which can only come about through a specific agreement (1998, 142). In Ted Humphrey's translation, the distinction is between visitor and permanent visitor (1983).

6. Habermas points out the difficulty of ensuring the enduring nature of the federation of states, given that it is a purely voluntary association (Bohman and Lutz-Bachmann 1997, 117).

7. Derrida was involved in the International Parliament of Writers' project to host, for one or two years, writers and artists who are persecuted in their countries. There are a range of these cities in Europe, North America, and Africa. Derrida also signed a petition saying he would host "illegal immigrants" in France.

8. Martha Nussbaum also connects Kant's view of cosmopolitanism with early Stoic cosmopolitans such as Cicero. She describes how Cicero took the Stoic belief that we must recognize and respect the personhood of all other human beings to "entail certain duties of hospitality to the foreigner and the other" (Bohman and Lutz-Bachmann 1997, 35). Nussbaum argues that Kant's and Cicero's ideas concerning hospitality are very close (Cicero *De Officiis* 1913, II, 64). Cicero says that it is creditable for a country to be hospitable, and advantageous in leading to influence abroad.

9. In "The right to philosophy from the cosmopolitan point of view," Derrida says that his reservations concerning Kant's concept of the cosmopolis are that it is "both too naturalist and too teleologically European" (2002, 15).

10. Arendt notes this problem of police dealing with the stateless in *The Origins of Totalitarianism* (1976, 287).

11. It should be noted that this treatment of asylum seekers was struck down by the High Court (case M70/2011). However, aspects of the Pacific Solution have been revived.

12. Derrida explains that he means by "hospitality is culture itself," in that any genuine culture will claim that it is hospitable (2001b, 97).

13. The situation is rather more complicated than Howard's claim acknowledges. At that time, Australia was third, after the United States and Canada, among the countries that have formal refugee settlement quotas. In terms of total numbers of refugees on a per capita basis, Australia ranked thirty-ninth in the world. See Do (2002). That ranking has continued to get lower and is now sixty-eighth (Tobin, 2010).

14. In contrast to Derrida's view, there are numerous philosophical proponents of completely free immigration. See Mertens (1996).

15. The reference to "constraints" indicates Derrida is not advocating the opening of all national borders.

16. Article 31 of the Geneva Convention and Protocol relating to the Status of Refugees (1951) also forbids the practice of imposing penalties on refugees who enter the country unlawfully.

17. See Marr and Wilkinson (2003, 140) for an analysis of the Australian government's strategy. Isaac (1996) argues that voluntary groups that support refugees can play an important role in making governments more hospitable.

18. Article 14 of the Universal Declaration of Human Rights is, "Everyone has the right to seek and to enjoy in other countries asylum from persecution" (1948). Benhabib believes that Arendt's reflections on this issue are inconclusive because "the right to be accepted by an organized human community cannot be based on any more fundamental philosophical principle" (Benhabib and Fraser 2004, 187).

19. In a short essay, Agamben argues that the situation of the refugee questions both the idea of "the rights of man" and the sovereignty of the state (1995).

20. Arendt says that action corresponds to the "human condition of plurality" (1998, 7).

21. See Australian Press Council (2001), and Mares (2002).

22. The demonstrations by "illegal" immigrants in the United States, such as students supporting the Dream Act, is a good example of people

claiming those rights for themselves. The Dream Act is legislation that would allow people who came to the United States as children to become citizens (Editorial, *New York Times,* 2010).

Chapter 6. Wonder, Radical Evil, and Forgiveness

1. Byron Williston makes the interesting point that for Descartes, reflecting on this separation may bring joy, since "[t]he agent realizes that it is precisely because she is generous that she is alienating herself from the object in question" (2003, 323).
2. See Schott's discussion of Beauvoir's multifaceted account of evil (Card 2003, 228–47).
3. Papastephanou points out that a view of "forgiveness with repentance" is evident in the literature of Ancient Greece (2003, 517–19).
4. In the following chapter, I will elaborate the distinction between forgiveness and reconciliation.
5. See Michael Levine's argument that psychiatrists, psychoanalysts, and judges in particular should avoid using the term *evil* (Mason 2006, 295–312).
6. "Extreme evil" is Badiou's preferred term for the Shoah (2001, 66).
7. Interestingly, Beauvoir says that lynching is an "absolute evil," but she means that it can never be justified or excused, rather than that it is radical evil (1997b, 146). Ferrara also gives a more general definition of radical evil as evil that we cannot bear to have connected with human life in any way, even as an emblem of what should not be done (Lara 2002, 186).
8. For example, Card says that her understanding of diabolical evil comes closer than Kant's "to the classic view of Satan as a corrupter" (2002, 212), although her intention is certainly not to glorify evil. In her more recent book, Card argues that we should understand diabolical evil as "doing one evil for the sake of another" (2010, 57). One example she gives is of forcing extermination camp inmates to take part in the murders themselves.
9. By contrast, Derrida claims, "Forgiveness has nothing to do with knowledge" (Caputo 2001, 70).
10. Michalson says it is not clear whether Kant means that all three are cases of moral evil, or only the last, as Kant says that we often have mixed

motives for acting (1990, 45). However, what Kant is concerned with in relation to "impurity" is the idea of acting only in conformity with duty, rather than from duty, as discussed in chapter 4.

11. So, for Kant, forgiveness is a conditional duty of love, rather than an unconditional duty of respect. I will discuss in both this and the following chapter some of the implications of this conditional character of forgiveness.

12. Allison argues that Arendt's view concerning the banality of evil is closer to Kant's of radical evil (Lara 2001). I think there is some truth in this point; however, Arendt's account concerns only one type of evil perpetrator, while Kant is giving a theory of evil in general.

13. Much of the material in the essay is republished in the book, but the essay contains different introductory remarks. Bernstein, after a comprehensive discussion of theories of radical evil, also concludes that "evil is an excess that resists total comprehension" (2002, 227).

14. Arendt notes that any work done in the camps could have been done better and more cheaply elsewhere, to support her view that they have another purpose (1948, 749). A great deal of productive work was carried out in the ghettoes, but these workers were all sent to concentration and extermination camps.

15. In the *Groundwork,* Kant writes: "In the kingdom of ends everything has either a *price* or a *dignity.* What has a price can be replaced by something else as its *equivalent*; what on the other hand is raised above all price and therefore admits of no equivalent has a dignity" (1996a, 4: 434).

16. Arendt adds farther on that this antiutility is only apparent, because the existence of concentration camps and people's treatment within them serves the purpose of keeping the population terrified (1976, 456). However, this purpose does not seem relevant to the camps, particularly extermination camps, in Germany during World War II, as war itself provides ways of subduing the population. Fine emphasizes the point that it is *difficult* to understand what happened in the Shoah within standard rationalistic and utilitarian frameworks (Lara 2001, 133).

17. In a letter to Jaspers, Arendt wrote, "For these crimes, no punishment is severe enough. It may be essential to hang Göring, but it is totally inadequate. That is, this guilt, in contrast to all criminal guilt, oversteps and shatters any and all legal systems" (1992, 54).

18. Whitebook, for example, connects Arendt's idea of omnipotence with psychoanalytic accounts of a primary stage of omnipotent perfection (Benhabib and Fraser 2004, 256–59).

19. Arendt makes this point in a letter to Gershom Scholem written in 1964 (1978).

20. Svendsen calls this stupidity and compares it to Dietrich Bonhoeffer's description of "foolishness"; in both cases, it refers to a lack of judgment (2010, 141–43).

21. Not all writers agree with Arendt that Eichmann was not motivated by virulent anti-Semitism. See, for example, Bernstein (2002, 270).

22. Bernstein notes this possibility: "The banality of evil is a phenomenon exemplified by only *some* of the perpetrators of radical evil—desk murderers like Eichmann" (2002, 222). Geddes also notes that Eichmann is one example of one kind of evil (2003, 108–109). However, Allison (Lara 2001, 87) argues that Arendt implies that such motivelessness characterizes the Nazi regime as a whole. He believes that Eichmann constitutes a limiting case of Kantian evil, because of his extreme neglect of the morally relevant features of his actions and extreme self-deception, rather than a different kind of evil (Lara 2001, 99). I believe Arendt could and probably did hold that many of the Nazi perpetrators were "banally evil" and that there are other kinds of evil.

23. This distinction roughly corresponds to the distinction between Erklären (explanation) and Verstehen (understanding) in hermeneutics. W. Dilthey is credited with developing the concept of understanding as "the process by which we recognize some inner content from signs received from the senses" (1976, 248). Another approach is that of Paul Formosa (2007), who argues that we can reach a *basic,* rather than full, understanding of evil actions by knowing what reasons motivated people to act, even if those reasons are not justified.

24. Other authors, such as Garrard (2002), directly argue that we *should* forgive the unforgivable, such as the crimes of the Shoah.

25. Jankélévitch (1903–1980) was Professor of Moral Philosophy, University of Paris.

26. Arendt's view that sadism was usually not a motive for the crimes, although in some cases it was, may seem utterly different from Améry's (1948, 758–59). Yet Améry is distinguishing existential sadism from pathological sexual sadism, of which he says, "In general, I don't believe that I encountered a single genuine sadist of this sort during my two years of imprisonment by the Gestapo and in concentration camps" (1980, 34).

27. See Thomas Brudholm (2008) for a detailed analysis and defense of Améry's refusal to give up his resentment.

28. Jean-Luc Nancy argues that evil is "unbearable and unpardonable"

(1993, 123) and defines evil as "*the hatred of existence as such*" (1993, 128).

29. Dooley characterizes Derrida's view thus: "To have a passion for the impossible or the unconditional means that you desire what you know to be impossible—due to the claim which language and tradition make upon you—so as to prevent the conditional from becoming *too* conditional" (Caputo 2001, 143). There is something worrying about having a passion or desire for the impossible because the impossible, as Derrida describes it, is dangerous and undesirable. In the case of hospitality, as I discussed in chapter 5, it is an ideal of self-destruction.

30. Light (1997, 54) claims that Jankélévitch's view is that the imprescriptible is of a different and worse, order, than the unpardonable, but he does not provide textual evidence. Jankélévitch's view in *Forgiveness* (*Le Pardon*) (2005) is that forgiveness is an act of grace that is beyond the realm of justice. However, he argues that it is important that the wrongdoer feels remorse (2005, 157).

31. One exception that Derrida notes is the *right of grace,* where a sovereign can pardon a criminal, in other words, forgive them in a way that goes beyond the law (2001, 46).

32. Derrida's view here suggests that of Levinas, where our responsibility to the Other implies a forgiving response (2001, 194–219).

33. Because Derrida defines forgiveness as forgiving the unforgivable, Papastephanou appears to *assume* that he believes we should forgive the unforgivable (2003, 507). Oliver argues that we can only supply the constant interrogation of the search for pure forgiveness by taking into account the unconscious (2003). Borradori claims the conclusion "is that the meaning of forgiveness remains enigmatic" and ineffable (2003, 144).

34. See Ott's biography of Heidegger for a discussion of his involvement with the Nazis in the 1930s (1994). Levinas says there are two conditions for forgiveness: "the good will of the offended party and the full awareness of the offender," and goes on to say, "It is difficult to forgive Heidegger," perhaps implying that Heidegger did not show full awareness of what he had done (1990, 25).

35. There is a disturbing note in Jankélévitch's essay when he says that juridical norms such as human rights can be dismissed when considering capturing and punishing Eichmann (1996, 557).

36. Kaposy (2005) has an interesting discussion of the two separate threads of Derrida's arguments concerning forgiveness, those related to meaning and those related to ethics.

37. Derrida even says we may have to be "forgiven forgiveness" because of that assertion (Caputo 2001, 22).

38. The concept of a "duty to forgive" would imply that all evil acts should be forgiven. Derrida does speak of a "right to forgive" as "the king's right to grant clemency" (Caputo 2001, 32).

39. See Hegel (1977, §670, 407–408). Speight compares Hegel's view of forgiveness with Butler's (2005).

40. Papastephanou observes that "there is no compelling argument supporting the view that forgiveness conditional on repentance is inescapably or exclusively committed to this kind of strategicality and exchange" (2003, 515). On the contrary, the victim's struggle to decide whether to forgive is independent of any strategic maneuvers, as Derrida himself implies by separating forgiveness from justice and politics. I believe that government apologies are important, and that is the subject of the next chapter.

41. Potter notes that often the oppressed are expected to forgive their oppressors (2001, 145).

42. See my paper "Envy and Resentment' (2001) for a discussion of ethical forms of resentment.

43. Narayan notes that we may still have negative feelings toward the offender, perhaps because we had negative feelings toward them prior to the offense, or our trust may be lessened, even though we have forgiven (1197, 171). See Hampton and Murphy for the distinction between forgiveness and justification, excusing, and being merciful (1988, 506).

44. In *Totality and Infinity,* Levinas discusses apology as a "primordial phenomenon of reason" where one justifies oneself before the other by apology. He says further, "Apology does not blindly affirm the self, but already appeals to the other" (1996, 252). It is as if we must all apologize for our very existence. Derrida takes up this theme, stating we will find in "Kant, Hegel, Nietzsche, and Heidegger" as well as Levinas, a problematic of guilt for merely existing, a guilt that is of course unforgivable and unexpiable, although we may hope for forgiveness (Caputo 2001, 43). Such an idea of fundamental guilt again emphasizes the religious aspect of apology and forgiveness.

45. Ricoeur refers suggestively to a "duty to forget," described as a "duty to go beyond anger and hatred" (1999, 11). The duty to forget is important and not the same as an injunction to forgive. Nietzsche writes that one cannot forgive if one forgets, and that strong natures are likely to forget in this way (1994, 23–24).

46. It should be noted that Kant thought that being forgiving is a form of the duty of love (1996b, 578).
47. Potter says that the "background condition" for forgiveness is that "it must be compatible with self-respect, respect for others as moral agents, and respect for the moral community" (2001, 139).
48. Although Kant states that it is "a duty of human beings to be *forgiving*" (Kant 1996, 6: 461), his reasons for thinking so are very different from mine. While he believes this because we are all guilty and because punishment should not be carried out in hatred, I am not relying on the idea that we are all guilty, and my conception of forgiveness is not related to punishment. See Sussman (2005) for a Kantian account of forgiveness understood in terms of God's grace.
49. In Card's discussion of Wiesenthal's dilemma, she accepts his nonforgiveness of Karl, but not his failure to tell Karl's mother about his actions (2002, 185).
50. Quinn, citing psychological evidence, argues that trying to forgive can actually be harmful for the victim (2004, 226).
51. Alice MacLachlan suggests that we should be less ideal in our thinking about forgiveness and acknowledge that forgiveness and continuing resentment can sometimes be mixed together (2009, 199).
52. Although see Zahavi (2010) for a discussion of exceptions.
53. Bartky's analysis of shame can usefully be brought into relation with Iris Marion Young's description of women's inhibited bodily comportment in "Throwing Like a Girl" (2005).

Chapter 7. Apology, Forgiveness, and Reconciliation

1. For example, the Japanese government apologized to Korean women who were forced to become prostitutes for Japanese soldiers during World War II and for its wartime aggression, and the Canadian government has apologized to indigenous communities for separating families and for native residential schools.
2. For example, this is Malcolm Fraser's interpretation: "An apology does not imply guilt. It implies a recognition that an injustice occurred" (Healey, 2001b, 17). Ahmed argues that an expression of regret is insufficient precisely because it is a refusal of responsibility (2004, 119).
3. The *Report* details the policy and practice of child removal based on the oral evidence of 535 indigenous witnesses, as well as the written

testimony of hundreds of others. As well as acknowledgment and apology, the report recommended that reparation should be made and should follow the van Boven principles to also include "guarantees against repetition, measures of restitution, measures of rehabilitation, and monetary compensation" (Human Rights and Equal Opportunity Commission 1997, Recommendation 3).

4. The *Report* argues that child removal involved the intention to destroy the independent identity of aboriginal people as a group and therefore constitutes genocide (Human Rights and Equal Opportunity Commission 1997, part 4). The Genocide Convention cites "forcibly transferring children of [a] group to another group with the intention of destroying the group" as one of the acts "committed with intent to destroy, in whole or in part, a national, ethnical, racial or religious group, as such," which constitute genocide (Genocide Convention 1948, Art. II). The policy, combined with the common belief that "full blood" indigenous Australians would "die out" anyway, seems to constitute an intention not just to destroy part of the group but to eventually destroy the whole group.

5. The *Report* states that "[e]vidence to the Inquiry establishes clearly that the childhood experience of forcible removal and institutionalization or multiple fostering makes those people much more likely to suffer emotional distress than others in the Indigenous community." Those separated are twice as likely to have these psychological problems as those who had close contact with their family and Aboriginal culture (Human Rights and Equal Opportunity Commission 1997, part 3).

6. Jankélévitch also says, "If everyone is guilty, no one is guilty" (1996, 563). See Schaap (2001) for a detailed discussion of Arendt's reasons for rejecting a "politics of guilt." She is partly responding to Jaspers's argument for collective political guilt (2001, ix–x).

7. Such is the case with the U.S. apology to Native Peoples (McKinnon 2009).

8. "Sorry books," both paper and electronic, were set up in Australia as a form of reconciliation during the period of the refusal to apologize. Lisa Guenther also stresses the ambivalence of shame, in that it can be both debilitating and a provocation to become ethically and politically active (2011).

9. Howard writes, "I feel deep personal sorrow for those of my fellow Australians who suffered injustices under the practices of past generations towards indigenous people. Equally, I am sorry for the hurt and

trauma many people many people continue to feel as a consequence of those practices.... Australians of this generation should not be required to accept guilt and blame for past actions and policies over which they had no control" (Healey 2001b, 7). Paradoxically, he offered a personal apology, which by his own logic should have been inappropriate. If a government is not responsible for the action of previous governments, an individual is even less likely to be responsible for a previous government's actions or the past actions of individuals.

10. In relation to how states should deal with past evil, Derrida argues that the decision whether to bring all past crimes to light is a contextualist one. What is appropriate for France is not necessarily appropriate for Algeria, for example. In Australia, we have the possibility of bringing past crimes to light and facing the need to make reparations. There seems no reason not to do so in this case, for fear that the country will be torn apart. Indeed, much of the past has come to light without unrest or in fact too little disturbance as a result.

11. During his visit to Australia in 2000, Derrida was asked by a journalist whether he thought the government should apologize. He was reluctant to give advice, but when pressed, he acknowledged its importance: —Yes, the government should apologize because that would be a promise to improve the situation, to change a terrible situation" (2001b, 64).

12. Another interpretation is that Derrida's account of the logic of unconditional forgiveness necessitates the forgetting of the original crime. See Verdeja 2004, 32–33.

13. Derrida argues that justice and law are heterogenous and indissociable (2001c, 87), and that conditional and unconditional hospitality are also in the same relation (2001a, 22–23).

14. Janna Thompson argues that we should try to approach true forgiveness but not to get too close to it, and that it is not clear if Derrida is morally prescribing unconditional forgiveness (2010, 272).

15. Bennett takes repentance as essential to forgiveness: "Insisting on the need for repentance is part of taking morality, and the wrongdoer as a moral agent, seriously" (2003, 74).

16. See Schaap for a discussion of "being politically disposed to forgive" (2003, 83).

17. Verdeja observes the asymmetry between victim and perpetrator in forgiveness, which makes it very different to a gift that can be given in

turn (2004, 29–30). Similarly, Ricoeur regrets that peoples or collectives cannot forgive (2004, 476–77).

18. The political journalist Paul Kelly argues that aboriginal people should forgive because "there will never be sufficient compensation to render justice" (Healey 2001b, 29). This seems to be a pragmatic recommendation to "move on" rather than an ethical reason. See Pettigrove for an argument that sometimes it is ethical to forgive in the absence of an apology, if there are no ethical objections and the consequences are beneficial (2004, 187–204).

19. For example, Govier and Verwoerd argue that apologies imply a request for forgiveness (2002, 67).

20. My focus is on the former, but the latter, although odd, is also possible. A person could request forgiveness while at the same time refusing to make the proper acknowledgment of their responsibility by apologizing.

21. It should be noted that Derrida, Ricoeur, and Arendt do not give *definitions* of forgiveness as such but rather broad characterizations. Arendt argues for the importance of forgiveness in politics in *The Human Condition* (1998, 236–43). Although space constraints prevent me from discussing her position in detail, I respond to her main contentions. See Schaap (2003) for a defense and application of Arendt's views.

22. In his reading of Arendt on self-expression in the public sphere, Schaap describes how, for her, "[w]hat counts is not so much the intentions or motivations of the actors, but the significance of the speech or deed itself insofar as it illuminates the common affairs of the polity" (2001, 763).

23. Thomas says that we do not necessarily do wrong in not forgiving, even if the person is worthy of forgiveness. While he claims it would be morally decent and admirable to forgive, if we do not do wrong, we do not fail in our responsibilities (2003, 201–30).

24. Digeser notes that "[a]s citizens, we should not forgive a government before it attempts to fulfill the demands of justice" (1998, 708). Even Elshtain, a supporter of what she calls "political forgiveness," concedes that expectations of forgiveness such as those Tutu urged on individuals during the TRC are problematic (2003, 63).

25. Gill observes that an apology can also be a catalyst for social change by publicly supporting a different moral standard (2002, 119).

26. Howard stated that "[t]he Government has always stressed that practical measures to address the profound economic and social disadvantage of

many indigenous Australians are at the heart of a successful reconciliation process" (Healey 2001b, 8).

27. See also Tutu (1999, 217). Moon notes that it was actually very difficult
for victims and perpetrators to meet as the TRC did not facilitate that
process (2004, 6).

28. Even Tutu speaks of hope, rather than the expectation of forgiveness for
the perpetrators of apartheid and accepts the importance of an apology:
"The victim, we hope, would be moved to respond to an apology by
forgiving the culprit" (Tutu 1999, 219).

29. Paul Coe, of the Redfern Aboriginal Legal Service also says, "The
term 'reconciliation' is premised on the notion of a pre-existing state
of goodwill between the invaders and Aboriginal people" (quoted in
Moores 1995, 283). Similarly, in the case of South Africa, relations
between victim and perpetrator "were narrated by the TRC as if they
were emerging out of a violent rupture to a previously harmonious
relationship" (Moon 2004, 187).

30. Govier differs from me in putting a great emphasis on forgiveness by
victims: "As for the victim role, what is required is not to forget, but to
forgive" (2002, 157).

Bibliography

ABC online. 2005. Sentence increased for sex abuse. http://www.abc.net. au/pm.

Agamben, G. 1999. *Remnants of Auschwitz: The witness and the archive.* Trans. Daniel Heller-Roazen. New York: Zone Books.

———. 1995. We refugees. *Symposium* 49, no. 2: 114–19.

Ahmed, S. 2004. *The cultural politics of emotion.* Edinburgh: Edinburgh University Press.

Alcoff, L. M. 2006. *Visible identities: Race, gender, and the self.* Oxford: Oxford University Press.

———. 1998. Racism. In *A companion to feminist philosophy*, ed. Alison M. Jaggar and Iris Marion Young, 475–84. Oxford: Blackwell.

Alexander, N. 1999. Rending Kant's umbrella: Kofman's diagnosis of ethical law. In *Enigmas: Essays on Sarah Kofman,* ed. Penelope Deutscher and Kelly Oliver. Ithaca: Cornell University Press.

Allen, E. 1997. On the reading of riddles: Rethinking Du Boisian "double consciousness." In *Existence in black: An anthology of black existential philosophy,* ed. Lewis Gordon, 49–68. London: Routledge.

Améry, J. 1980. *At the mind's limits: Contemplations by a survivor on Auschwitz and its realities.* Trans. Sidney Rosenfeld and Stella P. Rosenfeld. Bloomington: Indiana University Press.

Arendt, H. 2003. *Responsibility and judgment.* Ed. Jerome Kohn. New York: Schocken Books.

———. 1998. *The human condition.* 2nd ed. Chicago: University of Chicago Press.

———. 1995. *Men in dark times.* New York: Harcourt Brace.

———. 1994a. *Essays in understanding: 1930–1954.* Ed. Jerome Kohn. New York: Harcourt Brace.

———. 1994b. *Eichmann in Jerusalem: A report on the banality of evil.* New York: Penguin.

———. 1992. *Hannah Arendt/Karl Jaspers correspondence 1926–1969.* Trans. Robert and Rita Kimber. Ed. Lotte Kohler and Hans Saner. San Diego: Harcourt Brace.

———. 1982. *Lectures on Kant's political philosophy.* Ed. Ronald Beiner. Chicago: University of Chicago Press.

———. 1978a. *The life of the mind.* San Diego: Harcourt Brace Jovanovich.

———. 1978b. *The Jew as pariah: Jewish identity and politics in the modern age.* Ed. R. Feldman. New York: Grove Press.

———. 1976. *The origins of totalitarianism.* San Diego: Harcourt Brace.

———. 1968a. *Between past and future: Eight exercises in political thought.* 2nd ed. New York: The Viking Press.

———. 1968b. *Men in dark times.* San Diego: Harcourt Brace.

———. 1948. The concentration camps. *Partisan Review* 15, no. 7: 743–63.

Aristotle. 1984. *The complete works of Aristotle.* Vol. 2. Ed. Jonathon Barnes. Princeton: Princeton University Press.

Armour, E. T. 1998. American/French intersections: The play of race/class/politics in Irigaray. In *Reinterpreting the political: Continental philosophy and political theory,* ed. Lenore Langsdorf and Stephen H. Watson with Karen A. Smith, 209–29. Albany: State University of New York Press.

Australian Declaration towards Reconciliation. http://www.Austlii.edu.au/au/other/IndigLRes/car/2000.

Australian Government. Apology to Australia's indigenous peoples. http://australia.gov.au/about-australia/our-country/our-people/apology-to-australias-indigenous-peoples. May 23, 2012.

Australian Parliament. 1999. *Parliamentary debates: New series.* Canberra: Govt. Print.

Australian Press Council. 2001. http://www.presscouncil.org.au/pcsite/new/gpr249.html.

Backström, J. 2007. *The fear of openness: An essay on friendship and the roots of morality.* Åbo: Åbo Akademi University Press.

Badiou, A. 2002. *Ethics: An essay on the understanding of evil.* Trans. Peter Hallward. London: Verso.

Baier, A. C. 1995. *Moral prejudices: Essays on ethics.* Cambridge: Harvard University Press.

Bailey, A. 1998. Locating traitorous identities: Toward a view of privilege-cognizant white character. *Hypatia: A Journal of Feminist Philosophy* 13, no. 3: 27–43.

Bankovsky, M. 2005. Derrida brings Levinas to Kant: The welcome, ethics, and cosmopolitical law. *Philosophy Today* 49, no. 2: 156–71.

Barkan, E., and A. Karn, eds. 2006. *Taking wrongs seriously: Apologies and reconciliation*. Stanford: Stanford University Press.

Baron, M. 1997. Love and respect in the doctrine of virtue. *The Southern Journal of Philosophy* XXXVI: 29–44.

Bartky, S. L. 1990. *Femininity and domination: Studies in the phenomenology of oppression*. London: Routledge.

Beardsworth, R. 1996. *Derrida and the political*. London: Routledge.

Beauvoir, S. de. 2004. *The philosophical writings of Simone de Beauvoir*. Ed. Margaret A. Simons with Marybeth Timmerman and Mary Beth Mader. Chicago: University of Illinois Press.

———. 1998. *America day by day*. Trans. Carol Cosman. London: Victor Gollancz.

———. 1997a. *The second sex*. Trans. H. M. Parshley. London: Vintage. Also translated by Constance Borde and Sheila Malovany-Chevallier. New York: Knopf, 2010.

———. 1997b. *The ethics of ambiguity*. Trans. Bernard Frechtman. Secaucus: Citadel.

Benhabib, S. 2002. Judgment and the moral foundations of politics in Hannah Arendt's thought. In *Situating the self: Gender, community, and postmodernism in contemporary ethics*, 121–47. Cambridge: Polity.

———, and N. Fraser, eds. 2004. *Pragmatism, critique, judgment: Essays for Richard Bernstein*. Cambridge: MIT Press.

Bennett, C. 2003. Is amnesty a collective act of forgiveness? *Contemporary Political Theory* 2: 67–76.

Bergoffen, Debra. 2003. Failed friendship, forgotten genealogies: Simone de Beauvoir and Luce Irigaray. *Bulletin de la Société Americaine de Philosophie de Langue Française* XIII, no. 1: 16–31.

Bernasconi, R. 2003. Will the real Kant please stand up: The challenge of Enlightenment racism to the study of the history of philosophy. *Radical Philosophy* 117: 13–22.

———, ed. 2001. *Race*. Oxford: Blackwell.

———. 1999. The third party: Levinas on the intersection of the ethical and the political. *Journal of the British Society for Phenomenology* 30, no. 1: 76–87.

Bernstein, R. J. 2002. *Radical evil: A philosophical interrogation.* Cambridge: Polity.

———. 1996. Did Hannah Arendt change her mind? From radical evil to the banality of evil. In *Hannah Arendt: Twenty years later,* ed. Larry May and Jerome Kohn, 127–46. Cambridge: MIT Press.

Bloodsworth, M. K. 1999. Embodiment and ambiguity: Luce Irigaray, sexual difference, and "race." *International Studies in Philosophy* 31, no. 2: 69–90.

Bobbio, N. 2000. *In praise of meekness: Essays on ethics and politics.* Trans. Teresa Chataway. Oxford: Polity.

Bohemia, Princess Elisabeth of, and R. Descartes. 2007. *The correspondence between Elisabeth of Bohemia and René Descartes.* Trans. and ed. Lisa Shapiro. Chicago: University of Chicago Press.

Bohman, J., and Lutz-Bachmann, M., eds. 1997. *Perpetual peace: Essays on Kant's cosmopolitan ideal.* Cambridge: MIT Press.

Bono. 2010. In Ireland, Tuesday's Grace. *The New York Times,* June 19.

Bordo, S. 1990. Feminism, postmodernism, and gender-scepticism. In *Feminism/Postmodernism,* ed. Linda J. Nicholson, 133–56. New York: Routledge.

Borradori, G. 2003. *Philosophy in a time of terror: Dialogues with Jürgen Habermas and Jacques Derrida.* Chicago: University of Chicago Press.

Boss, J. 1997. Throwing pearls to the swine: Women, forgiveness, and the unrepentant abuser. In *Philosophical Perspectives on Power and Domination,* ed. Laura Duhan Kaplan and Laurence F. Bove, 235–47. Amsterdam: Rodopi.

Brownback, S. 2008. Brownback applauds passage of Native American Apology Amendment to Indian Health Bill. http://brownback. senate. gov/pressapp.recotd.cfm?id=293090.

Brudholm, T. 2008. *Resentment's virtue: Jean Améry and the refusal to forgive,* Philadelphia: Temple University Press.

Butler, J. 1993. *Bodies that matter: On the discursive limits of "sex."* London: Routledge.

———. 1992. Contingent foundations: Feminism and the question of "postmodernism." In *Feminists Theorize the Political,* ed. Judith Butler and Joan W. Scott, 3–21. New York: Routledge.

———. 1990. *Gender trouble: Feminism and the subversion of identity.* London: Routledge.

Cagle, R. 2005. Becoming a virtuous agent: Kant and the cultivation of feelings and emotions. *Kant-Studien* 96: 452–67.

Caldwell, A. 1997. Fairy tales for politics: Unworking Derrida through Irigaray. *Philosophy Today* 41, no. 1: 40–50.

Campion-Smith, B. 2008. Harper officially apologizes for native residential schools. *TheStar.Com.* June 11.

Caputo, J. 1997. *Deconstruction in a nutshell: A conversation with Jacques Derrida.* New York: Fordham University Press.

———, M. Dooley, and M. J. Scanlon, eds. 2001. *Questioning God.* Bloomington: Indiana University Press.

Card, C. 2010. *Confronting evils: Terrorism, torture, genocide.* Cambridge: Cambridge University Press.

———. 2002. *The atrocity paradigm: A theory of evil.* Oxford: Oxford University Press.

———. 1999. *On feminist ethics and politics.* Lawrence: University of Kansas Press.

———, ed. 2003. *The Cambridge companion to Simone de Beauvoir.* Cambridge: Cambridge University Press.

Cash, M. 2002. Distancing Kantian ethics and politics from Kant's views on women. *Minerva—An Internet Journal of Philosophy* 6: 1–21.

Castle, S. 2001. Europe's apology for slavery rules out reparations. *The Independent.* September 8.

Celan, P. 1988. Todtnauberg. In *Poems of Paul Celan,* trans. Michael Hamburger, 292–93. New York: Persea Books.

Chandler, D. 2003. The cosmopolitan paradox: Response to Robbins. *Radical Philosophy* 118: 25–30.

Chanter, T. 1995. *Ethics of Eros: Irigaray's rewriting of the philosophers.* New York: Routledge.

Cheah, P., and E. Grosz. 1998. The future of sexual difference: An interview with Judith Butler and Drucilla Cornell. *Diacritics* 28, no. 1: 19–42.

———, and B. Robbins, eds. 1998. *Cosmopolitics: Thinking and feeling beyond the nation.* Minneapolis: University of Minnesota Press.

Cicero, M. T. 1913. *De officiis.* Trans. Walter Miller. London: William Heinemann.

Cohoon, C. 2011. Coming together: The six modes of Irigaray eros. *Hypatia: A Journal of Feminist Philosophy* 26, no. 3: 478–96.

Cordner, C. 2002. *Ethical encounter: The depth of moral meaning.* Basingstoke: Palgrave.

Covell, C. 1998. *Kant and the law of peace: A study in the philosophy of international law and international relations.* Basingstoke: MacMillan.

Critchley, S. 2000. Remarks on Derrida and Habermas. *Constellations* 7, no. 4: 455–65.

———. 1999a. *The ethics of deconstruction: Derrida and Levinas.* 2nd ed. West Lafayette: Purdue University Press.

———. 1999b. *Ethics, politics, and subjectivity: Essays on Derrida, Levinas, and contemporary French thought.* London: Verso.

Custer, O. 1998. Exercising freedom: Kant and Foucault. *Philosophy Today* 42 Supp: 137–47.

Daly, M. 1973. *Beyond God the father: Toward a philosophy of women's liberation.* Boston: Beacon Press.

David, A. 1997. Le Dœuff and Irigaray on Descartes. *Philosophy Today* 41, no. 3/4: 367–82.

Derrida, J. 2005. *Rogues: Two essays on reason.* Trans. Pascale-Anne Brault and Michael Naas. Stanford: Stanford University Press.

———. 2002a. Ethics and politics today. In *Negotiations: Interventions and interviews, 1971–2001,* trans. Elizabeth Rottenberg, 295–314. Stanford: Stanford University Press.

———. 2002b. *Ethics, institutions, and the right to philosophy.* Trans. Peter Pericles Trifonas. Lanham, MD: Rowman and Littlefield.

———. 2001a. *On cosmopolitanism and forgiveness.* Trans. Mark Dooley and Michael Hughes. London: Routledge.

———. 2001b. *Writing and difference.* Trans. Alan Bass. London: Routledge.

———. 2001c. Justice, colonisation, translation. In *Deconstruction engaged: The Sydney seminars,* ed. Paul Patton and Terry Smith, 81–91. Sydney: Power Publications.

———. 2000. *Of hospitality: Anne Dufourmantelle invites Jacques Derrida to respond.* Trans. Rachel Bowlby. Stanford: Stanford University Press.

———. 1999. *Adieu to Emmanuel Levinas.* 1997. Trans. Pascale-Anne Brault and Michael Naas. Stanford: Stanford University Press.

———. 1997. *The politics of friendship.* Trans. George Collins. London: Verso.

———. 1992a. Force of Law: The "Mystical Foundation of Authority." Trans. Mary Quaintance. In *Deconstruction and the possibility of justice,* ed. Drucilla Cornell, Michel Rosenfeld, and David Gray Carlson, 3–67. London: Routledge.

———. 1992b. *Given time: 1. Counterfeit money.* Trans. Peggy Kamuf. Chicago: The University of Chicago Press.

———. 1988. *Limited inc.* Ed. Gerald Graff. Evanston: Northwestern University Press.

———. 1976. *Of grammatology.* Trans. Gayatri Chakravorty Spivak. Baltimore: The John Hopkins University Press.

Descartes, R. 1984–1991. *The philosophical writings of Descartes.* Vols. 1–3. Trans. John Cottingham, Robert Stoothoff, Dugald Murdoch, and Anthony Kenny. Cambridge: Cambridge University Press.

———. 1989. *The passions of the soul.* Trans. Stephen H. Voss. Indianapolis: Hackett.

Deutscher, P. 2008. *The philosophy of Simone de Beauvoir: Ambiguity, conversion, resistance.* Cambridge: Cambridge University Press.

———. 2003. Already lamenting: Deconstruction, immigration, colonialism. *Studies in Practical Philosophy* 3, no. 1: 4–19.

———. 2002. *A politics of impossible difference: The later work of Luce Irigaray.* Ithaca: Cornell University Press.

———. 1998. Mourning the other, cultural cannibalism, and the politics of friendship (Jacques Derrida and Luce Irigaray). *differences: a journal of feminist cultural studies* 10, no. 3: 159–84.

Digeser, P. 1998. Forgiveness and politics: Dirty hands and imperfect procedures. *Political Theory* 16, no. 5: 700–24.

Dikeç, M. 2002. Pera peras poros: Longings for spaces of hospitality. *Theory, Culture and Society* 19, no. 1–2: 227–47.

Dillon, R. S. 2001. Self-forgiveness and self-respect. *Ethics* 112, no. 1: 53–85.

———. 1997. Self-respect: Moral, emotional, political. *Ethics* 107, no. 2: 226–49.

Dilthey, W. 1976. *Selected writings.* Ed. and trans. H. P. Rickman. Cambridge: Cambridge University Press.

Diprose, R. 2002. *Corporeal generosity: On giving with Nietzsche, Merleau-Ponty, and Levinas.* Albany: State University of New York Press.

Do, T. 2002. Statistics: Refugees and Australia's contribution. In *Refugees and the myth of the borderless world,* 41–48. Canberra: National Library of Australia.

Dostal, R. J. 1984. Judging human action: Arendt's appropriation of Kant. *Review of Metaphysics* 37: 725–55.

Du Bois, W. E. B. 1986. *W. E. B. Du Bois: Writings.* New York: The Library of America.

Dummett, M. 2001. *On immigration and refugees.* London: Routledge.

Du Toit. 2009. *A philosophical investigation of rape: The making and unmaking of the feminine self.* London: Routledge.

Editorial. 2010. Courage in Arizona. *The New York Times,* May 19.

Elshtain, J. B. 2003. Politics and forgiveness. In *Burying the past: Making peace and doing justice after civil conflict,* ed. Nigel Biggar, 45–64. Washington: Georgetown University Press.

Engels, F. 1968. The origin of the family, private property, and the state. In *Karl Marx and Frederick Engels: Selected Works,* 455–593. London: Lawrence and Wishart.

Fanon, F. 1967. *Black skin, white masks.* New York: Grove Press.

Feder, E. K., M. C. Rawlinson, and E. Zakin, eds. 1997. *Derrida and feminism: Recasting the question of woman.* London: Routledge.

Flikschuh, K. 2000. *Kant and modern political philosophy.* Cambridge: Cambridge University Press.

Formosa, P. 2007. Understanding evil acts. *Human Studies* 30, no. 2: 57–77.

Foucault, M. 1997. *Ethics: Subjectivity and truth.* Trans. Robert Hurley and others. In *Essential Works of Foucault 1954–1984,* ed. Paul Rabinow. Vol. 1. London: Penguin.

Fraser, N. 1997. *Justice interruptus: Critical reflections on the "postsocialist" condition.* New York: Routledge.

Freedman, J. 2008. Women's right to asylum: Protecting the rights of female asylum-seekers in Europe? *Human Rights Review* 9: 413–33.

Freud, S. 1964. Femininity. In *The standard edition of the complete psychological works of Sigmund Freud.* Vol. 22. Trans. James Strachey. London: Hogarth.

———. 1961. Some psychical consequences of the anatomical distinction between the sexes. In *The standard edition of the complete psychological works of Sigmund Freud.* Vol. 19. Trans. James Strachey, 243–58. London: Hogarth.

Frierson, P. R. 2002. Learning to love: From egoism to generosity in Descartes. *Journal of the History of Philosophy* 40, no. 3: 313–38.

Frye, M. 2001. White woman feminist 1983–1992. In *Race and Racism,* ed. Bernard Boxhill, 83–100. Oxford: Oxford University Press.

———. 1983. *The politics of reality: Essays in feminist theory.* Freedom: Crossing Press.

Fuss, D. 1989. *Essentially speaking: Feminism, nature, and difference.* New York: Routledge.

Gaita, R. 2000. *A common humanity: Thinking about love and truth and justice.* Melbourne: Text Publishing.

———. 1991. *Good and evil: An absolute conception.* London: Macmillan.

Garrard, E. 2002. Forgiveness and the Holocaust. *Ethical theory and Moral Practice* 5: 147–75.

Geddes, J. L. 2003. Banal evil and useless knowledge: Hannah Arendt and Charlotte Delbo on evil after the Holocaust. *Hypatia: A Journal of Feminist Philosophy* 18, no. 1: 104–15.

Gill, K. A. 2002. The moral functions of an apology. In *Injustice and Rectification,* ed. Rodney C. Roberts, 111–23. New York: Peter Lang.

Gilligan, C. 1993. *In a different voice: Psychological theory and women's development.* 2nd ed. Cambridge: Harvard University Press.

Glover, J. 2001. *Humanity: A moral history of the twentieth century.* London: Pimlico.

Golding, M. P. 1984–85. Forgiveness and regret. *The Philosophical Forum* 16: 121–37.

Gourevitch, P. 1998. *We wish to inform you that tomorrow we will be killed with our families: Stories from Rwanda.* New York: Farrar Straus and Giroux.

Govier, T. 2002. *Forgiveness and revenge.* London: Routledge.

———, and W. Verwoerd. 2002. The promise and pitfalls of apology. *Journal of Social Philosophy* 33: 67–82.

Grosz, E. 1994a. The hetero and the homo: The sexual ethics of Luce Irigaray. In *Engaging with Irigaray: Feminist philosophy and modern European thought,* ed. Carolyn Burke, Naomi Schor, and Margaret Whitford, 335–50. New York: Columbia University Press.

———. 1994b. *Volatile bodies: Toward a corporeal feminism.* Sydney: Allen and Unwin.

Guenther, L. 2011. Shame and the temporality of social life. *Continental Philosophy Review* 44, no. 1: 23–39.

Guyer, P. 2010. Moral feelings in the *Metaphysics of Morals*. In *Kant's Metaphysics of Morals: A critical guide,* ed. Lara Denis, 130–51. Cambridge: Cambridge University Press.

Hampton, J., and J. Murphy. 1988. *Forgiveness and mercy.* Cambridge: Cambridge University Press.

Haslanger, S. 2005. You mixed? Racial identity without racial biology. In *Adoption matters: Philosophical and feminist essays,* ed. Charlotte Witt and Sally Haslanger, 265–89. Ithaca: Cornell University Press.

———. 2000. Gender and race: (What) are they? (What) do we want them to be? *Nous* 34, no. 1: 31–55.

Hayward, J. 2011. Harper tours migrant ship, vows crackdown on human smuggling. *The Canadian Press,* February 21.

Healey, J., ed. 2001a. *Issues in society: The stolen generations* 156. Sydney: The Spinney Press.

————. 2001b. *Issues in society: Towards reconciliation* 140. Sydney: The Spinney Press.

Hegel, G. W. F. 1977. *Phenomenology of spirit.* Trans. A. V. Miller. Oxford: Oxford University Press.

————. 1970. *On Christianity: Early theological writings.* Trans. T. M. Knox. Gloucester: Peter Smith.

Heinämaa, S. 2003. *Toward a phenomenology of sexual difference: Husserl, Merleau-Ponty, Beauvoir.* Lanham: Rowman and Littlefield.

————. 1999. Wonder and (sexual difference): Cartesian radicalism in phenomenological thinking. *Acta Philosophica Fennica* 64: 277–96.

Hepburn, R. W. 1984. Wonder. In *"Wonder" and other essays: Eight studies in aesthetics and neighbouring fields,* 131–54. Edinburgh: Edinburgh University Press.

Hodge, J. 2003. Feminism and utopia: Irigaray reading Kant. *Women: a cultural review* 14, no. 2: 195–209.

hooks, b. 1987. Feminism: A movement to end sexist oppression. In *Feminism and equality,* ed. Anne Phillips, 62–76. Oxford: Blackwell.

Human Rights and Equal Opportunity Commission. 1997. *Report of the national inquiry into the separation of aboriginal and Torres Strait islander children from their families (Bringing them home report).*

Human Rights First. 2009. *Background briefing note: The detention of asylum seekers in the United States: Arbitrary under the ICCPR.* http://www.humanrightsfirst.org/asylum/asylum_03.htm.

Huntington, P. 1997. Fragmentation, race, and gender: Building solidarity in the postmodern era. In *Existence in black: An anthology of black existential philosophy,* ed. Lewis R. Gordon, 185–202. London: Routledge.

Hutchings, K. 1996. *Kant, critique, and politics.* London: Routledge.

Ignatieff, M. 1996. Articles of faith. *Index on Censorship* 5: 110–22.

Irigaray, L. 2008a. *Sharing the world.* London: Continuum.

————. 2008b. *Conversations.* London: Continuum.

————. 2002a. *Between east and west: From singularity to community.* Trans. Stephen Pluháček. New York: Columbia University Press.

————. 2002b. *The way of love.* Trans. Heidi Bostic and Stephen Pluháček. London: Continuum.

————. 2000a. *Democracy begins between two.* Trans. Kirsteen Anderson. London: Athlone Press.

————. 2000b. *To be two.* Trans. Monique M. Rhodes and Marco F. Cocito-Monoc. London: Athlone Press.

————. 2000c. *Why different? A culture of two subjects: Interviews with Luce*

Irigaray. Ed. Luce Irigaray and Sylvère Lotringer. Trans. Camille Collins. New York: Semiotext (e).

———. 1998. The feminine mystique. Interview by Jennifer Wallace. *The Times*, 18 September.

———. 1996. *I love to you: Sketch of a possible felicity in history*. Trans. Alison Martin. New York: Routledge.

———. 1995a. Je—Luce Irigaray: A meeting with Luce Irigaray. Interview by Elizabeth Hirsch and Gary A. Olson. *Hypatia* 10, no. 2: 93–115.

———. 1995b. The question of the other. *Yale French Studies* 87: 7–19.

———. 1993a. *An ethics of sexual difference*. Trans. Carolyn Burke and Gillian C. Gill. Ithaca: Cornell University Press.

———. 1993b. *Je, tu, nous: Toward a culture of difference*. Trans. Alison Martin. London: Routledge.

———. 1993c. *Sexes and genealogies*. Trans. Gillian C. Gill. New York: Columbia University Press.

———. 1992. *Elemental passions*. Trans. Joanne Collie and Judith Still. New York: Routledge.

———. 1991. *The Irigaray reader*. Ed. Margaret Whitford. Oxford: Blackwell.

———. 1985a. *Speculum of the other woman*. Trans. Gillian C. Gill. Ithaca: Cornell University Press.

———. 1985b. *This sex which is not one*. Trans. Catherine Porter with Carolyn Burke. Ithaca: Cornell University Press.

Isaac, J. 1996. A new guarantee on earth: Hannah Arendt on human dignity and the politics of human rights. *American Political Science Review* 90, no. 1: 61–74.

Jaggar, A. 1979. On sexual equality. In *Philosophy and women*, ed. Sharon Bishop and Marjorie Weinzweig, 77–87. Belmont, CA: Wadsworth.

Jankélévitch, V. 1996. Should we pardon them? *Critical Inquiry* 22: 552–72.

———. 1967. *Le pardon*. Paris: Aubier-Montaigne. *Forgiveness*. Trans. Andrew Kelley. Chicago: University of Chicago Press, 2005.

Jaspers, K. 2001. *The question of German guilt*. Trans. E. B. Ashton. New York: Fordham University Press.

Jones, R. 2011. *Irigaray*. Cambridge: Polity.

Joris, P. 1988. *Celan/ Heidegger: Translation at the mountain of death*. http:// wings.buffalo.edu/epc/authors/joris/t.

Joy, M. 2000. Love and the labour of the negative: Irigaray and Hegel. In *Resistance, flight, creation: Feminist enactments of French philosophy*, ed. Dorothea Olkowski, 113–123. Ithaca: Cornell University Press.

Joyce, R. 1999. Apologizing. *Public Affairs Quarterly* 13: 159–73.

Kant, I. 2000. *Critique of the power of judgement.* Trans. Paul Guyer. Cambridge: Cambridge University Press.

———. 1996a. *Practical philosophy.* Trans. and ed. Mary J. Gregor. Cambridge: Cambridge University Press.

———. 1996b. *Lectures on ethics.* Trans. Peter Heath. Cambridge: Cambridge University Press.

———. 1996c. *Religion and rational theology.* Trans. and ed. Allen W. Wood and George di Giovanni. Cambridge: Cambridge University Press.

———. 1991. *Political writings.* Trans. H. B. Nisbet. Ed. H. S. Reiss. Cambridge: Cambridge University Press.

———. 1986. *Critique of pure reason.* Trans. Norman Kemp Smith. London: Macmillan.

———. 1957. *Perpetual peace.* Ed. Lewis White Beck. New York: The Liberal Arts Press.

Kaposi, D. 2010. Descartes on the excellent use of *admiration.* In *Philosophy begins in wonder: An introduction to early modern philosophy, theology, and science,* ed. Michael Funk Deckard and Péter Losonczi, 107–18. Eugene: Pickwick.

Kaposy, C. 2005. "Analytic" reading, "continental" text: The case of Derrida's "On Forgiveness." *International Journal of Philosophical Studies* 13, no. 2: 203–26.

Kateb, G. 2001. The judgment of Arendt. In *Judgment, imagination, and politics: Themes from Kant and Arendt,* ed. Ronald Beiner and Jennifer Nedelsky, 121–38. Lanham, MD: Rowman and Littlefield.

Katz, C. E. 2001. For love is as strong as death. *Philosophy Today* 45, no. 5: 124–32.

Kearney, R. 2003. *Strangers, gods, and monsters: Interpreting otherness.* London: Routledge.

———, and M. Dooley. 1999. *Questioning ethics: Contemporary debates in philosophy.* London: Routledge.

Kofman, S. 1982. The economy of respect: Kant and respect for women. *Social Research* 49: 383–404.

Kort, L. F. 1975. What is an apology? *Philosophy Research Archives* 1, no. 1055: 78–87.

La Caze, M. 2002. *The analytic imaginary.* Ithaca: Cornell University Press.

———. 2001. Envy and resentment. *Philosophical Explorations* IV, no. 1: 31–45.

———. 2000. Sublimation, love, and creativity. In *The analytic Freud: Philosophy and psychoanalysis,* ed. Michael Levine, 261–76. London: Routledge.

————. 1994. Simone de Beauvoir and female bodies. *Australian Feminist Studies* 20: 91–105.

————, D. Cox, and M. Levine. 2003. *Integrity and the fragile self.* Aldershot: Ashgate.

Lara, M. P. 2001. *Rethinking evil: Contemporary perspectives.* Berkeley: University of California Press.

Le Dœuff, M. 2003. *The sex of knowing.* Trans. Kathryn Hamer and Lorraine Code. London: Routledge.

————. 2002. Bringing us into twenty-first century feminism, with joy and wit. Interview with Pamela Anderson and Meena Dhanda. *Women's Philosophy Review* 30: 8–39.

————. 1993. On some philosophical pacts. *The Journal of the Institute of Romance Studies* 2: 395–407.

————. 1991. *Hipparchia's choice: An essay concerning women, philosophy, etc.* Trans. Trista Selous. Oxford: Blackwell.

————. 1989. *The philosophical imaginary.* Trans. Colin Gordon. London: Athlone.

Levi, P. 2000. *The periodic table.* Trans. Raymond Rosenthal. London: Penguin.

Levinas, E. 2001. *Totality and infinity: An essay on exteriority.* Trans. Alphonso Lingis. Pittsburgh: Duquesne University Press.

————. 1994. *Beyond the verse: Talmudic readings and lectures.* Trans. Gary D. Mole. London: Athlone.

————. 1990. *Nine Talmudic readings.* Trans. Annette Aronowicz. Bloomington: Indiana University Press.

Levine, M. P. and T. Pataki, eds. 2004. *Racism in mind.* Ithaca: Cornell University Press.

Light, S. 1997. Vladimir Jankélévitch and the *imprescriptible. International Studies in Philosophy* 29, no. 4: 51–57.

Lloyd, G. 2000. No one's land: Australia and the philosophical imagination. *Hypatia* 15, no. 2: 26–39.

Lu, C. 2000. The one and many faces of cosmopolitanism. *The Journal of Political Philosophy* 8, no. 2: 244–67.

Lucashenko, M. 1994. No other truth: Aboriginal women and Australian feminism. *Social Alternatives* 12, no. 4: 21–24.

MacLachlan, A. 2009. Practicing imperfect forgiveness. In *Feminist ethics and social and political philosophy: Theorizing the non-ideal,* 185–203. New York: Springer.

Manne, R. 2001. In denial: The stolen generations and the right. *Quarterly Essay* No. 1.

Mares, P. 2002. *Borderline*. Sydney: University of New South Wales Press.

Marr, D., and M. Wilkinson. 2003. *Dark victory*. Sydney: Allen and Unwin.

Marshall, J. 1998. *Descartes's moral theory*. Ithaca: Cornell University Press.

Martin, A. 2004. A European initiative: Irigaray, Marx, and citizenship. *Hypatia* 19, no. 3: 20–37.

Marx, K. 1967. *Capital*. Trans. Eden and Cedar Paul. London: Dent.

Mason, T., ed. 2006. *Forensic psychiatry: Influences of evil*. Totowa, NJ: Humana.

McDonald, D. N. 1998. Moving beyond the face through eros: Lévinas and Irigaray's treatment of the woman as alterity. *Philosophy Today* 42 (Supp.): 71–76.

McKinnon, J. D. 2009. U.S. offers an official apology to Native Americans. *The Wall Street Journal*, December 22.

Mertens, T. 1996. Cosmopolitanism and citizenship: Kant against Habermas. *European Journal of Philosophy*, 4, 3: 328–47.

Michalson, G. E. 1990. *Fallen freedom: Kant on radical evil and moral regeneration*. Cambridge: Cambridge University Press.

Mill, J. S. 1970. The subjection of women. In *Essays on Sex Equality*, ed. Alice Rossi, 123–242. Chicago: University of Chicago Press.

Millet, K. 1969. *Sexual politics*. London: Rupert Hart-Davis.

Moi, T. 1999. *What is a woman? And other essays*. Oxford: Oxford University Press.

———. 1994. *Simone de Beauvoir: The making of an intellectual woman*. Oxford: Blackwell.

Montaigne, M. de. 1976. *The complete essays of Montaigne*. Trans. Donald M. Frame. Stanford: Stanford University Press.

Moon, C. 2004. Prelapsarian state: Forgiveness and reconciliation in transitional justice. *International Journal for the Semiotics of Law* 17: 185–97.

Moores, I. 1995. *Voices of aboriginal Australia: Past, present, future*. Springwood: Butterfly Books.

Morgan, V. G. 1994. *Foundations of Cartesian ethics*. New Jersey: Humanities Press.

Murphy, J. G. 1995. Kant on theory and practice. In *Theory and practice*, ed. Ian Shapiro and Judith Wagner DeCew, 47–78. New York: New York University Press.

Nancy, J-L. 1993. *The experience of freedom*. Trans. Bridget McDonald. Stanford: Stanford University Press.

Narayan, U. 1997. Forgiveness, moral reassessment, and reconciliation. In *Explorations of value*, ed. Thomas Magnell, 169–78. Amsterdam: Rodopi.

Nietzsche, F. 1994. *On the genealogy of morality*. Ed. Keith Ansell-Pearson. Trans. Carol. Diethe. Cambridge: Cambridge University Press.

———. 1982. *Daybreak*. Trans. R. J. Hollingdale. Cambridge: Cambridge University Press.

Nobles, M. 2008. *The politics of official apologies*. Cambridge: Cambridge University Press.

Nye, A. 1999. *The princess and the philosopher: Letters of Elisabeth of the Palatine to René Descartes*. Lanham, MD: Rowman and Littlefield.

Okin, S. M. 1998. Feminism and political theory. In *Philosophy in a feminist voice: Critiques and reconstructions*, ed. Janet A. Kourany, 116–44. Princeton: Princeton University Press.

Oliver, K. 2007. Vision, recognition, and a passion for the elements. In *Returning to Irigaray: Feminist philosophy, politics, and the question of unity*, ed. Maria C. Cimitile and Elaine P. Miller, 121–35. Albany: State University of New York Press.

———. 2003. Forgiveness and subjectivity. *Philosophy Today* 47, no. 3: 280–87.

———. 2001. *Witnessing: Beyond recognition*. Minneapolis: University of Minnesota Press.

Ott, H. 1994. *Martin Heidegger: A political life*. Trans. Allan Blunden. London: Fontana.

Papastephanou, M. 2003. Forgiving and requesting forgiveness. *Journal of Philosophy of Education* 37, no. 3: 503–524.

———. 2002. Kant's cosmopolitanism and human history. *History of the Human Sciences* 15, no. 1: 17–37.

Perpich, D. 1998. A singular justice: Ethics and politics between Levinas and Derrida. *Philosophy Today* 42 (Supp): 59–70.

Pettigrove, G. 2004. Unapologetic forgiveness. *American Philosophical Quarterly* 41: 187–204.

Pettman, J. 1992. *Living in the margins: Racism, sexism, and feminism in Australia*. Sydney: Allen and Unwin.

Phelps, J. et al. 2009. *Detained lives: The real cost of indefinite immigration detention*. London: London Detainee Support Group.

Plato. 1999. *The collected dialogues*. Ed. Edith Hamilton and Huntington Cairns. Princeton: Bollingen.

Potter, N. 2001. "Is refusing to forgive a vice? In *Feminists Doing Ethics*, ed. Peggy DesAutels and Joanne Waugh, 135–50. Lanham, MD: Rowman and Littlefield.

Potter, N. T. 2002. Kant and capital punishment today. *The Journal of Value Inquiry* 36, no. 2–3: 267–82.

Quinn, C. 2004. On the virtue of not forgiving: When withholding forgiveness is morally praiseworthy. *International Journal of Applied Philosophy* 18, no. 2: 219–29.

Rawls, J. 1975. Fairness to goodness. *Philosophical Review* 84, no. 4: 536–54.

Rich, A. 1976. *Of woman born: Motherhood as experience and institution.* London: Virago.

Ricoeur, P. 2004. *Memory, history, forgetting.* Trans. Kathleen Blamey and David Pellauer. Chicago: University of Chicago Press.

———. 1999. Memory and forgetting. In *Questioning ethics: Contemporary debates in philosophy,* ed. Richard Kearney and Mark Dooley, 5–11. London: Routledge.

Robbins, B. 2002. What's left of cosmopolitanism? *Radical Philosophy* 116: 30–37.

Rorty, A. O. 1992. Descartes on thinking with the body. In *The Cambridge companion to Descartes,* ed. John Cottingham, 371–392. Cambridge: Cambridge University Press.

Rothfield, P., ed. 2003. *Kant after Derrida.* Manchester: Clinamen.

Rubenstein, M-J. 2011. *Strange wonder: The closure of metaphysics and the opening of awe.* New York: Columbia University Press.

Sandford, S. 2001. Feminism against "the feminine." *Radical Philosophy* 105: 6–14.

Sartre, J-P. 2003. *Being and nothingness: An essay on phenomenological ontology.* Trans. Hazel E. Barnes. London: Routledge. *L'Être et le néant.* Paris: Gallimard, 1943.

———. 1999. *Anti-Semite and Jew.* Trans. George J. Becker. New York: Schocken Books.

Savage, C. 2009. U.S. will settle Indian lawsuit for $3.4 billion. *New York Times,* December 9.

Scarth, F. 2004. *The other within: Ethics, politics, and the body in Simone de Beauvoir.* Lanham, MD: Rowman and Littlefield.

Schaap, A. 2003. Political Grounds for Forgiveness. *Contemporary Political Theory* 2: 77–87.

———. 2001. Guilty subjects and political responsibility: Arendt, Jaspers, and the resonance of the "German question" in politics of reconciliation. *Political Studies* 49: 749–66.

Scholl, I. 1983. *The white rose: Munich 1942–1943.* Hanover, NH: Wesleyan University Press.

Schor, N. 1995. *Bad objects: Essays popular and unpopular.* Durham: Duke University Press.

Schwirtz, M. 2010. Putin marks Soviet massacre of Polish officers. *The New York Times,* April 7.

Sereny, G. 1995. *Albert Speer: His battle with truth.* London: Picador.

———. 1974. *Into that darkness: From mercy killing to mass murder.* London: Deutsch.

Simons, M. 1999. Richard Wright, Simone de Beauvoir, and *The Second Sex.* In *Beauvoir and* The Second Sex*: Feminism, race, and the origins of existentialism,* 167–84. Lanham, MD: Rowman and Littlefield.

Sparrow, R. 2000. History and collective responsibility. *Australasian Journal of Philosophy* 78, no. 3: 346–59.

Speight, C. A. 2005. Butler and Hegel on forgiveness and agency. *The Southern Journal of Philosophy* XLIII: 299–316.

Spelman, E. 1988. *Inessential woman: Problems of exclusion in feminist thought.* Boston: Beacon Press.

Stone, A. 2006. *Luce Irigaray and the philosophy of sexual difference.* Cambridge: Cambridge University Press.

Sussman, D. 2005. Kantian forgiveness. *Kant-Studien* 96: 85–107.

Svendsen, L. 2010. *A philosophy of evil.* London: Dalkey Archive Press.

Thomas, L. 2003. Forgiving the unforgivable? In *Moral philosophy and the Holocaust,* ed. Eve Garrard and Geoffrey Scarre, 201–30. Aldershot: Ashgate.

Thompson, J. 2010. Is apology a sorry affair? Derrida and the moral force of the impossible. *The Philosophical Forum* 41, no. 3: 259–74.

———. 2000. Historical obligations. *Australasian Journal of Philosophy* 78, no. 3: 334–45.

Thompson, K. 2009. Senate backs apology for slavery. *Washington Post,* June 19.

Tobin, J. 2010. Australia tops miser ranking on refugees. *The Age.* August 6.

Tutu, D. 1999. *No future without forgiveness.* London: Rider.

UNHCR. 2001. The international protection of refugees: Interpreting Article 1 of the 1951 Convention relating to the status of refugees. *Refugee Survey Quarterly* 20, no. 3: 77–104.

United Nations. 1967. Protocol relating to the status of refugees of 1967. *Treaty Series,* Vol. 606, No. 8791.

———. 1951. Convention relating to status of refugees of 1951. *Treaty Series.* Vol. 189, No. 2545.

———. 1948. Convention on the prevention and punishment of the crime of genocide. Article I, 78, U.N.T.S. 229. December 9.

United Nations General Assembly. 1948. Universal declaration of human rights.

Van Roermund, B. 2001. Rubbing off and rubbing on: The grammar of reconciliation. In *Lethe's law: Justice, law, and ethics in reconciliation,* ed. Emilios Christodoulidis and Scott Veitch, 153–90. Oxford: Hart Publishing.

Velleman, J. D. 1999. Love as a moral emotion. *Ethics* 109: 338–71.

Venn, C. 2002. Altered states: Post-Enlightenment cosmopolitanism and transmodern socialities. *Theory, Culture & Society* 19, no. 1: 65–80.

Verdeja, E. 2004. Derrida and the impossibility of forgiveness. *Contemporary Political Theory* 3: 23–47.

Villa, D., ed. 2000. *The Cambridge companion to Hannah Arendt.* Cambridge: Cambridge University Press.

White, R. 1999. Elemental passions and the nature of love. *Philosophy Today* 43, no. 1: 43–48.

Wiesenthal, S. 1998. *The sunflower: On the possibilities and limits of forgiveness.* Revised Edition. New York: Schocken Books.

Williston, B. 2003. The Cartesian sage and the problem of evil. In *Passion and virtue in Descartes,* 301–31. New York: Humanity Books.

Wingenbach, E. C. 1996. Sexual difference and the possibility of justice: Irigaray's transformative politics. *International Studies in Philosophy* 28, no. 1: 117–34.

Wittgenstein, L. 1993. A lecture on ethics. In *Philosophical occasions 1912–1951,* ed. James C. Klagge and Alfred Nordmann, 37–44. Indianapolis: Hackett.

Wollstonecraft, M. 1988. *A vindication of the rights of woman.* 2nd ed. New York: Norton.

Wood, A. 1999. *Kant's ethical thought.* Cambridge: Cambridge University Press.

Young, I. M. 2005. *On female body experience: Throwing like a girl and other essays.* Oxford: Oxford University Press.

———. 1997. *Intersecting voices: Dilemmas of gender, political philosophy, and policy.* Princeton: Princeton University Press.

———. 1990. *Justice and the politics of difference.* Princeton: Princeton University Press.

Young-Bruehl, E. 1996. *The anatomy of prejudices.* Cambridge: Harvard University Press.

Zack, N. 2005. *Inclusive feminism: A third wave theory of women's commonality.* Lanham, MD: Rowman and Littlefield.

———. 1998. *Thinking about race.* Belmont, CA: Wadsworth.

Zahavi, D. 2010. Shame and the exposed self. In *Reading Sartre: On phenomenology and existentialism,* 211–26. London: Routledge.

Ziarek, E. P. 2001. *An ethics of dissensus: Postmodernity, feminism, and the politics of radical democracy.* Stanford: Stanford University Press.

Ziarek, K. 2000. Proximities: Irigaray and Heidegger on difference. *Continental Philosophy Review* 33: 133–58.

Zutlevics, T. L. 2002. Reconciliation, responsibility, and apology. *Public Affairs Quarterly* 16: 63–75.

Index

Achilles, 106

Aesthetics, 99, 100, 102–103, 106, 213n23

Afghanistan, 114

African Americans, 3, 76, 82, 167, 199n16, 209n24

Agamben, Giorgio, 145, 216n19

Ahmed, Sara, 162, 172, 222n2

Alcoff, Linda Martín, 60, 74, 81, 82, 208n21; *Visible Identities*, 82

Alexander, Natalie, 205n38

Allen, Ernest, 76

Algeria, 224n10

Allen, Ernest, 209n25

Allison, Henry, 218n12, 219n22

Alwyn, Patricio, 181

Améry, Jean, 9, 137, 143–144, 149–150, 164, 193, 219n26; *At the Mind's Limits*, 143. *See also* trust

Amnesty, 181, 182

Analytic Imaginary, The, 3, 199n18

Ancient Greece, 217n3

Apologies, 3, 9, 10, 86, 111, 151, 156, 159, 160, 164, 167, 169, 171, 173, 174, 176, 177, 178, 179, 181, 182, 183, 184, 185, 189, 191, 194, 209n29, 221n44, 223n3, 224n9, 224n11, 225n19–20, 225n25, 226n28; official apologies, 3, 9, 10, 165,

166, 167, 168, 170, 174, 175, 179, 181, 183, 185, 186, 187, 194, 195, 223n7; Sorry, 168, 186, 223n8–9

Arendt, Hannah, 3, 7, 9, 10, 72, 84, 85, 86, 93, 94, 99, 100, 103–107, 108, 110, 114, 127, 130–131, 132, 136, 137, 138–142, 143, 144–148, 149, 151, 152, 155, 156, 157, 158, 163, 164, 165, 166, 167, 170, 171, 172, 180, 185, 191, 192, 193, 200n28, 205n39, 210n3, 210n7, 213n26–28, 214n29–30, 216n10, 216n18, 216n20, 218n12, 218n14, 218n16–18, 219n19, 219n21–22, 219n26, 223n6, 225n21–22; action, 130, 132; *Eichmann in Jerusalem*, 9, 157; labor, 130; natality, 141; plurality, 142; *Responsibility and Judgment*, 85, 165; superfluousness, 145, 146; *The Human Condition*, 107, 139, 145, 213n26, 225n21; *The Origins of Totalitarianism*, 7, 9, 105, 130, 131, 141, 216n10; thoughtlessness, 145. *See also* evil; the right to have rights

Aristotle, 11, 15, 26, 42, 50, 52, 81, 105, 107, 197n5, 198n7, 199n25, 203n28, 213n28; *Metaphysics*, 197n5; *Nichomachean Ethics*, 52, 213n28; *Rhetoric*, 198n5

Armour, Ellen, 70

247

Ferrara, Alessandro, 138–139, 217n7

Fine, Robert, 218n16

Flikschuh, Katrin, 118

Forgiveness, 7, 8, 9, 10, 46, 86, 94, 97,
99, 100, 102, 109, 111, 120, 135, 136,
137, 138–141, 143, 147–149, 150–164,
165, 166, 167, 173, 175, 177–181, 182,
183, 184, 185, 189, 191, 192, 193, 194,
195, 213n22, 213n26, 217n3–4217n9,
218n11, 220n30–34, 220n36, 221n37–
41, 221n43–45, 222n46–51, 224n14–17,
225n1821, 225n23–24, 226n28, 226n30;
the unforgivable, 8, 9, 137, 142, 148–151,
153, 155, 158, 159, 164, 174, 176,
219n24, 220n33, 221n44

Formosa, Paul, 219n23

Foucault, Michel, 108, 213n23, 214n31

France, 122, 129, 149, 215n7, 224n10;
occupation of France, 182

Fraser, Malcolm, 222n2

Fraser, Nancy, 64, 68, 206n2, 216n18,
218n18

Freedman, Jane, 129

Freedom, 26, 29, 30, 37, 87, 88, 90, 145,
211n9; reproductive, 16

Free will, 8, 15, 26, 29–30, 40, 136, 200n4,
210n1

Friendship, 5, 16, 37, 38, 48, 49–53, 107,
110, 184, 190, 203n27, 203n28, 204n28,
204n30, 204n34, 204n35

Frierson, Patrick, 200n4, 201n4, 201n7

Freud, Sigmund, 15, 20, 44, 46, 204n31;
penis envy, 19

Frye, Marilyn, 62, 63, 80, 81; *The Politics of
Reality*, 62

Fuss, Diana, 206n4, 209n32

Gaita, Raimond, 183

Garrard, Eve, 156, 158, 219n24

Geddes, Jennifer L., 219n22

Generosity, 1, 2, 5, 6, 7, 8, 10, 11, 12, 23, 25,
26, 29, 31, 32, 33, 35, 37, 38, 39, 46, 48,
53, 56, 57–58, 59, 60, 63, 64, 65, 66, 67,
68, 71, 79, 85, 86, 90, 93, 94, 103, 107,
108, 109, 110, 111, 113, 114, 117, 119,
120, 122, 124, 125, 128, 131, 132, 133,
135, 136, 137, 142, 143, 144, 146, 147,
148, 150, 158, 159, 160, 161, 162, 163,
164, 165, 166, 167, 169, 170, 173, 175,
176, 177, 181, 183, 184, 185, 187, 189,
191, 192, 193, 194, 195, 199n21, 199n22,
208n19; and ethics, 25–30; *generosité*, 2,
25; and wonder, 30–34, 71–77, 80–84

Genius, 101–102, 213n23

Genocide, 137, 139, 144, 146, 155, 156,
162, 193, 223n4

Germany, 72, 139, 191, 218n16; The White
Rose, 211n11

Gift, the, 120, 121, 148

Gill, Kathleen A., 225n5

Gilligan, Carol, 16, 201n5

God, 15, 20, 97, 98, 136, 138, 151, 182,
201n4, 222n48

Golding, Martin, 168

Gourevitch, Philip, 126

Government, 9, 78, 79, 91, 92, 105, 118,
122, 123, 125, 130, 131, 132, 133, 165,
166, 167, 168, 169, 170, 171, 172, 173,
174, 178, 181, 182, 183, 185, 186, 192,
194, 216n17, 224n9, 224n11, 226n26;
world government, 94, 127, 129

Govier, Trudy, 160, 175, 181, 184, 225b19,
226n30

Gratitude, 40

Grosz, Elizabeth, 21, 65, 198n15

Guenther, Lisa, 223n8

Guilt, 9, 10, 106, 148, 151, 162, 163, 168,
172–173, 174, 185, 218n17, 221n44,
222n48, 223n6, 224n9; collective guilt,
10, 166, 170, 171, 172, 223n6

Guyer, Paul, 201n10

Habermas, Jürgen, 215n6

Habit, 14, 25, 31, 32, 45, 136